HOUSEKEEPING
MANAGEMENT

HOUSEKEEPING
MANAGEMENT

SECOND EDITION | **MATT A. CASADO**

WILEY

JOHN WILEY & SONS, INC.

Library of Congress Cataloging-in-Publication Data

Casado, Matt A., 1937-
    Housekeeping management / Matt A. Casado. – 2nd ed.
        p. cm.
    Includes index.
    ISBN 978-1-118-07179-3 (cloth)
    1. Hotel housekeeping–Management.   I. Title.
    TX928.C37 2012
    647.068–dc23

                                    2011016028

Printed in the United States of America
V10007025_122018

CONTENTS

Although hospitality is timeless, the industry, along with every other aspect of our society, has changed dramatically since the first edition of this book was published. Students in community colleges and four-year hotel programs must keep abreast of new technologies, be aware of updated procedures for security, and respond to trends such as the current focus on environmental impact and sustainability. At the same time, the structure of management is changing with the consolidation of middle-management positions, leaving future managers to cover more territory. Executive housekeepers who once oversaw only the cleaning of guest quarters are now expected to be capable of directing the housekeeping department by themselves without direct supervision by upper management, and also of understanding basic engineering concepts and energy conservation.

Housekeeping Management, *Second Edition*, includes updates on:

- *Technology* and *security*.
- A *new chapter on sustainability*; this important topic is also covered through additional application problems and case studies.
- A *new chapter on energy conservation* that includes basic knowledge about water, electricity, and HVAC systems from both the housekeeping and engineering departments' perspectives, allowing instructors of lodging management programs to teach elements of engineering that students need before joining the hospitality industry.

ORGANIZATION OF THE TEXT

This book presents the three types of expertise required to become an ideal executive housekeeper: *management of resources*, *administration of assets*, and knowledge of *housekeeping technical operations*. The book is divided into six parts, as outlined below:

Part 1: Introduction to Housekeeping Management is geared toward preparing future executive housekeepers as department heads, covering management concepts and responsibilities as they apply to the housekeeping department.

Part 2: Organization of the Housekeeping Department deals with housekeeping structural planning for large properties, including an effective model for staffing the department by teams.

Part 3: Technical Skills Management discusses the technical skills needed for running the housekeeping department, including descriptions of material, inventory techniques, linen and laundry room management, and the function of cleaning.

Part 4: Human Resources Management covers aspects of personnel administration, including employee motivation, worker satisfaction, and cultural diversity issues.

Part 5: Administrative Controls focuses on budgeting, cost control, and productivity issues as they relate to the housekeeping department.

Part 6: Risk and Environmental Issues in Lodging Properties addresses risk management and environmental issues in lodging. Chapter 10: Safety, Security, and Infectious Diseases addresses the issues of safety, security, and infectious diseases from the housekeeping and engineering departments' perspectives. Chapter 11: Energy and Water Conservation in Lodging Properties focuses on energy conservation and presents elements of engineering in lodging properties. Finally, Chapter 12: Environmental Management and Sustainability describes issues related to environmental management and sustainability, the topic of green properties, and green certification for lodging establishments.

A unique feature of this book is the **application of its theoretical content through presentation of practical case studies** in each chapter. I devised these operational examples from experience gained throughout my extensive career as hotel rooms division director and general manager, and as a hospitality educator. The book can also be used as a professional resource for lodging industry practitioners.

NEW TO THIS EDITION

Housekeeping Management, Second Edition has been revised and updated. New and updated content includes:

- A new Chapter 11: Energy Conservation in Lodging Properties, focusing on *energy conservation methods and techniques specifically with regard to the engineering field.*
- A new Chapter 12: Environmental Management and Sustainability, covering *lodging sustainability through additional application problems and case studies.*
- An *updated section on security* in Chapter 10: Safety, Security, and Infectious Diseases in Property Operations.
- A *new section on international terrorism as it pertains to lodging establishments* in Chapter 10: Safety, Security, and Infectious Diseases.
- A *new section on risk and environmental issues* from both housekeeping and engineering departments' perspectives in Chapter 12: Environmental Management and Sustainability.
- *Detailed OSHA and HazComm regulations* in Chapter 5: Characteristics of House-keeping Equipment and Supplies.
- *Updated section on electronic equipment in guestrooms* in Chapter 5: Characteristics of Housekeeping Equipment and Supplies.
- Description of *most recent communication tools in housekeeping* in Chapter 1: The Housekeeping Department in Lodging Operations.
- *Revised section on staffing the housekeeping department* in Chapter 3: Structural Planning of the Housekeeping Department.
- Math problems made clearer with additional example sets.
- New glossary.

TEXT FEATURES

Each chapter of *Housekeeping Management, Second Edition* includes the following features:

Learning Objectives help students identify the skills and knowledge they will acquire upon completing the chapter.

The **Chapter Overview** summarizes the content and topics covered in each chapter.

Key Terms highlight the specialized terminology in each chapter. A full list of key terms in each chapter is also provided at the end of each chapter, and key terms are fully defined in the new Glossary.

Discussion Questions are included at the end of each chapter to foster class discussion or be used as homework assignments.

Situational **Minicases** focus on realistic day-to-day, practical problems hospitality managers face.

Operational **Case Studies** provide scenarios involving technical dilemmas executive housekeepers need to solve when managing the department.

ADDITIONAL RESOURCES

An **Instructor's Manual** (ISBN 978-1-118-15216-4) is available to professors who have adopted this textbook. The **Instructor's Manual** contains teaching suggestions, sample syllabi, and test questions and answers. An electronic version of the **Instructor's Manual** is available to qualified instructors on the companion Web site at www.wiley.com/college/casado. The Web site also includes PowerPoint slides.

The **Test Bank** for this text has been specifically formatted for **Respondus**, which is easy-to-use software for creating and managing exams that can be printed to paper or published directly to Blackboard, WebCT, Desire2Learn, eCollege, ANGEL, and other eLearning systems. Instructors who adopt *Housekeeping Management* can download the **Test Bank** free. Additional Wiley resources also can be uploaded into your LMS course at no charge. To view and access these resources and the Test Bank, visit www.wiley.com/college/casado, click on the "Visit the Companion Sites" link, then click the link for "Instructor Companion Site."

ACKNOWLEDGMENTS

The author would like to thank Mary Natali for her editing help and consistent support. To the companies that provided photographs to be included in this edition: Marriott Corporation, Starwood Hotels and Resorts, Drury Hotels, Sloane Valve, Ecolab, and InterContinental Hotels Group.

To the reviewers of the manuscript for their suggestions:

Jane A. Broden, Wake Technical Community College
Akita Brooks, Walnut Hill College
Jodi Fisher, Anne Arundel Community College
Paula Kirch Smith, Cincinnati State Technical and Community College
Kathleen Krahn, Northern Arizona University

Matt A. Casado, Ed.D., C.H.A., C.H.E.
Professor
Northern Arizona University

Introduction to Housekeeping Management

PART

1

CHAPTER

1

The St. Regis New York
Courtesy of Starwood Hotels & Resorts Worldwide, Inc.

The Housekeeping Department in Lodging Operations

CHAPTER OBJECTIVES

- Discuss the history of the lodging industry.
- Describe the classification of lodging establishments.
- Define the management structure of lodging operations.
- Explain the elements of the rooms division.
- State the importance of the housekeeping department.
- Discuss the interaction of the housekeeping department with other property units.

OVERVIEW

This chapter explains the origins of lodging operations and describes the development of the lodging industry in the United States. The industry encompasses several types of establishments whose goal is to attract the different segments of the hospitality market.

Lodging establishments can be classified by size and type of service, ranging from the small, humble bed-and-breakfast inn to colossal megahotels and resorts offering luxurious accommodations and services. These lodging properties can be independently owned, franchised, or run by management companies. Students in hotel and restaurant management programs must be aware of the advantages and disadvantages of working for small companies as well as for multi-unit corporations.

The structure of lodging operations is also explained in this chapter, together with a description of the position of the housekeeping department in the organizational chart of large hotels. The chapter ends with a discussion of the interaction necessary between housekeeping and the property's operational and support units.

HISTORY AND STRUCTURE OF LODGING OPERATIONS

Lodging operations are an intrinsic part of the hospitality trade and perhaps the most important of the segments into which this industry is divided. To *lodge* means to furnish guests with room or quarters, generally on a temporary basis. This broad definition implies that the lodging industry is quite diverse, for the renting of living space can range from a simple room in a boarding house to a spacious suite in a luxury hotel, or a bungalow in a lavish resort.

Since the beginning of recorded time, people have traveled and therefore have been in need of lodging. For instance, the excavated ruins of Pompeii in Italy show houses of rest and solace where, up to A.D. 79, wayfarers and seamen of the time were able to relax and be entertained for a fee. Lodging facilities used for economic purpose were built along transportation routes where traveling parties found it convenient to make rest stops en route to their destinations. In Marco Polo's time, rest areas were strategically placed at a distance of a day's ride by caravan. Polo was able to travel from Venice to the Mongol Empire of Kublai Khan in Central Asia by making scheduled stops along the way, where food and safe shelter were available.

Chaucer's *The Canterbury Tales*, written around 1390 in England, contains lively descriptions of inn-keeping practices of the time. In *Don Quixote*, many of Cervantes' ideals are put into practice at an inn in La Mancha, Spain. What we know today as **inns** had their origin in England some centuries ago, the name meaning "a public house that provides lodging for travelers and others." These taverns with rooms for rent were usually located along highways to provide a convenient overnight stay for those traveling by coach. The introduction of railways in the nineteenth century created the need for a large number of these hostelries along the numerous lines that crisscrossed the country. Today, the term inn implies a small hotel, although properties called "inns" often contain a large number of rooms; for example, the Holiday Inn San Francisco Golden Gateway has 499 guestrooms.

The term **hotel** derives from the French *hostel*. The modern French word hôtel suggests "a more or less commodious establishment with up-to-date appointments," although this was not necessarily true one hundred years ago. Today, the term hotel defines a lodging establishment offering accommodation, food and beverage, and amenities to guests. The New Orleans

Windsor Court Hotel, which consumers have rated as one of the best hotels in the United States, advertises meeting facilities, an outdoor pool, a health club, ballrooms, concierge services, a five-diamond dining room, chamber music, and 24-hour suite service. Nightly advertised rates at the Windsor Court range from $190 to $625 for regular guestrooms, to $620 for a club floor suite.

The first **spas** were operated in Europe and consisted of resorts located by mineral springs, which were believed to have curative powers. Today, spas offer a wide array of health-related services ranging from curative massage and mud baths to weight-loss programs.

THE LODGING INDUSTRY IN AMERICA

The first American inns were similar to England's inns of the 1700s. In colonial times, many of the American inns bore such names as "King's," "Queen's," and "Red Lion," but the revolt of the colonies produced a change, and these "royal" names gave place to those in harmony with the spirit of the time. A portrait of George Washington replaced that of George III on the swinging signs as these once quiet taverns became the meeting-places of patriots. Inns were often the backdrop for historic events that took place during and immediately following the Revolution. George Washington was a guest of the City Tavern, Philadelphia (1775), and the Bunch of Grapes Tavern, Boston, where he enjoyed "an elegant dinner provided at the public expense, while joy and gratitude sat on every countenance and smiled in every eye." He stayed at a tavern in East Chester when he was ill, and it was in the assembly room of Fraunces Tavern that Washington bade farewell to the faithful men who, with him, had achieved the liberty of the States. The East Chester Tavern later played a part in U.S. history once again, when President John Adams made it a temporary seat of government by staying there during the yellow fever epidemic in the capital.

In 1794, the seventy-three-room City Hotel was built in New York City. The National Hotel was opened in Washington in 1827, and at once became the home of eminent public men. The Tremont House, which opened in Boston in 1829, was the grandest hotel in the land, boasting a lobby where guests could register instead of doing so at the bar. It was even claimed to be the largest and most elegant hotel in the world at the time, and certainly there was nothing equal to it in England. In 1833, the United States Hotel opened in New York, followed by the Louisville Hotel in 1834 and the Galt House in Louisville in 1835. In 1836, New York opened its rival to the Tremont of Boston, the Astor House, which was built of massive granite. In 1841, the Planters' House, St. Louis—known as the largest hotel west of the mountains—was opened. Charles Dickens stopped there in 1842, and even spoke favorably of it in his *American Notes*. In 1859, the Fifth Avenue Hotel, New York, was completed, and its claim to fame was the first passenger elevator.

At the turn of the century there were an estimated 43,500 hotels in the United States, which provided employment to over 3 million persons.

At this time, hotels in America were either first class or quite rudimentary, and for this reason, the need for modern, hospitable, inexpensive commercial hotels became imperative. Ellsworth Statler, justly regarded as the father of commercial hotels, pioneered a new concept in lodging establishments. His **Statler Hotels**, built in Buffalo, Boston, Cleveland, and New York, at the beginning of the twentieth century, offered the traveler a series of conveniences and services not previously available. Amenities such as light switches, private baths, full-length mirrors, and free morning newspapers were instantly appreciated by guests, who from then on expected to find them wherever they traveled. There was a boom in the hotel industry during the 1920s and a large number of hotels were erected around the country. After a severe slump during the Great Depression, the lodging industry entered an era of extreme intensity. The fact that many people had to travel during World War II and the prosperous postwar years accelerated the need for yet more hotels. Additional new hotels and motor inns were built, including several chains of establishments still in business today. Hilton, Sheraton, and Marriott Hotels, and Wilson's Holiday Inns soon spread nationwide.

In the 1950s, **motels**, which for some time had been catering only to the motoring public, began to gain in popularity. Motels, which offered convenient access by automobile, lower prices than those charged by hotels, and basic but sufficient services, became a favorite form of accommodation, especially for families traveling long distances by automobile.

Air travel, and the fact that people had increasingly substantial disposable incomes, allowed large numbers of travelers to take vacations in distant places during the 1960s and 1970s. This prompted the appearance of **resort** hotels near natural attractions and sporting locations, or in places with balmy, tropical weather. Present-day resorts offer a full range of services aimed at providing guests with every necessity—and luxury—even in remote locations. The Phoenician Resort in Scottsdale, Arizona, offers guestrooms sheathed in Italian marble, with Berber carpets and rattan furniture. Guests staying at the Phoenician have a choice of four restaurants, tiered pools with waterfalls, and golf courses and tennis courts amid 130 acres of desert, garden, and mountain.

The end of the Cold War and the constant advances of technology continued to create new opportunities for business and leisure. Today, as globalization advances, an increasing number of people from all parts of the world are traveling for business and leisure purposes, which further increases the demand for lodging facilities. American hospitality corporations are acquiring properties on every continent, especially South America, Eastern Europe, and Southeast Asia. China, the old Soviet Union countries, and the rest of Asia are sure to follow.

The future of the hospitality industry could not be brighter. Travel and tourism, of which lodging is an integral component, is the country's second largest employer. Domestic and international travelers inject billions of dollars in the U.S. economy every year, and this bonanza is very likely to continue growing due to the increasing number of Americans traveling for business and leisure purposes and to the booming international travel market.

TYPES OF LODGING ESTABLISHMENTS

Besides hotels, motels, and resorts, the lodging industry today offers a variety of establishments aimed at fulfilling the needs of the current market. The most common are:

- Bed-and-breakfast inns
- Time-share condominiums
- Cruise ships
- Institutional lodging establishments
- Casinos

Bed-and-breakfast inns are usually small, privately owned establishments located in suburban and rural locations. They are often uniquely appointed converted private homes that cater to travelers seeking a homey, personal environment. **Time-share condominiums** are apartments, villas, or bungalows usually built near popular vacation spots (such as ski resorts, beaches, or Disney World, for example) that are sold to individual owners who use them or rent them out to transient guests. Time-share owners also have the option of trading with other owners of units located in different parts of the country or the world.

Cruise ships can be described as floating luxury hotels/resorts that provide most of the same services and amenities as properties located on land. Having become quite popular in the vacation and convention markets, cruise ships are one of the fastest growing segments of the hospitality industry.

Institutional lodging is provided by housing facilities that are integral parts of institutional organizations, such as hospitals, retirement homes, universities, and colleges. In some cases this type of lodging requires limited services, such as weekly cleaning or catered meals, which may be provided by contracting companies.

With the adoption of gaming by a large number of Native American tribes, **casinos** have grown in popularity in many states of the United States. Casinos are generally first-class hotels that provide elaborate facilities for gambling, ranging from the ubiquitous slot machine to the sophisticated baccarat or roulette tables. These highly profitable establishments often offer luxurious lodging and lavish entertainment at low cost to attract potential customers.

Lodging properties can be **independently owned**, owned by a **multi-unit chain**, **franchised**, or managed by a **management company**. Properties that are independently owned are not affiliated with any multiple-property entity and are usually managed by their owners. This type of property still represents the largest segment of the lodging industry. A typical independently owned establishment is small in size and is located in a relatively small community. There are advantages and disadvantages to independent operation: on the positive side, independent lodging establishments can provide guests with unique, personalized service while saving royalty and management fees that otherwise would have to be paid to franchisors and/or management companies. On the negative side, such properties may not have name recognition for travelers, they lack collective advertising power, and they are unable to benefit from a national/international reservation system. Often, independently owned and managed properties join reservation referral systems and marketing associations, such as Best Western International, Leading Hotels of the World, or Utell International, which incorporates 3,000 establishments in 130 countries.

Chain properties operate under the direct control of the chain's headquarters. Establishments belonging to the same chain display the same logo and offer identical services by category. For instance, a Hilton four-star hotel must provide similar service and amenities whether it is located in Florida or in Oregon. This assures guests of consistency in price, room layout, menus, sports facilities, and so on. There exist a large number of chains in the world, such as Ritz-Carlton and Loews in the United States, Four Seasons in Canada, and Grupo Sol Melia in Spain.

An effective way for owners of lodging properties to take advantage of the marketing and central reservation power of chain systems is to contract the right to conduct business displaying the logo of the chain by franchising. However, once the franchise is granted, the franchisee must comply with the corporation's requirements regarding service and amenities to be provided to guests.

When hotel owners lack the operative expertise necessary to manage their properties efficiently, they may choose to contract with a management company. In this case, the owner signs a contract delegating the property's operations to such a company in exchange for either paying a basic fee or allowing the management company to retain an agreed-upon percentage of the revenue or income, or a combination of the two.

CLASSIFICATION BY SIZE

Lodging facilities can also be categorized by size. An arbitrary classification could be:

Small: up to 75 rooms

Medium: from 75 to 200 rooms

Large: from 200 to 500 rooms

Very large: more than 500 rooms

The size of a property can be used to estimate the amount of work required of the housekeeping department on a daily basis to maintain the property. For instance, while a 100-room property can be serviced with a relatively small number of housekeeping employees, the Sheraton Hotel & Towers in New York City, with 1,750 rooms, will require over one hundred section housekeepers to service the guestrooms at 100 percent occupancy. Add to that the supervisors, housepersons, public area attendants, linen room attendants, laundry personnel, and other support employees, and it is clear that the number of workers in the housekeeping department of a large hotel such as this can be astounding. This will be covered in greater detail in Chapter 3.

CLASSIFICATION BY TYPE OF SERVICE

Lodging properties can also be categorized by service. **Economy** or budget properties focus on meeting the basic needs of the traveling public—that is, clean, comfortable rooms that are not expensive. The market segments typically attracted to economy properties are guests traveling with children, bus tours, and budget-minded retirees. Many of these properties do not offer food and beverage services except for breakfast, although they all feature TV and some have a swimming pool, a whirlpool, and tennis courts.

Mid-market properties offer all the amenities expected in a "home-away-from-home setting." Restaurants, coffee shops, bars, luggage service, meeting rooms, health club, and room service are generally offered in such properties. The quality of bed linen, towels, room furniture, lobby décor, and customer service must be good or very good. Travelers who frequent properties of this type are business-people, individual tourists, conventioneers, and guests wishing to receive a guaranteed level of excellent service. Often, mid-market properties feature suites that consist of a bedroom, adjacent living room, and a kitchenette with refrigerator. Suites are very appealing to families with children or to two couples traveling together.

Luxury properties offer world-class service, which includes any type of convenience that would be expected by any traveler in any country in the world. Committed to the ultimate in hospitality, luxury properties may feature extravagant amenities like Godiva or other imported chocolates, specialty toiletry items, slippers, silk robes, and special services like executive floors, concierge, foreign language translators, a nanny, and a private

Marriott Renaissance, Bangkok, Thailand
Courtesy of Marriott International, Inc.

secretary. The American Automobile Association (AAA) is the most common rater of lodging establishments in the United States. As a service to its members, this organization provides travel guides that are updated annually describing the properties and evaluating their services. The ratings are determined by field inspectors who base their decisions on thorough evaluations of the properties' design, décor, fittings, comfort, and levels of service, cleanliness, and upkeep. In general, AAA awards three diamonds to economy establishments, while mid-market properties are assigned four diamonds. Invariably, luxury hotels and resorts receive a rating of five diamonds. The Mobil Travel Guide awards stars to lodging establishments, providing the background of the ratings for the benefit of travelers. Their inspectors evaluate objective criteria, including housekeeping and guestroom amenities, before providing the star status that guests can depend on. Every hotel, resort, or bed and breakfast that has a Mobil star rating is recommended. The star system ranges from five to one star, depending on the facilities, service level, and overall experience the property provides. In some countries, an official branch of the government performs the classification of lodging properties to ensure that the quality of their lodging establishments is consistent. Outside the United States, stars are usually used instead of diamonds to designate the ratings.

IMPORTANCE OF THE HOUSEKEEPING DEPARTMENT

A characteristic common to all lodging establishments, regardless of size and category, is the need for housekeeping services, which can range from very sophisticated to a simple matter of

Lobby, CasaMagna Marriott Puerto Vallarta, Mexico
Courtesy of Marriott International, Inc.

"refreshing" rooms once a week. For instance, a luxury hotel, casino, or resort usually requires that the rooms be impeccably clean, that the bed linen be changed every time the bed is used, and that turndown service be provided daily. On the other hand, the service for a university residence room might consist in just providing the tenant with a fresh set of sheets every Monday morning. Mid-range service hotels generally require that guestrooms be thoroughly cleaned daily, that bed and bathroom linen be changed every day, and that 24-hour housekeeping service be provided seven days a week. In any case, because housekeeping services must always be provided, the management of the housekeeping department in every lodging establishment is of critical importance to the success of the property.

It is essential that future graduates of hospitality programs understand the options that the industry offers regarding housekeeping management positions. Graduates wishing to achieve the position of executive housekeeper in a relatively short period of time should keep in mind that a small or medium-sized property generally offers the best option for candidates to reach this goal. In large or very large establishments, where housekeeping operations are quite complex, it will take longer for candidates to become managers of the department. In any case, the position of executive housekeeper will always be a challenging and rewarding one, as well as an adequate springboard from which to work toward the goal of becoming the property's general manager.

When looking for their first job, hospitality graduates should understand the differences among working for properties that are independently or chain-owned, franchised, or run by management companies. An independently owned establishment might not offer substantial opportunities for advancement, as the owners do not usually have any other properties. In this case, the waiting period for reaching an executive position can be a long one. On the other hand, chains offer limitless job opportunities, as these corporations generally expand nationally and internationally by building new places or merging with other companies. If a management company manages a large number of properties, the possibilities for advancing could be as large as those offered by chains. However, it is not unusual for these companies to be rather small, in which case not many openings will occur regularly. Often, independent operators own franchised properties. In this case, working for a "Marriott" or "Sheraton" hotel doesn't mean that you will be working for these corporations, as the owners have merely contracted with the chains for the right to display their commercial names.

THE ROOMS DIVISION

Lodging is an integral part of the **hospitality industry**. Hospitality involves the reception of guests and the provision of services to them with liberality and kindness. The task of providing hospitality and services to guests in a friendly and efficient manner falls mainly on the property's **rooms division**.

The overall success of an operation depends on the profitability of the rooms division, which generally accounts for a large share of a hotel's sales while generating a gross profit percentage from 70 to 80 percent of the revenue. Besides providing lodging and professional services such as check-in, luggage handling, and room upkeep, rooms division personnel must provide the "home-away-from-home" feeling so cherished by travelers who are temporarily separated from their families. Offering tastefully decorated guestrooms and

FIGURE 1.1 Sample Division Chart of Large Property

public areas and impeccable cleanliness in a subdued, relaxing atmosphere is also of the utmost importance.

Large properties are divided into operational units called divisions. Two of these divisions—Rooms, and Food and Beverage—are **revenue-generating centers**, while the others are considered to be **support centers**. The executive in charge of the rooms division is the **Rooms Division Director**, who in some properties may be called resident manager, executive manager, or senior assistant manager. Figure 1.1 shows the breakdown of divisions in a large property. The rooms division director reports directly to the property's general manager. As a member of the **executive committee**, the rooms division director takes an active part in policy-making decisions related to operations. Other members of this committee generally include: the food and beverage director, in charge of the food and beverage division; the sales director, who deals with sales, marketing, and public relations; the controller or chief financial officer; the human resources director, in charge of personnel matters;

and the plant manager, responsible for the engineering and maintenance needs of the property.

Figure 1.2 shows the rooms division divided into departments. Of these, the **front office** and **housekeeping departments** are of critical importance to the property. The **executive housekeeper** is the head of housekeeping and is, therefore, directly responsible for managing what is in most cases the largest department of the establishment. The position of executive housekeeper in the organizational chart is that of **department head**, equal in rank to the front office manager, the security manager, and the remaining managers in charge of departments in

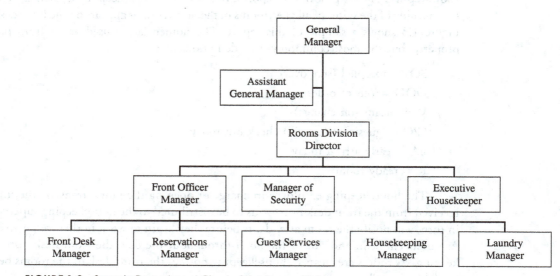

FIGURE 1.2 Sample Department Chart of the Rooms Division

other divisions. In smaller properties, the division directors do not exist; instead, department heads manage the different units and report directly to the general manager.

INTERACTION BETWEEN HOUSEKEEPING AND OTHER DEPARTMENTS

The housekeeping department is an integral part of all the areas into which a lodging operation is divided. Although housekeeping's primary communication takes place with the front office and engineering departments, a strong relationship must exist with all the other units of the property as well. For instance, room service, a department in the food and beverage division that delivers food to guestrooms, must be in direct contact with housekeeping for the removal of trays and carts. The sales department, which often must have access to ready rooms to be shown to meeting planners or tour operator representatives, must communicate this need to the housekeeping department. There is an extensive variety of software programs that graduates will find when they join the lodging industry. These user-friendly programs can be learned on site with just a basic computer knowledge on the part of the new employees.

COMMUNICATION WITH THE FRONT OFFICE

Guestrooms in lodging properties are sold by the front office. The front desk must know at every given moment what rooms have been cleaned and are available for occupancy. Housekeeping must provide the front desk with a listing of rooms that are ready for occupancy so guests can be checked in. If the communication between the two departments is poor or breaks down, delays in guest check-in will occur, or people will be checked into rooms that are thought to be ready but that in fact are occupied or not ready. If this happens often, the property's reputation will suffer.

The cycle of communication begins early each day, when the front desk provides the housekeeping department with a computer-generated or written report called the **night clerk's room report**. The purpose of this report is to inform the housekeeping department very early in the morning of the status of all guestrooms in the property as it appears on the front desk records. Figure 1.3 shows a sample of this report. The nomenclature used varies from property to property, but the most commonly used definitions are:

SO = occupied (stay over)

OOO = out of order

V = vacant (on change)

C/O = guest has (or will) check out today

EA = early arrival today

R = ready room

The housekeeping employee in charge of opening the house transfers the information received from the front desk into forms to be distributed to the housekeeping supervisors who, in turn, will notify the room attendants before they begin to work in their respective sections. As guests check in and out of the hotel throughout the day, the front desk notifies housekeeping. As rooms are cleaned, housekeeping notifies the front desk of the rooms being made available for selling.

FIGURE 1.3 Sample of Night Clerk's Report to Housekeeping

Night Clerk's Report

Date: _____ Prepared By: _____

Total Rooms Occupied: _____

Check-Outs: _____

Stay Overs: _____

Out of Order: _____

Room	Status	Room	Status	Room	Status	Room	Status
1001	SO	2001	OOO	3001	SO	4001	V
1002	SO	2002	SO	3002	SO	4002	OOO
1003	C/O	2003	SO	3003	R	4003	SO
1004	V	2004	C/O-EA	3004	R	4004	R
1005	SO	2005	V	3005	C/O	4005	R
Room	Status	Room	Status	Room	Status	Room	Status
1001	SO	2001	OOO	3001	SO	4001	V
1002	SO	2002	SO	3002	SO	4002	OOO
1003	C/O	2003	SO	3003	R	4003	SO
1004	V	2004	C/O-EA	3004	R	4004	R
1005	SO	2005	V	3005	C/O	4005	R

The report indicates that rooms 1001, 1002, 1005, 2002, 2003, 3001, 3002 and 4003 are occupied and staying over. Rooms 1003, 2004 and 3005 are checkouts. Rooms 2001 and 4002 are out of order. Rooms 1004, 2005 and 4001 are vacant and not ready. Rooms 3003, 3004, 4004 and 4005 are ready to be sold. There is a scheduled early arrival in room 2004.

As soon as it is possible, an A.M. **guestroom check** is performed by housekeeping to ascertain whether the information provided in the night clerk's report was accurate. When discrepancies are found between the status of rooms received from the night clerk and the physical inspection of the rooms, the front desk is immediately notified. For instance, if the front desk reports that a certain room is vacant and housekeeping finds it occupied, a discrepancy exists and the front desk should be notified. There are several reasons why discrepancies may occur. The most common are:

A guest switches from one room to another and the front desk neglects to change its records.

An error is made by the night clerk when filling out the night clerk's report.

A guest is given the wrong room key by mistake.

The room was used by an unauthorized employee.

The room was sold by the front desk without being recorded, and the money pocketed by the clerk.

A guest checks in or out between when the report is made and when the check is conducted.

The P.M. **room check** is conducted by the housekeeping department just before the end of the morning shift. This guestroom check consists of entering every room in the house at approximately the same time in order to generate a report showing the status of all guestrooms. The report is made available to the front desk and compared with the front desk records. As with the A.M. report, if discrepancies are found, they are immediately investigated and the records corrected. Besides reporting whether rooms are occupied, vacant, out of order, or ready, the report should provide the front desk with information that can help this department better control the guest records. The most common symbols used are:

B = slept out (guest did not use the room but baggage is still in the room)

NB = occupied, no baggage

DND = do-not-disturb sign on door

LO = lock out (room has been locked by management so that guest cannot reenter)

As the evening progresses and the room attendants on the evening shift continue to clean rooms from late check-outs and day-rate occupancy, the front desk is notified of the rooms available for sale.

Other communications between the front office and the housekeeping department involve information about occupancy forecasts, the arrival of VIPs, the early check-in of groups, the closing of certain sections for deep cleaning or repairs, delivery of guest laundry, lost and found items, special guest requests, and so on. The communication between the housekeeping department and the front desk is greatly improved when the property uses a computerized system. For instance, when a guest checks out, the front desk clerk enters the departure in the computer and it appears instantly in the housekeeping monitor. When housekeeping has rooms ready to be sold, the information is entered in the system and it too shows up quickly in the front desk terminal.

There are an increasing number of digital programs that can help lodging professionals communicate within and outside the department very effectively. For example, OPTii Solutions offers a hand-held device that can instantly modify the status of guestrooms as well as update guestroom-service schedules. The touch-screen interface can send and receive timely communications and generate reports on rooms cleaned without the need to use computer screens or make telephone calls between the front desk and the housekeeping department. OPTii's Web site is: www.optiisolutions.com.

COMMUNICATION WITH MAINTENANCE

The relationship between housekeeping and the maintenance department must be as close as that with the front office. Every piece of equipment, fixtures, and furniture in the guestrooms, hallways, linen and laundry rooms, public areas, and employee locker rooms must be in perfect working order at all times. The number of items that may be in need of repairs in a single guestroom can be substantial: beds, chairs, desks, TVs, radios, lights, doors, toilets, faucets, walls, heating, air conditioning, and so on. It is, therefore, imperative that good communication between the two departments exists at all times. For instance, if a guestroom lock is broken, maintenance must be notified, the room put out of order, the work performed, the area cleaned, and the room put back in vacant-ready status. As with the front desk, a computerized system or hand-held electronic devices should be used for instant message delivery.

There are two types of maintenance performed by the engineering department in hospitality properties. **Regular maintenance** is performed when an item is broken and needs

FIGURE 1.4 Sample Maintenance Request Form

MAINTENANCE REQUEST

By _____ Date _____

Location _____

Problem _____

Assigned To _____

Date Compl. _____ Time Spent _____

Completed By _____

Remarks _____

Original: Originator Canary: Maintenance; Manila: Maintenance

D105–106

to be repaired. In this case, a three-part **work order form** is filled out by a housekeeping employee, who forwards two copies to engineering and keeps the third copy filed until the work is completed. When work is completed, one of the copies is returned to housekeeping for comparison, the work is inspected, and the area cleaned. When a problem is urgent and engineering does not promptly address it, housekeeping generates a **second request** work order to remind that department that the work must be completed. If the repair needs to be done in order to be able to sell the room that day, an urgent request is sent to engineering so that the work is given priority over other nonessential jobs. Figure 1.4 is a standard form used for requesting repair and maintenance services from the engineering department.

The orderly flow of information between housekeeping and engineering about items or areas in need of attention is of critical importance. As the housekeeping department staff is directly involved in cleaning most sections of the property, they are in the best position to find areas in need of maintenance or repair.

Preventive maintenance consists of inspecting guestrooms and other areas on a regular basis to identify repair and maintenance needs. In most hotels, the executive housekeeper and the chief engineer cooperate in combining room cleaning with preventive maintenance programs. This involves conducting a thorough maintenance inspection of all rooms in the property two or three times a year. Figure 1.5 is a sample **maintenance checklist** used to perform maintenance inspections. The form contains a list of every item that could be in need of repair. After the preventive maintenance inspection has been completed, a check mark will indicate that the standards of operation have been met, while an "x" mark will indicate that the item in question is in need of repair. Preventive maintenance programs are essential to ensure that guests staying in the property find the rooms in perfect working order.

COMMUNICATION WITH HUMAN RESOURCES

Communication between the housekeeping and human resources departments is necessary when considering personnel staffing. When an employee is needed in the housekeeping department, an *employee requisition* is filled out and sent to human resources to initiate the process. Most

FIGURE 1.5   Sample Maintenance Checklist

- Doors
- A/C Unit
- Floor
- Television
- Drapes

- Lights
- Walls
- Furniture
- Telephone
- Closet

- Electrical
- Ceiling
- Windows
- Mirrors
- Bed

Bathroom:
- Lights
- Tub
- Caulking

- Paint
- Vanity
- Drains

- Air Vent
- Shower
- Toilet

Remarks:
- Doors
- A/C Unit
- Floor
- Television
- Drapes

- Lights
- Walls
- Furniture
- Telephone
- Closet

- Electrical
- Ceiling
- Windows
- Mirrors
- Bed

Bathroom:
- Lights
- Tub
- Caulking

- Paint
- Vanity
- Drains

- Air Vent
- Shower
- Toilet

Remarks:
- Checked
- Needs Repair
Room Number: _____

properties have software linking the two departments. Figure 1.6 is a sample employee requisition that provides human resources with the necessary information for the job in question. After receiving the request, human resources advertises for the position, prescreens the candidates, conducts the first interview, and checks references. The final candidates are then sent to housekeeping for a second interview and hiring selection.

Human resources is usually also involved in the orientation of new housekeeping employees, at which time the company's philosophy, compensation package, pay schedule, and rules and regulations are explained in detail to the new worker. This department also ensures that the new employee fills out all necessary forms related to legal residency, income tax, and personal information. Good communication with human resources will result in hiring the right employees to fill housekeeping vacancies.

COMMUNICATION WITH FOOD AND BEVERAGE

Food and beverage is the second major revenue center in the property after the rooms division. The food and beverage division in large hotels comprises the property's kitchens, restaurants, coffee shops, cafeterias, bars, lounges, banquets, catering services, clubs, and room service. In large hotels, the housekeeping department should only be indirectly involved in the cleaning of

FIGURE 1.6   Sample Employee Requisition

Date: _____ Department: _____

Position: _____

New: _____ Replacement: _____ Number required: _____

Classification: _____

(Full-time, Part-time, Temporary, Pool)

Working hours: _____ Estimated no. of hours/week: _____

Desired starting date: _____

Starting rate of pay: _____ Base rate: _____

Specification (general description of duties): _____

Special qualifications (desired or required): _____

food and beverage outlets. However, the communication between food and beverage and housekeeping is necessary in some specific areas.

There must be good cooperation regarding the pickup of room service material from guestroom areas. Housekeeping must see to it that hallways are free of trays and carts placed there by guests and section housekeepers; therefore, calls to room service must be regularly placed to

King room, Sheraton Aloft Montreal
Courtesy of Starwood Hotels & Resorts Worldwide, Inc.

remind this department to clear all areas. The laundry room must provide the food and beverage department with clean napery on a daily basis. This often means that the laundry manager must request that the soiled linen be delivered to the laundry room on time, properly sorted out, and free from food scraps and table debris. Furnishing clean uniforms to cooks, waiters, and bartenders is also usually the responsibility of the housekeeping department. As communication with food and beverage service personnel is traditionally difficult, efforts must be made to establish good relationships between departments.

COMMUNICATION WITH SALES AND MARKETING

The primary goal of the sales and marketing division is to sell the products and services offered by the property. Given that cleanliness is one of the most important reasons that guests choose a particular lodging property, the onus of providing this critical service falls on the housekeeping department. There must be good communication between sales and housekeeping if customer satisfaction is to be achieved. For instance, if sales and marketing has guaranteed late check-out to a large group of guests attending a convention without notifying housekeeping, some of the rooms might not be cleaned in time to be available for a tour group scheduled to check in that same evening. If sales and marketing has promised that 40 rooms will be available for early check-in to a company attending a conference at the property and housekeeping has not been notified, there might not be enough manpower that morning to clean the rooms on time.

Communication between sales and housekeeping is also necessary when specific rooms or suites must be available for inspection to meeting planners who are considering the property for a possible convention. If the rooms in question have not been impeccably cleaned, the company executive might take their business elsewhere.

COMMUNICATION WITH THE ACCOUNTING OFFICE

It is seldom acknowledged that communication between housekeeping and the accounting office is of great importance, yet there are several reasons why this is so. For instance, in large properties, the purchasing agent often reports to the controller; therefore, the executive housekeeper is communicating with the accounting office when placing orders for equipment and supplies for the department. Also, housekeeping must provide accounting with all information regarding wages and salaries—for instance, informing the office of pay increases, hours worked per week, overtime, bonuses awarded to workers, and so on. The executive housekeeper must also provide accounting with monthly inventory information in order to ascertain expenses of controllable goods to work out cost percentages.

KEY TERMS

A.M. guestroom check
Bed-and-breakfast
Casinos

Cruise ships
Department head
Economy property

Employee requisition
Executive committee
Executive housekeeper
Franchised property
Front office
Hospitality industry
Hotel
Housekeeping department
Independently owned property
Inn
Institutional lodging
Luxury property
Maintenance checklist
Management company
Mid-market property
Motel

Multi-unit chain
Night clerk's room report
P.M. guestroom check
Preventive maintenance
Regular maintenance
Resort
Revenue-generating center
Rooms division
Rooms division director
Second request
Spa
Statler hotels
Support center
Time-shared condominiums
Work order

DISCUSSION AND REVIEW QUESTIONS

1. What is the origin of the word inn? Is there a difference between the meaning of inn some centuries ago and the meaning of inn today?

2. How would you define the word hotel? Is there a difference between hotels and inns in today's market?

3. In which way were inns and taverns associated with the American Revolution?

4. Why is Ellsworth Statler considered the father of commercial hotels?

5. List the most common types of lodging properties in today's market.

6. How would you describe institutional lodging?

7. What is the difference between a franchised property and a property run by a management company?

8. What are the three categories in which lodging properties are generally classified by type of service?

9. Explain why the rooms division is considered a revenue center rather than a support center.

10. Indicate the purpose of the A.M. guestroom check report conducted by housekeeping.

11. Give two reasons why communication between the housekeeping and maintenance departments must be kept efficient.

12. As an executive housekeeper, what department would you contact to solve a problem arising from unacceptable presorting of napery items?

MINICASES

SITUATION 1

As a student about to graduate from a hotel/restaurant management program, you receive three job offers from three different companies recruiting at your university. The first company offers you a position as assistant housekeeping manager paying $33,000 per year. The company is a partnership that owns five Holiday Inn–franchised properties. The second company is the Marriott Corporation, which owns a large number of hotels and resorts around the world. The position offered to you is that of housekeeping manager trainee at a salary of $31,500 per year. The third company would like to hire you as assistant executive housekeeper and is offering you a salary of $34,000 per year. This is a management company that runs 150 properties in 16 states. (a) Which job would you rather accept? (b) What are the reasons that you would provide in support of your decision?

SITUATION 2

As housekeeping supervisor in a resort, you are in the process of preparing the A.M. guestroom check report when you discover that room 2004 is occupied, although the night clerk's report that you received early in the morning indicated that the room was vacant. (a) What do you think could have happened for the discrepancy to exist? (b) What do you do from there?

SITUATION 3

It is 7:30 P.M. As supervisor of the housekeeping evening shift, you receive a computer message from the engineering department indicating that the painting job in the out-of-order room 2008 has been completed. The hotel will be at 100 percent occupancy that evening. (a) What steps will you take after receiving the information from engineering?

SITUATION 4

Mary Lee is the executive housekeeper of a small resort on the Pacific coast where she has worked for the last twelve years. The property has a new general manager who has been promoted from the ranks into the position. It is time to start working on departmental budgets for the next fiscal year, but the resort's chief engineer has been taken ill and will not return for the next month or so. Believing that he will not be able to compile the final comprehensive budget on time, the general manager decides to ask Miss Lee to put together the engineering department budget because of, as he puts it, Mary's industry experience. (a) If you were the executive housekeeper of the resort, would you agree to compile the budget? (b) Explain the reasons for your decision.

CASE STUDY

The Makings of a Housekeeping Manager

Shanequa Palm was hired by a lodging company after three successful interviews during her senior year in a hotel and restaurant management program. The need for supervisors in the company was extreme and she was assigned to the position of assistant executive housekeeper after two weeks of initial training. While in charge of the department on a Sunday morning, she received a call from two laundry workers scheduled to work that day. One explained that she was having car trouble and that it would take her two to three hours to get to work. The second said that she couldn't find a babysitter to take care of her two children. The hotel was very busy that morning, with many check-outs and an early check-in of a tour group. The laundry room was in a state of collapse with soiled linen piling up quickly in the sorting area. On the floors, section housekeepers were running out of clean items to make up the guestrooms.

Shanequa understood that someone needed to start washing linen immediately. She asked Rene, a public area attendant, to start the machine and take care of the washing. Rene refused, arguing that he didn't know how to operate the washing machine and that it was not his job to wash anything. In a panic, Shanequa begged a team supervisor to ask a section housekeeper to help in the laundry room. She refused, explaining that the rooms in her section needed to be cleaned and that it was not in a section housekeeper's job description to wash linen.

At that point, the manager remembered the emphasis that most of her college professors put on treating employees nicely. Specifically, she recalled that the main management premise was to influence the activities of subordinates to *willingly* accomplish goals and that a manager must be concerned about tasks *and* human relations. Her solution was to solve the problem by abandoning the office and washing the linen herself. Three hours later, one of the laundry workers arrived and took over the job.

On returning to the office, she was handed four written complaints from guests about poor service. One of them stated that it had taken 45 minutes to get two extra clean towels in room 707. Shanequa began to wonder if she had made the right decision by abandoning the supervision of the department to wash the linen herself.

Assignment

1. How would you judge Shanequa Palm's management role in that specific situation?

2. How effective do you think her management approach will be in the long run?

3. How would you have dealt with this situation?

Sheraton Hotel Ankara, Turkey
Courtesy of Starwood Hotels & Resorts Worldwide, Inc.

The Executive Housekeeper as Department Manager

CHAPTER OBJECTIVES

- Learn how management concepts apply to the position of executive housekeeper.
- Discuss the necessity of achieving high productivity in housekeeping while also considering the needs of the employees in the department.
- Understand the role of the executive housekeeper as department head.
- Explain the role of the executive housekeeper as department coordinator.
- List the managerial responsibilities of the executive housekeeper.

OVERVIEW

This chapter explains how management concepts can be applied to the role of executive housekeeper. As a manager, you must be able to combine concern for production and concern for people in order to run the department effectively. The traditional functions of management can be followed as a guide to organize and coordinate the department, plan and direct activities, and control results.

As a department head, the executive housekeeper must be proficient in technical, people-related, and conceptual skills. As a manager, the executive housekeeper must understand the concepts of time management, problem resolution, quality control, and decision making, and operate within the precepts of industry-accepted codes of ethics.

MANAGEMENT CONCEPTS AS THEY APPLY TO THE EXECUTIVE HOUSEKEEPER

It is the responsibility of a manager to create and maintain an environment in which people can work toward the goals of the company. As the manager of the largest department in the lodging property, the executive housekeeper must possess strong managerial skills in order to perform this task well. Members of a management staff must be concerned with the productivity of the work force and people, and must be able to efficiently coordinate effort in the workplace.

CONCERN FOR PRODUCTION

The overall goal of management in a profit-making operation is to increase the owner's equity by maximizing profits. So, in turn, one of the major concerns of the executive housekeeper should be to maximize the productivity and efficiency of housekeeping employees. Theoretical production and efficiency methods in the workplace were first explored at the turn of the century by **Frederick W. Taylor**, whose **classic scientific management** concepts, although developed under industrial conditions, can still be applied today in the lodging industry. Taylor analyzed jobs systematically to determine the amount of work that each employee could produce. He did so by measuring the performance of workers in a given period of time. This allowed management to set standards of production and require employees to reach the pre-established levels of performance in a certain number of hours. If the productivity levels were above the standard, management could choose to pay bonuses to workers as an incentive to maintain productivity quotas. If the productivity levels were below the standard, production methods had to be improved.

This approach is still followed in well managed housekeeping operations. For instance, the executive housekeeper can analyze the time required to efficiently clean one of the property's guestrooms and use that time as the department's standard for that task. When productivity and quality exceed the standards, special recognition or extra compensation can be given for maintaining the productivity quotas. If performance falls below preestablished levels, the section housekeepers would need to be retrained or the method used to clean guestrooms reevaluated. This approach can foster productivity and increase the profits of the company, which in turn could pay its employees higher wages.

CONCERN FOR PEOPLE

Frederick Taylor's classic scientific management approach dealt with techniques to increase productivity in the workplace. At the time, workers had little reason to improve their productivity; on the contrary, they viewed the introduction of new machines and equipment to improve efficiency as a direct threat.

Toward the end of the 1920s, a new management approach developed as a result of experiments conducted in the workplace by **Elton Mayo**. The study concluded that factors other than the physical aspect of a job can have an effect on productivity, namely, the workers' social interactions and personal relationships. Mayo's study demonstrated that in order to increase productivity in the workplace, human relations factors must be considered. That is, an organization consists first and foremost of the people working in it and management must be greatly concerned with the social and psychological aspects of the relationship between the company and its employees. As a result, the **human relations management** approach was developed.

This approach can be easily understood and applied from a housekeeping management perspective. For instance, if the department manager does not consider the social needs of the workers a priority, workers in turn will not develop a sense of loyalty for their manager. If a houseperson who is scheduled to work the morning shift cannot find a babysitter for mornings, management should do everything possible to schedule this worker in the evening. If this were done, the employee would feel gratitude and therefore be more willing to return the favor by improving productivity. In other words, productivity can be greatly improved if management takes care of its workers.

The human relations theory allowed an understanding of the dynamics of human behavior that led to the premise that management must be aware that workers, besides being units of production, are social entities in their own right.

COMBINING CONCERN FOR PRODUCTION AND CONCERN FOR PEOPLE

Mayo's work provided a needed addition to scientific movement. Management, which until then perceived employees as mechanistic elements in the productive system, was now viewing workers as human components in the organization's social system. Although it is true that executive housekeepers must develop a keen sense for production in the workplace (after all, the main reason for lodging companies to stay in business is to generate a profit), they must also see housekeeping employees as individuals. Yet, without adequate productivity in the workplace, profits will be diminished, forcing management to pay insufficient wages and to provide inferior benefits.

Clearly, then, adding concern for people to the management equation is imperative. However, the real skill lies in finding a proper balance; for example, an executive housekeeper determined to please workers at any cost may not be totally successful, for employees easily sense when a manager is a "softy," not tough enough to have the work done fairly but efficiently. A case in point would be an executive housekeeper agreeing to pay too much overtime or allowing employees to call in with any excuse not to show up for work.

COORDINATION OF EFFORT IN THE WORKPLACE

Another function of management is to see to it that all parts of a working unit are integrated as a whole. **Henri Fayol**, of France, theorized that certain management principles can be applied to any type of business as well as to the various levels within the business.

These principles apply, therefore, to the lodging industry in general and to the housekeeping department in particular. Fayol's book, *Administration Industrielle et Générale*, originally published in 1916, was not adopted in the United States until three decades later. Fayol proposed that a manager must practice the following functions of management:

Planning
Organizing
Directing
Coordinating
Controlling

Planning

One of the main functions the manager of the housekeeping department must perform is deciding what tasks are essential at any given time to keep the department running at peak efficiency. As the occupancy of the property varies from month to month, and even from day to day, forecasting labor and supplies needs must be done in advance to minimize costs. The definition of planning is simple: deciding where one should go and how to get there. Planning, however, is not always easy, for it requires the predetermination of strategies and policies necessary to fulfill company goals. When forecasting employees, for instance, the executive housekeeper must skillfully plan the scheduling of employees according to the property's upcoming occupancy. If the hotel is full, all employees are needed, but only part of the staff is required when the occupancy is low. Regarding material, lack of planning might result in purchasing excessive amounts of guest supplies, for example, which means tying up cash that might be needed to pay salaries or to buy new bed linens. On the other hand, underestimating future occupancy may result in understocking supplies and running out of them when they are most needed.

Creativity is an important element of the planning function; it requires the ability of a manager to develop and implement different, more efficient solutions to operational problems. A creative executive housekeeper is flexible in judging employee initiatives, encouraging workers to develop new ways to improve the efficiency of the department. A highly structured, bureaucratic housekeeping department might be efficient in production but would stifle or limit innovation. Creativity in planning should allow for diversity of ideas without attempting to rigidly structure the behavior of employees.

Planning involves the achievement of short- and long-range objectives. A **short-range objective** might be to bring down the labor cost by one percentage point next month. A **long-range objective** might be to increase the productivity of section housekeepers by 5 percent over last year's results by the end of the current fiscal year.

Organizing

The organization of housekeeping is necessary in order to establish a pattern of relationships with other operational units and among the different components of the department itself. The organization of housekeeping includes the determination of tasks, skills, and personnel necessary to achieve the objectives of the department. It is the responsibility of the executive housekeeper to structure the department so that all work can be finished efficiently and on time. The first necessary step when structuring the housekeeping department is to determine the pattern of authority by drawing an organizational chart. This follows the principle of **unity of command** proposed by Fayol, which states that workers should be given orders only by their own supervisor. To this effect, the **span of control** must be clearly defined; this relates to the number of subordinates that a supervisor can oversee effectively. In the housekeeping department, when employees are well trained and dependable, the span of control can be quite broad. In the case of new or untrained employees, the span of control should be narrow, usually four or five workers.

Defining relationships within the department is also important because a strong cooperation must exist among its different units. For instance, a sufficient amount of clean linen must be made available to section housekeepers during the morning shift to set up guestrooms as quickly as possible. However, if the soiled linen is not brought to the laundry room to be washed, dried, and ironed early in the day, the clean linen will not be ready on time.

Another organizational task is that of creating descriptions of the jobs to be done (list of tasks) and the qualifications of workers who are to perform the jobs. Matching the right person to each job that must be accomplished is a priority in the organization of the housekeeping department. For instance, section housekeepers in lodging properties must clean between 12 and 20 rooms on average in one eight-hour shift. The importance of selecting people who are physically able to perform this strenuous job is obvious.

Guestroom, Marriott Cannes, France
Courtesy of Marriott International, Inc.

Directing

This managerial function involves achieving the goals of the department by explaining to employees what needs to be accomplished, then facilitating their efforts to do the job. Crucial to directing effectively is the ability of the manager to train, motivate, supervise, and discipline employees. Competent executive housekeepers will be able to attain higher levels of productivity from the housekeeping work force than managers who are not adequately trained to direct people.

Without proper direction, employees tend to duplicate efforts, focus on the wrong priorities, and relate efforts to the wrong purpose. An example of improper direction may be allowing section housekeepers to clean every guestroom (checkout and stay-over rooms alike) early in the morning when there are incoming guests waiting in the lobby to be checked in. Another example of poor management would be to play favorites with employees, which would lead to discontent among them. As a manager, an efficient executive housekeeper should emphasize both the economic-technical system and the human aspects of administration.

Coordinating

If we compared the housekeeping department to an orchestra, coordinating would be the act of bringing all the instruments together to produce a fine piece of music, that is, matching the individual work of the staff to the common goals of the operation. The executive housekeeper must coordinate the procurement and distribution of materials, working schedules, and overall communication among the different units of the department. This function is carried out through a series of briefings, meetings, and committee work where daily operational matters, intradepartmental issues, and hotel-wide concerns are addressed.

Lodging operations require a large degree of interdepartmental coordination. It is the job of the executive housekeeper to integrate the department in the operation as a whole, making sure that communication flows to and from housekeeping and the different operational units of the property. A case in point would be attending a meeting in which the arrival of a large convention to the hotel is discussed. It would be up to the executive housekeeper to learn about the number of people in the group, arrival time, the type of accommodation booked, and other requirements, and to communicate this information in due course to the housekeeping supervisors for proper follow-up.

Coordination can be achieved by linking all activities together under a central authority. In the housekeeping department, however, it would be difficult to cope individually with all the coordinating problems that might arise every day. The coordinating function must be supported by a system of procedures designed to carry out much of the routine work automatically, for instance, using forms, memos, and routing slips. It is also important to achieve voluntary coordination on the part of the housekeeping employees. If they see the need for coordination and they are willing to find means to integrate their activities with those of other participants, departmental coordination will be accomplished.

Controlling

The purpose of control is to make operations more efficient and cost-effective. This function involves measuring actual with expected standards established during the planning process and effecting necessary corrections if deviations from the standards are found. Feedback is an essential component in the control process. In housekeeping departments, feedback should be sought from guests, employees, and other departments of the lodging operation. Figure 2.1 is an

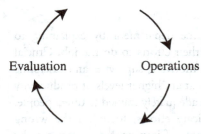

Evaluation   Operations

FIGURE 2.1 The Cycle of Control

example of the control process, in which standards are set during the planning function, operations take place, feedback is obtained from different sources, an evaluation of results is conducted, and new standards are prescribed. For example, let's suppose that you decide that each one of your section housekeepers is to clean 15 rooms in an eight-hour shift. One month after having set this standard you get feedback from guests that the rooms are not very clean. In this case, the standard of 15 rooms per shift should be reevaluated and perhaps lowered to 14 rooms to be cleaned in eight hours. Then, the cycle of control is set into motion again.

The responsibility of executive housekeepers to control the activities of their department represents an important management function. Without controls there is no way of evaluating the degree to which the objectives set during the planning function are met. In other words, the actual results need to be compared to desired or anticipated goals and standard of performance. Labor cost percentages are typical standards of control; if the labor cost was set in the budget at 18 percent of revenue and the actual labor cost is running at 22 percent, the results are over budget and some corrective measures must be taken.

Controlling also refers to the need to regulate and protect material and equipment. This can be accomplished by implementing stock pars and taking protective measures against theft, pilferage, and misuse. Effective quality control can also lead to significant saving in costs. For instance, controlling the quality of cleaning materials to be used in the housekeeping department can result in substantial savings of time spent in having the job done.

THE EXECUTIVE HOUSEKEEPER AS DEPARTMENT HEAD

The position of executive housekeeper in the organizational structure of lodging operations is that of **department head** or member of the middle management team. In small properties, executive housekeepers report directly to the general manager of the establishment, while in large properties they report to the rooms division director.

Today's successful executive housekeeper requires skills beyond those of a person who is just in charge of keeping the place clean. An effective manager of the housekeeping department must be object-, people-, and idea-oriented.

TECHNICAL, PEOPLE, AND CONCEPTUAL SKILLS

Executive housekeepers cannot concentrate their managerial ability on technical skills alone—material, budgets, equipment. They also must concern themselves with people and with the conceptualization of notions about the resolution of management-related issues. Executive housekeepers must have a thorough knowledge of how the job is done and how the equipment works, and also be able to exercise leadership and influence people to have the work done while being sensitive to the employees' needs. At the same time, they must be able to analyze situations, implement change, and effect innovative ideas in the workplace.

SUPERVISION

A supervisor is anyone whose responsibility is to supervise; therefore, every manager is a supervisor. The definition of supervision is quite similar to that of management in that it is concerned with directing, facilitating, and monitoring the work of others in order to have the job done. The executive housekeeper's field of supervision encompasses three major components: the company's assets, the employees, and the guests. Poor supervision of employees may lead to preparing guestrooms inefficiently, which in turn may create customer disloyalty and an eventual loss of profits.

Executive housekeepers can effect supervision tightly or loosely. Supervision can be exacted by following prescribed rules and regulations or by allowing teamwork and decision making by line employees. In the latter case, workers are expected to exercise initiative and self-coordination. Whether to use one style or the other should depend on the composition of the work force. When there is a substantial turnover of employees and their working skills are weak, supervision should be tighter than when the work force is well trained and reliable.

LEADERSHIP

Providing leadership is one aspect of management. Leadership can be defined as "the ability to lead people to willingly perform in ways to achieve the organization's goals." One commonly encountered problem in the lodging industry is that of indifferent employees. Some of the reasons for this are the inadequate wages, poor benefits, part-time positions, and insufficient training so common in the industry. In spite of these obstacles, it is the task of hospitality managers to create an appropriate environment in which employees willingly display a positive attitude toward guests and fellow workers. This can be achieved through proper leadership.

There are three leadership styles generally used by leaders in human situations. In the **authoritarian style**, the manager who dictates the tasks to be performed and the ways to accomplish them assumes the determination of policies; input from subordinates is not sought. **The democratic style** of management takes place when all policies are reached after group discussion and decision, encouraged and facilitated by the manager. In the **laissez-faire style,** subordinates have complete freedom for group or individual decisions where the manager does not take part in matters related to work. An executive housekeeper exerting the same leadership style in all circumstances will most likely fail to achieve optimum results in the workplace. As different problems require different solutions, a flexible approach should be used when leading people. For instance, if a houseperson refuses to perform a task necessary for the normal operation of the department, the manager should compel the worker to do the job. On the other

Lobby, The St. Regis Hotel, New York
Courtesy of Starwood Hotels & Resorts Worldwide, Inc.

hand, if the same houseperson is performing the job satisfactorily, the manager should allow the worker to do the job without interfering.

Several studies conducted to identify leadership traits have yielded a series of attributes inherent to their personalities. Successful business managers generally are well educated, self-assured, decisive, risk takers, power seekers, problem solvers, and good in their relationships with people. Besides these attributes, executive housekeepers should be good motivators, good communicators, good delegators, and good administrators of their invested power/authority.

COMMUNICATION

The fundamental function of communication is to link people together in organizations in order to achieve a common purpose. The activity of a group would be impossible without good communication because without it coordination could not be effected. One of the attributes executive housekeepers must have is the ability to determine when and what to communicate to whom, as well as to know the available means for information transfer, including the use of both formal and informal avenues.

Communication depends on the way different people perceive messages, and even ideas. Workers of diverse geographical or ethnic backgrounds might interpret differently concepts such as "clean," "on time," or "efficient." Executive housekeepers must have the ability to convey messages to all employees so that they are unequivocally understood.

Housekeeping managers spend most of their working time talking and listening to others; in some cases communicating represents about 80 percent of the work day. This volume and intensity of communication requires that hospitality students become proficient in sharing meaning and understanding with others. There are four types of verbal communication: speaking, listening, writing, and reading. Speaking and writing are used to send messages, while listening and reading are used to receive them. Of all these, face-to-face communication is the most effective. Hospitality students should work toward becoming proficient in these communication skills before graduating from college.

In order to avoid one-way communication, managers should strive to convey their message in such a way that employees feel free to express their feelings as well. There is a difference between getting someone to agree with the message sent and showing a willingness to accept possible disagreement. In the first case, we are trying to communicate one way; in the second, we are being open to receive the employee's feedback in return.

Another condition for two-way communication is the ability to understand what someone is trying to say from that person's point of view. In other words, being able to empathize during a conversation is the key element for two people to understand each other.

There can be several roadblocks to effective communication. The **status barrier** can undermine willingness to listen patiently to workers who are perceived as having low social status, as in, for example, the communication process that may take place between a section housekeeper and an engineer who might consider the former "unworthy" to listen to. In this case, it is better to use an impersonal mechanism like a work order to avoid any friction between departments. The **psychological barrier** can cause communication distortion when one of the communicators has a preconceived negative perception of the other person. If front-office personnel perceive housekeeping room attendants as "members of the cleaning brigade," they will always find reasons not to listen attentively to them. In this case, cross-training between the two departments will be necessary for all to understand the importance of the type of job performed by section housekeepers.

Communication breakdowns can also occur when people pass judgment in haste (shooting from the hip), when they seem unapproachable, or when they show displeasure at being interrupted. Cutting in with a quick judgment while workers are explaining something only shows a manager's inability to listen properly and will discourage two-way communication. Not having an open-door policy will discourage workers from engaging in informal conversation, which can be an effective way of learning what is on employees' minds. Interruptions are often nothing but unscheduled exchanges of important information.

Although many managers are good top-down communicators, they often don't have the patience or interest to listen to dissenting views or they don't have good listening skills. In the first case, managers must understand that any views expressed by any employee in the organization might be worth listening to. Managers who are incapable of listening should develop listening skills. Several types of listening are appropriate for different circumstances. **Active listening**, for instance, is necessary when an employee requests information leading to the resolution of a problem. In **passive listening**, on the other hand, the listener expects a nonjudgmental answer or acknowledgment. An employee who is complaining about the lack of cleanliness in the locker rooms requires active listening and specific answers. A worker lamenting the loss of a relative calls for passive listening and perhaps a word of encouragement.

POWER/AUTHORITY

Power is the ability a person has to influence the behavior of others. When power is institutionalized in organizations, the ability to influence the behavior of others becomes a right. This established power is referred to as authority. The use of power should be administered wisely, for individuals generally cannot grow and develop in an atmosphere of overwhelming authority. However, for repetitive work such as housekeeping's, well-defined procedures and a rather strong power base may be most appropriate.

Some managers may have an innate ability to do or affect something; others may resort to their invested authority to get things accomplished. Managers may exert their authority by coercion, reward, suggestion, persuasion, or emulation. **Coercive** and **reward power** refer to situations in which the manager administers punishment or recompense depending on the employee's behavior. Rewards and punishments should be administered fairly and be based on the behavior modification they may effect when applied to workers. **Suggestion** applies when the leader places an idea or proposition before a worker for consideration and possible action. If suggestion doesn't work, the manager may resort to **persuasion**, that is, advising or urging (rather than forcing) a person to do something. The best source of leader power is **emulation**, in which workers want to equal or excel the behavior of a superior. Executive housekeepers who are experts in their fields and possess charismatic behavior generally fit this type of leadership.

DELEGATION

No one should attempt to accomplish effectively the duties of executive housekeeper without delegating to others some of the functions involved in the management of the department.

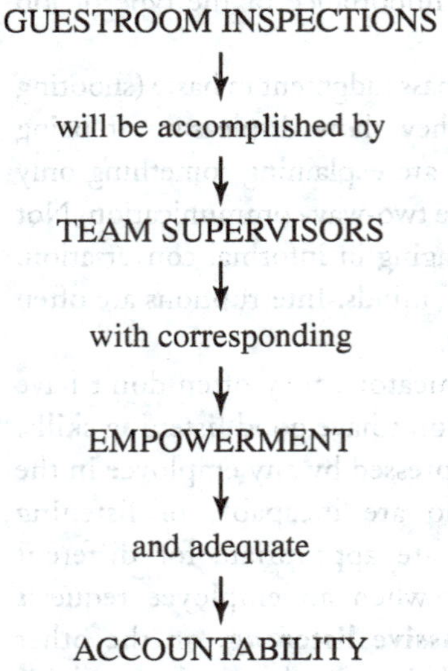

GUESTROOM INSPECTIONS

↓

will be accomplished by

↓

TEAM SUPERVISORS

↓

with corresponding

↓

EMPOWERMENT

↓

and adequate

↓

ACCOUNTABILITY

FIGURE 2.2 Delegation Diagram

Carrying out the responsibility of managing the housekeeping department requires the completion of numerous tasks, most of which are performed by assistants, supervisors, and hourly employees.

Delegation can be defined as the process of assigning work with the necessary authority and accountability to accomplish it effectively. In practice, the process of delegation involves the creation of a relationship in which authority and responsibility are shared between manager and employee to get the job done. When delegation takes place effectively, the manager is left free to coordinate the different activities of the department. There are four steps that must be followed when delegating tasks: defining the task, designating who is to perform the job, empowering the employee to do the job, and requiring accountability for it. Figure 2.2 is a delegation diagram showing a simple delegation process.

Several methods of delegation can be used in the housekeeping department. The manager may decide to define the results expected after the task is accomplished. For instance, the section housekeepers will clean 15 guestrooms efficiently in one eight-hour shift. The manager may set performance standards to be met after the completion of tasks, for example, using guestroom inspection forms indicating levels of cleanliness and décor. The manager may also establish specific procedures to do the job; for instance, breaking down the way to clean a bathtub into components to be followed sequentially by section housekeepers. Some managers find it difficult to delegate authority to others, for reasons that may include lack of trust in employees, unwillingness to invest any of their authority in others, and enjoying hands-on work.

Executive housekeepers must understand that, although authority and responsibility may have been delegated, they are ultimately responsible for the acts of their subordinates. For this very reason, the process of delegation must always be carefully and efficiently administered. Responsibility is ultimately the superior's obligation and cannot be shifted to subordinates. The manager of housekeeping, employed by the company, cannot avoid total responsibility for the results of the department. If employees are negligent in their duties or upset guests, the executive housekeeper must answer to the rooms division director or general manager for these actions.

MANAGEMENT RESPONSIBILITIES OF THE EXECUTIVE HOUSEKEEPER

Beginning with Henri Fayol's proposition 100 years ago, the functions of management have been repeatedly listed with some variations, as planning, organizing, directing, and controlling. There are, however, several other management abilities that executive housekeepers must master to effectively fulfill the numerous responsibilities inherent in their positions. Among those, the management of time, the solution of operational and personnel problems, the achievement of quality, the practice of values, and the ability to make decisions are the most manifest.

TIME MANAGEMENT

Time must be managed proactively by managers in order to be ready for upcoming events rather than having to react to crises. The tasks to be accomplished in the housekeeping department are so numerous that managers often find, to their dismay, that 8, 10, and even 12 hours of work per day are not enough to get the job done. In most cases, too many hours on the job leads to burnout and ultimately even resigning the position.

Job demands in the housekeeping department generally can be categorized into short-term, intermediate-term, or long-term time frames. The short-term demands include day-to-day matters of an operational nature, such as ensuring that the guestrooms are cleaned well and on time, that the soiled linen and napery are processed prior to distribution deadlines, that public areas and offices are cleaned before or after rush hour, and so on. Short-term demands usually require an intense interaction with employees as a large number of activities take place at the same time.

Intermediate-term demands require planning and organizing activities necessary to maintain the cohesiveness and efficiency of the housekeeping department. The training and development of housekeeping employees and the preparation of labor and supply forecasts for upcoming events are typical examples of intermediate-term activities. These activities require not only downward communication but also lateral interaction with other departments of the property. For example, the arrival next month of a large convention would require a review with the sales and front desk departments of the specific steps necessary to coordinate this event.

Long-range forecasting is another important task for executive housekeepers, specifically in the preparation of annual budgets. This process requires the provision of resources for both capital and operational expenditures and foreseeing essential major maintenance and refurbishing projects. Long-term demands require substantial upward communication with the rooms division director, lateral communication with the controller and plant manager, and downward communication with the department supervisors.

The first step in managing time is to chart it. Having a time log, such as a computer program or wall bulletin board where the day's and week's activities are entered, helps one to plan ahead and to be aware of how much time each activity requires to be completed. Computer software such as Microsoft Outlook can be equally effective. Tickler-file systems and phone call screening are some practices that can save precious time.

PROBLEM SOLVING

A problem in the workplace can be defined as any impediment or difficulty that interferes with the regular achievement of goals. Considering the unpredictability and immediacy of situations, the type of employees, and the pace of housekeeping operations, executive housekeepers must possess an extraordinary ability to solve problems swiftly and effectively without resorting to the "shoot-from-the-hip" approach.

The first step to effective problem solving is to identify the real issue. For instance, if the laundry department is chronically behind in producing clean linen, the laundry workers might be blamed for it, although the real cause could be obsolete laundry equipment. Once problems have been clearly identified, their solution can be attempted individually or collectively. When the solution seems clear and the manager does not see any need for the input of others, problems should be solved by the managers themselves. Such is the case when dealing with inanimate economic and technical aspects of operating the department. When the problem deals with human aspects, the task becomes more difficult and judgmental and usually needs the involvement of others. In collective problem solving, the manager's role is to foster ideas, then guide the process to its conclusion. Brainstorming is an effective technique aimed at eliciting group input by discussion in order to find solutions to problems.

The solution of problems can be facilitated by *empowering* employees to do whatever is necessary, within reason, to resolve problems for the guest rather than to shift the problem upward to management. Some workers may be reluctant to solve problems for fear of making mistakes or assuming too much authority. In these cases, employees need to be invested with some leeway to make their own decision in uncomplicated cases.

TOTAL QUALITY MANAGEMENT (TQM)

Quality control has been a major concern in American businesses for a very long time, since companies long ago realized that quality standards for any given product are ultimately established by the customer. However, while manufacturing companies in general concern themselves mainly with the quality of mechanical processes, lodging operations must concern themselves with both product and service quality.

The principles of total quality management (TQM) that apply to housekeeping operations are: understanding customer requirements, measuring customer satisfaction, empowering employees, and focusing on the continuous improvement of the search for quality. Housekeeping managers in lodging operations must be aware of the expectations of the traveling public when staying in their properties. Cleanliness, firm mattresses, fluffy towels, appropriate amenities, and friendly service are generally ranked as top requirements for the American traveler. In locations where the customer base is different from the norm, surveys should be conducted to find out guests' expectations. For instance, a property that regularly receives large numbers of tourists from Japan may want to know what pleases Japanese guests, whose tastes might differ from those of, say, Canadian customers.

Guests' input should be sought regularly to find out whether they are pleased with the accommodations and services offered. Comment cards and personal interaction with guests will provide the information the department needs to measure guest satisfaction. Although I have stayed in numerous lodging properties, including four- and five-star hotels and resorts, I have never been approached by a housekeeping manager or supervisor to find out if my room was prepared to my liking. These relationships with guests should be the rule in lodging operations rather than the exception.

Empowering employees to take initiative in customer satisfaction is essential to quality management. In order to achieve this, employees should be given greater decision-making latitude and be given twice the necessary training to enable them to make reasonable decisions. This TQM approach generally results in a streamlined chain of command and in workers taking responsibility for their own work performance.

The concept of TQM also implies that the process of striving for excellence is not finite—it is about constantly improving and innovating. Avoiding errors, not fixing them, should be a never-ending process. Well-implemented TQM programs can also provide tangible savings to housekeeping operations. For instance, section housekeepers who are committed to quality could conduct the final inspection of their own rooms before giving them to the front desk for occupation, thus eliminating the need for a designated inspector.

Suite Hotel Indigo San Diego, IHG
Courtesy of Six Continents Hotels, Inc.

ETHICAL VALUES

It is the manager's obligation to follow those lines of action that are acceptable in terms of the values of society. The concept of ethics should, therefore, be mainly concerned with the social responsibilities of managers. The reality of this, however, is quite difficult to grasp because there are no nationally recognized ethical standards. With regard to the behavior of executive housekeepers as department managers, "ethics" could be referred to as high standards of professional conduct, affecting matters such as sexual harassment, equal opportunity, privacy rights, racial discrimination, and making decisions that affect people's lives: all these fall within the realm of values in the workplace.

Some guidelines for ethical behavior in the workplace include:

1. Be honest in relationships with others.
2. Enhance the human dignity of workers.

3. Respect employees as individual human beings.
4. Understand the needs and concerns of employees.
5. Observe the law.
6. Be accountable for your decisions.
7. Create a good reputation as a manager.
8. Be fair and equitable.
9. Show integrity in business transactions.

The ethical reputation of companies is often determined by the behavior of the managers who work for them. Housekeeping managers should make reasonable efforts to foresee possible negative ethical consequences that would mar the reputation of their companies, their guests, and their subordinates.

DECISION MAKING

Choosing from among alternatives for a course of action is called decision making. One of the executive housekeeper's central jobs is to prioritize what needs to be done, who will do it, where, and even how. The process of decision making involves the identification of what needs to be accomplished, the search for possible alternatives, the evaluation of these alternatives, and the selection and implementation of the best one by which the job can be done. Managers should avoid making rapid-fire decisions that often fall short of the desired target.

Good managers often decide to accomplish a job cost-effectively in order to maximize profits; however, the needs, attitudes, and prejudices of people must be taken into account. For example, an executive housekeeper may decide to improve the labor cost percentage of the department by laying off two full-time workers and hiring four part-time employees without benefits to do the same job. While the results may be positive in the short run, the reaction of the remaining full-time workers may be quite negative, as they might perceive the company as not taking the welfare of its people into account.

One way to improve decision making is by getting employees involved in the process. This method usually draws on different viewpoints and motivates people to be cooperative in carrying out an idea. Indeed, some companies use the concept of **quality circles**, in which total worker involvement is sought in the decision-making process as well as in matters related to production and quality.

KEY TERMS

Active listening	Democratic leadership style
Authoritarian leadership style	Elton Mayo
Classic scientific management	Emulation
Coercive power	Frederick Taylor

Henri Fayol
Human relations management
Laissez-faire management style
Long-range objectives
Persuasion power
Psychological barrier
Quality circles

Reward power
Short-range objectives
Span of control
Status barrier
Suggestive power
Unity of command

DISCUSSION AND REVIEW QUESTIONS

1. Why should executive housekeepers have great concern for production as well as for people in the workplace?

2. When planning activities in the housekeeping department, what could be a short-range objective? A long-range objective?

3. Describe the principle of unity of command and explain why it should be adopted in housekeeping operations.

4. Give a practical example of the control process as a management function in housekeeping operations.

5. When managing employees, what is the difference between authoritarian and laissez-faire styles?

6. When communicating verbally with employees, when would you listen actively and when passively?

7. What are the advantages and disadvantages of empowering hourly employees in the housekeeping department?

8. Explain a practical way of implementing total quality management (TQM) in the housekeeping department.

9. In your opinion, why should executive housekeepers follow an ethical code of professional conduct in the workplace?

10. Describe both an ethical example and an unethical example of professional conduct of a housekeeping manager.

11. Why would you, as an executive housekeeper, adopt quality circles in your department?

MINICASES

SITUATION 1

George Sandoval, housekeeping manager at the Royal Hotel, wrote the following memo regarding operations in the laundry department of the hotel: "The level of productivity of laundry workers has been very low lately. On two occasions, there has not been enough linen to go around and the section housekeepers have had to wait for sheets and pillowcases to set up the beds. Beginning today, the 30-minute mid-morning break will be reduced to 15 minutes in order to increase productivity. I will be checking the laundry room often to make sure that everyone is on task at all times. We must have the clean linen out fast every morning!" (a) How would you evaluate George's attitude regarding his concern for production? (b) How would you evaluate George's attitude regarding his concern for people? (c) What would you have done in George's place?

SITUATION 2

After graduating from a hotel and restaurant management school, Christie Wilson accepted the position of assistant to the executive housekeeper at a mid-market hotel on the East Coast. Christie's responsibilities included supervising 80 housekeeping employees, filling in for team supervisors when they called in sick, conducting inventories, preparing weekly time cards, and assisting her boss in the overall management of the department. The first month was spent becoming familiar with the department procedures and getting acquainted with her fellow employees. After the training period, Christie got more and more involved with the routine duties of the housekeepers, housepersons, and laundry workers. If they had a problem, she would immediately get personally involved in finding the solution. In time, her performance began to deteriorate as she had to deal with the tasks described in her job description plus the problems her subordinates were having.

After a while, complaints began to pour in from the accounts department, the front desk, and top management about paperwork being backlogged and errors being committed regularly. Christie began to find herself becoming jumpy and restless at the onset of any minor crisis. Her employees started filing complaints with the executive housekeeper, who thought that Christie would work out her problems as she continued to gain experience on the job. This turned out not to be the case. After six months on the job, Christie had a nervous breakdown and decided that it was a mistake to have accepted the assistant manager position. (a) What did Christie do wrong from the beginning? (b) What recommendation do you have for Christie as she begins to look for another job with a lodging company?

SITUATION 3

You are a housekeeping manager in a resort in the Southwest. You have received several complaints about supervisor Johnson repeatedly asking female employees for dates after work. After discussing the problem with Johnson, he becomes defensive, saying that he will quit the job if you keep bothering him about his personal relationships with his fellow workers. Because Johnson is a very dedicated, productive employee, you decide not to pay any attention to the complaints lest you end up losing this otherwise excellent supervisor. (a) Are you behaving ethically in this particular situation? (b) Why or why not?

CASE STUDY 1

The Need to Maximize Productivity in the Housekeeping Department

Once upon a time, there was a donkey standing knee-deep in a field of carrots, contentedly munching away. The farmer wanted the donkey to pull a loaded cart but the donkey would not walk over to it. The farmer stood by the cart and held a bunch of carrots for the donkey to see, but the donkey continued to munch away on the carrots on the field.

Once upon a time, a farmer had four donkeys and a barn full of carrots that she kept under lock and key. At the end of the day of cart pulling, the farmer looked over the day's performance of each donkey. To one of the donkeys she said: "You did an outstanding job; here are six carrots for you." To two of the others she said: "Your performance was average;

here are three carrots.'' To the last donkey she said: ''You didn't pull the share of the load; here is one carrot.''

Assignment

Pretend that the farmer in this case was the executive housekeeper of a large hotel.

1. Why did she act this way?
2. What would the top donkey, average-performing donkeys, and worst-performing donkey think before beginning to work the following day?
3. Compose a similar situation in a housekeeping setting where the above story can be applied.

CASE STUDY 2

Ethical Behavior of Housekeeping Managers

Tom Armenta is executive housekeeper of a small resort in a small town in the Midwest. The establishment has an excellent reputation and no direct competition. As a result, business is good and the income before taxes for the last five years has been above the industry average. Tom is considered a very good manager by the company and receives substantial bonuses for achieving, and sometimes bettering, the departmental budgeted bottom line. Tom considers himself very lucky to be operating in an area of abundant worker supply because of the absence of other resorts in the area. The property as a whole has been able to maintain very low expenses in the categories of salaries and employee benefits.

The hourly employees in the department, however, do not consider themselves so fortunate. Those in need of medical care cannot easily cover their health expenses with the wages paid by the resort. Last week, a group of employees representing all hourly workers asked to meet with Tom to request that the company offer medical insurance benefits as part of the compensation package. After making the necessary calculations, the executive housekeeper determined that the departmental profit before income taxes would diminish from 27 to 23 percent. This reduction would prevent Tom's receipt of his 12 percent bonus.

After consultation with the resort's general manager, both decided that the supply of local workers would guarantee a sufficient number of applicants willing to work for the compensation the resort currently offers. Tom's thinking was that as a manager, his job is to maximize profit while complying with existing labor laws.

Assignment

1. Discuss the case and decide whether Tom Armenta behaved ethically.
2. Did the resort general manager act ethically by denying the housekeeping workers medical benefits to maintain the 27 percent departmental income?
3. What would the reaction of the employees be?

CASE STUDY 3

Reward Power in a Housekeeping Operation

Kristin Rivkin was a successful executive housekeeper in a downtown hotel in Toledo, Ohio. One of the reasons for her commendable achievements as a leader was the system of rewards that she had had approved by the general manager and put in place to compensate employee performance. She had established a bonus scale that was tied to a point system in which workers received extra money for good performance—for example, arriving to work on time, lack of absenteeism, going the extra step to service guests, suggesting ways to improve operations, and higher-than-average productivity. Employees worked very hard to obtain points that translated into extra cash over their minimum wages at the end of the pay period. Kristin had demonstrated to her superiors that the bonus system in place was well worth the high productivity achieved, the better-than-average employee retention, and the achievement of superior customer service. In fact, the profit percentage of her department was the highest of all the company's properties. Considered to be a star, Kristin was asked to manage the housekeeping department of a larger hotel that the company was opening in Phoenix, Arizona. Kristin accepted and was transferred with a substantial raise in salary.

A new manager was quickly hired to replace Kristin. Although relatively new in the industry, Bryan Samuelson held a degree from a hotel and restaurant management program and was proud of having finished his academic work with a 3.8 GPA in hi major. On taking over the management of the department, Bryan was surprised to find in place the bonus/compensation system initiated by Kristin. He remembered from his college courses that rewards could be used with employees in some occasions but that this type of management power was likely to erode if workers expected to be rewarded for any extra effort put in their jobs. He decided to get rid of the system and replace it with a more equitable way of rewarding performance.

Knowing that it would be difficult to take away a recompense system that had been in place for a long period of time, Bryan decided to increase employee wages across the board before eliminating the bonus/performance method. His goal was to motivate employees to put extra effort in their work by paying them a better wage.

Three months into the implementation of his plan, Bryan realized that his system had failed; productivity was down, absenteeism was up, and customer satisfaction had deteriorated to dangerous levels. Bryan was flabbergasted, wondering what had gone wrong in the process.

Assignment

1. Discuss this case and determine how reward power was used by the two managers.
2. In your opinion, who was a better administrator, Kristin Rivkin or Bryan Samuelson?
3. Explain what you would have done if you had replaced Kristin as a manager.
4. Determine what Bryan should do after finding out that his changes had not worked as expected.

Organization of the Housekeeping Department

Chapter 3: Design of the Housekeeping Department

PART

2

Section housekeeper, Shanghai Marriott
Courtesy of Marriott International, Inc.

Design of the Housekeeping Department

CHAPTER OBJECTIVES

- Define the areas of housekeeping responsibility in large properties.
- Discuss the need for establishing area cleaning inventories, frequency schedules, and performance standards.
- Describe the process of dividing the guestroom cleaning staff into teams.
- Explain the composition of a staffing matrix for a large hotel.
- Describe the process of setting up a Housekeeping Need table.
- Explain how to set up standing schedules for the different housekeeping teams.
- Describe how the number of workers is adjusted daily based on occupancy.
- Discuss the alternative methods of scheduling employees in the housekeeping department.
- Describe technology associated with the housekeeping department.

OVERVIEW

This chapter describes the design of the housekeeping department, beginning with the definition of its areas of responsibility. Although in small properties executive housekeepers may be in charge of servicing most areas, in large establishments the areas of responsibility should be limited to guestrooms, offices, public areas, back-of-the-house spaces, employee locker rooms and cafeteria, laundry, and linen rooms.

Once the areas of responsibility have been established (what is to be cleaned), the executive housekeeper needs to determine how often they are to be cleaned, and to what degree. The purpose of this planning activity is to provide workers with specific guidelines about how the different cleaning tasks should be performed. The property's guestrooms should then be divided into sections and the sections grouped into teams, determining how many teams will be needed to service the property while giving employees two days off every week. An example of a staffing matrix for large hotels is provided in this chapter.

The housekeeping department must prepare the rooms for incoming guests as soon as possible. Although guests are expected to check out around noon and to check in after 2 P.M., this does not always happen. It is not uncommon for convention and resort properties to have most of the guestrooms in the house depart at midday and receive a large number of guests right at the same time. When one considers that the rooms must be thoroughly cleaned and inspected in such a short period of time, it is clear that the scheduling of employees in lodging properties can be very difficult indeed. Because labor is the largest housekeeping expense, the executive housekeeper must be sure not to overschedule the department's workforce, for calling too many employees to work results in decreased departmental profit. On the other hand, not having enough section housekeepers to quickly turn over ready rooms to the front desk will result in incoming guests having to wait in the lobby until enough rooms are available for check-in. Thus, understaffing the department to save on labor expense may also cause guest dissatisfaction and an eventual loss of business. When scheduling workers, the executive housekeeper must combine the need to provide adequate coverage to clean the guestrooms effectively with ensuring fairness to employees and achieving an adequate departmental profit. This chapter ends with a brief review of housekeeping management systems available.

AREAS OF HOUSEKEEPING RESPONSIBILITY

When organizing the internal structure of lodging properties, the identification of cleaning and maintenance responsibilities for every area of the hotel is a prerequisite. All spaces of the property must be assigned by upper management to the different operating departments that are then charged with keeping their respective areas in a perfect state of cleanliness and maintenance. Ideally, in order not to leave any space unassigned, the various cleaning and maintenance area boundaries are marked on a copy of the property's blueprint.

The areas of responsibility of the housekeeping department will be different depending on the size of the property. In small lodging operations the executive housekeeper is usually in charge of the cleaning and upkeep of most areas. In this particular case, very close cooperation between housekeeping and other departments is necessary to have the job done efficiently. For instance, if housekeeping is in charge of cleaning the banquet rooms, the manager needs to know the type and time of functions in order to provide the necessary service. In some cases, because the preparation and service of food begin very early in the morning and end quite late in the evening, the cleaning function in food and beverage areas must be provided late at night.

In large properties, the division of work by area is spread out among the different operating departments. Often some of the cleaning functions—such as cleaning the kitchen, restaurant, and grounds—are contracted out to outside companies. Before contracting out cleaning tasks, it is important to obtain cost estimates from two or three different sources based on the size of the areas and the type and frequency of the cleaning desired. Once the contract has been signed, it is essential to check the quality of the work performed by the contractor. In no case should the cost of the services contracted be substantially higher than the cost of the same services performed by in-house personnel. An ideal division of work in large properties would keep the housekeeping department from having to clean areas that are operated by the food and beverage or engineering divisions. There are several reasons for this: the housekeeping department usually does not have the necessary technical resources, the time, or the expertise to clean ovens, walk-in refrigerators, kitchen hoods, and swimming pools, or to prune palm trees and trim rose bushes. An ideal distribution of cleaning and maintenance responsibilities in large hotels may be:

Area	Department Responsible
Guestrooms, including hallways, ending areas, elevators, stairwells, and floor closets	Housekeeping
Public areas, including lobbies, front desk, main entrance, corridors, restrooms, game and exercise rooms, and shops	Housekeeping
Offices	Housekeeping
Employee areas, including locker rooms, cafeterias, and restrooms	Housekeeping
Laundry room	Housekeeping
Linen room	Housekeeping
Housekeeping storage areas	Housekeeping
Recreation areas, including pools, tennis courts, volleyball courts, etc.	Engineering
Grounds, including parking lot, parking garages, trees, landscaping, and sidewalks	Engineering
Maintenance shop	Engineering
Food and beverage service, including restaurants, coffee shops, bars, and cocktail lounges	Food & Beverage*
Kitchens	Food & Beverage*
Banquets, including ballrooms, meeting rooms, and exhibition halls	Banquets

*Often these outlets are contracted out to outside cleaning contractors. Cleaning areas of difficult accessibility, such as windows in high-rise buildings, may also be assigned to outside cleaning services.

Once the cleaning and maintenance responsibilities for all the areas of the property have been established, the respective department heads must plan the activities necessary for the upkeep of their areas, secure sufficient resources, and provide personnel to service them effectively.

AREA CLEANING INVENTORIES

The first step in planning the upkeep of the different areas assigned to the housekeeping department is to establish a list of the items that need to be regularly cleaned and maintained. A cleaning inventory list for guestrooms, for instance, will include all items that need to be cleaned, checked, and maintained in each room. The list should follow the sequence that section housekeepers keep when servicing guestrooms, for example, beginning with the entrance door to the rooms, standing lamps, window sills, furniture, and so on, and ending with vacuuming the carpet. Another example of cleaning inventory would be that drawn for the lobby of the hotel, which might include not only furniture and fixtures but also water fountain, plants, bookcase, chandelier, and so on. Area cleaning inventories should be combined with cleaning frequency schedules, including what needs to be cleaned and how often the items must be cleaned in one single document.

CLEANING FREQUENCY SCHEDULE

Once the area cleaning inventory lists have been prepared, the frequency for cleaning and maintenance of each item should be established. Figure 3.1 shows a sample area cleaning inventory and frequency schedule. Generally, items need to be cleaned daily, biweekly, weekly, monthly, and so on. An example of items in need of daily service in the lobby area would be the windowsills; plants could be dusted twice a week, the water fountain polished once a week, the air vents on the wall once a month, and so forth. Besides cleaning items on a regular basis, most areas are **deep cleaned** once or twice a year. In this case, the cleaning crews scrape and scrub every nook and cranny until all surfaces are spotless. Deep-cleaning projects generally coincide with low-occupancy periods and are coordinated with repairs being done in the area by the engineering department.

PERFORMANCE STANDARDS

After compiling cleaning inventories and frequency schedules, performance standards must be established. Performance standards are used to inform subordinates of the equipment and

FIGURE 3.1 Sample Area Cleaning Inventory and Frequency Schedule—Lobby

ITEM	ACTIVITY	FREQUENCY
Carpet	Vacuumed	Daily
Furniture	Dusted	Daily
Furniture	Polished	Daily
Chandelier	Dusted	Bimonthly
Lamps	Dusted	Bimonthly
Wood Paneling	Polished	Monthly
Sconces	Dusted	Weekly
Water Fountain	S/S Cleaned	Biweekly
Sand Ashtrays	Cleaned	Twice daily
Air Vents	Dusted	Monthly
Hallway	Stripped/Waxed	Monthly

Holiday Inn Express & Suites Costa Mesa, IHG
Courtesy of Six Continents Hotels, Inc.

supplies they must use to clean an item, of the method or way of doing the job, and of the expected cleaning outcomes. It is not good enough to tell section housekeepers and public areas attendants to "clean well." "Cleaning well" may mean different levels of cleanliness to different people. An example of a performance standard to clean a vanity top could be: "Spray all-purpose cleaner on the vanity top and wipe the surface clean with a sanitized rag, wiping it dry until no spots, marks, or specks remain."

The development of cleaning performance standards should be established keeping in mind the direct input of the workers who are assigned to do the cleaning. The written cleaning standards should be a part of the department's **standard operating procedures** (SOPs) and strictly observed during the training period of new employees. Properties that have written cleaning standards in place are able to measure employee performance by comparing the worker cleaning outcomes with the established standards.

DIVISION OF GUESTROOMS

The assignment of guestrooms for daily cleaning is usually done randomly in small hotels. That is, the section housekeepers are gathered at the beginning of the shift and given a number of rooms to service on an individual basis. In large hotels, however, **housekeeping teams** should be formed to which the same sections of rooms are consistently assigned. There are several

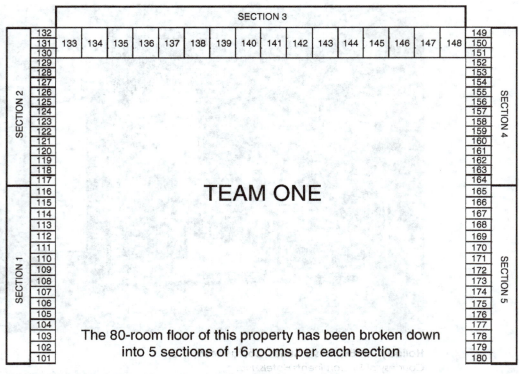

FIGURE 3.2 Sample Guest Room Breakout into Cleaning Sections

advantages to allotting the guestrooms to teams. Individual housekeepers take ownership of the rooms they clean day in and day out, showing pride in the work they perform, which increases their morale. Teams create a sense of unity, of common interests and responsibilities (esprit de corps) by which room attendants are less likely to let their partners down by calling in sick, thus improving attendance. A team may consist of four or five **section housekeepers**, a **team supervisor**, and a **houseperson**. The section housekeeper cleans guestrooms, while the supervisor coordinates the work of the teams and inspects rooms. The housepersons assist in the work by providing the team with supplies, hauling the trash, vacuuming the hallways, moving heavy objects around, and so on.

Guestrooms are divided by creating a pictorial representation of all rooms and allocating a certain number of them to every section housekeeper of each team. Figure 3.2 shows a floor plan layout of a large hotel in which the sections have been delimited to include 16 rooms per room attendant. The criteria for guestroom cleaning workload vary from hotel to hotel depending on the size of the rooms, the number of furniture and fixture pieces to be cleaned, and the level of quality that management wishes to provide. Generally, a property with small rooms (such as Motel 6 or Econolodge) allocates about 18 rooms per section housekeeper for an eight-hour shift. Properties with average-size rooms assign around 16, while establishments with large rooms or suites allocate about 12 units per shift.

As an example, a 400-room property that assigns 16 rooms to one section housekeeper and that groups the section housekeepers in teams of five would have the following workload distribution at 100 percent occupancy:

Number of teams: **5** ($400 \div 16 = 25$; $25 \div 5 = 5$)

Number of section housekeepers: **25** ($400 \div 16 = 25$)

Number of team supervisors: **5** (one per team)

Number of housepersons: **5** (one per team)

In this particular example, the assignment of five teams to clean the rooms works perfectly. But what would happen if the hotel continues to operate at 100 percent occupancy for some time? As the workers need to be given two days off per week to avoid overtime, the department will need a larger number of workers to substitute for those who are off. The problem becomes more complicated if the property operates an **on-premise laundry**. Let us suppose that this is the case and that the laundry is operated by one full team consisting of five section housekeepers, one supervisor, and one houseperson. In this case, as the hotel is open seven days a week and the employees work only five, the total number of teams, section housekeepers, supervisors, and housepersons needed to clean the guestrooms and operate the laundry will be as follows:

25 section housekeepers needed to clean the rooms + 5 to operate laundry = 30 workers

30 workers × 7 days per week of operation = 210 man/days

210 man/days ÷ 5 days per week employees work = 42 workers needed

The minimum number of teams and workers needed to cover guestroom cleaning and laundry operation is now:

Number of teams: **8** ($42 \div 5 = 8$)

Number of section housekeepers: **42**

Number of supervisors: **8**

Number of housepersons: **8**

The distribution of teams on any given day that the hotel is full will be:

Teams assigned to guestroom cleaning: **5** ($400 \div 16 = 25$; $25 \div 5 = 5$)

One team to operate laundry: **1**

Two teams off duty: **2**

Total teams: **8**

This example property will need eight teams to operate efficiently.

STAFFING MATRIX

The internal organization of the housekeeping department follows the same pattern as that of the property as a whole. The chain of command begins with the executive housekeeper and goes on to encompass all employees in the department. Figure 3.3 is a typical organization chart for the housekeeping department of a large hotel.

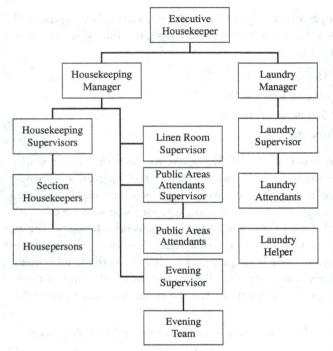

FIGURE 3.3 Sample Organizational Chart for the Housekeeping Department

Besides the section housekeepers, supervisors, and housepersons needed to clean the guestrooms, and the laundry room workers, the housekeeping department needs additional personnel to service other areas of the property, such as offices, public and back-of-the-house sections, and linen room. The employees in the department's work force can be classified into **management, fixed, evening, laundry, and guestroom cleaning teams**. The executive housekeeper, housekeeping manager (assistant to the executive housekeeper), and laundry manager fall under management. These employees are salaried and are required to work a minimum of 40 hours each week. The housekeeping fixed employees are the public areas attendants and the linen room attendants. These workers are usually hourly employees who are guaranteed five days' work regardless of guestroom occupancy. The reason for guaranteeing fixed work is that whether or not the guestrooms have been sold out, lobbies, offices and other front and back-of-the-house public areas must be serviced on a daily basis. The evening team takes over the duties of the department at the end of the morning shift when all regular teams clock off. The jobs generally assigned to the evening shift are cleaning late checkout and day-rate guestrooms, providing turndown service, counting soiled linen, servicing public and back-of-the-house areas, preparing carts for the morning shift, washing guestroom glasses, and filling out guest requests as the evening progresses. As with the public areas attendants, the evening team is composed of hourly employees who are guaranteed five days of work regardless of occupancy. The guest room cleaning and laundry teams are also composed of hourly employees, but the number of hours they are scheduled to work depends on the number of guestrooms sold daily. For instance, if the hotel is full, all section housekeepers who are not off duty that day will be needed to clean all guestrooms, but if the occupancy drops to 80 percent, only enough section housekeepers to clean 80 percent of the guestrooms will be called to work. Figure 3.4 is a sample staffing matrix for a hotel with on-premise laundry that needs five regular teams to clean guestrooms, one laundry team, and two relief teams to cover days off.

SECTION HOUSEKEEPER NEED TABLE

The scheduling of employees for guestroom cleaning and laundry operation is done taking into account the property's daily occupancy. If the establishment is full today and at three-fourths occupancy tomorrow, all guestroom-cleaning and laundry personnel will be scheduled to work tomorrow but only 75 percent of the workers should be asked to work the day after. For example, a 400-room property having 16 of its rooms cleaned by one

FIGURE 3.4 Sample Staffing Matrix for the Housekeeping Department of a Large Property.

Management
  1 Executive housekeeper
  1 Housekeeping manager
  1 Laundry manager
Fixed
  1 Linen room supervisor
  1 Public areas attendant
  4 Public areas attendants
Evening Team
  1 Evening supervisor
  2 Section housekeepers
  2 Public areas attendants
  1 Houseperson
Regular Team One
  1 Housekeeping team supervisor
  5 Section housekeepers
  1 Houseperson
Regular Team Two
  1 Housekeeping team supervisor
  5 Section housekeepers
  1 Houseperson
Regular Team Three
  1 Housekeeping team supervisor
  5 Section housekeepers
  1 Houseperson

Regular Team Four
  1 Housekeeping team supervisor
  5 Section housekeepers
  1 Houseperson
Regular Team Five
  1 Housekeeping team supervisor
  5 Section housekeepers
  1 Houseperson
Laundry Team
  1 Laundry supervisor
  5 Laundry attendants
  1 Laundry helper
Relief Team One
  1 Housekeeping supervisor
  5 Section housekeepers
  1 Houseperson
Relief Team Two
  1 Housekeeping supervisor
  5 Section housekeepers
  1 Houseperson

This staffing matrix covers all housekeeping positions for a lodging property with on-premise laundry that needs five regular teams, a laundry team, and two relief teams to operate. The property would also need a fixed team to service public areas, back of the house and offices, and an evening team.

section housekeeper in one 8-hour shift will schedule the room attendants on a particular week as follows:

Day of the week	% Occupancy	Rooms to be cleaned	Section housekeepers
Monday	80	?	?
Tuesday	100	320 (400 × .80)	20 (320: 16)
Wednesday	75	400 (400 × 1.0)	25 (400: 16)
Thursday	90	300 (400 × .75)	19 (300: 16)
Friday	40	360 (400 × .90)	23 (360: 16)
Saturday	40	160 (400 × .40)	10 (160: 16)
Sunday	90	160 (400 × .40)	10 (160: 16)
Monday	?	360 (400 × .90)	23 (360: 16)

TABLE 3.1 Sample Section Housekeeper Needs[a]

Percent of Occupancy	Rooms to Be Cleaned	Section Housekeepers Needed/Day	Hours/ Day	Hours/ Week	Hours/ Month
100 (400 × 1.0)	400 (÷ 16)	25 (× 8)	200 (× 7)	1,400	6,000
95 (400 × .95)	380 (÷ 16)	24 (× 8)	192 (× 7)	1,344	5,760
90 (400 × .90)	360 (÷ 16)	22 (× 8)	176 (× 7)	1,232	5,280
85 (400 × .85)	340 (÷ 16)	21 (× 8)	168 (× 7)	1,176	5,040
80 (400 × .80)	320 (÷ 16)	20 (× 8)	160 (× 7)	1,120	4,800
75 (400 × .75)	300 (÷ 16)	19 (× 8)	152 (× 7)	1,064	4,560
70 (400 × .70)	280 (÷ 16)	17 (× 8)	136 (× 7)	952	4,080
65 (400 × .65)	260 (÷ 16)	16 (× 8)	128 (× 7)	896	3,840
60 (400 × .60)	240 (÷ 16)	15 (× 8)	120 (× 7)	840	3,600
55 (400 × .55)	220 (÷ 16)	14 (× 8)	112 (× 7)	784	3,360
50 (400 × .50)	200 (÷ 16)	12 (× 8)	96 (× 7)	672	2,880
45 (400 × .45)	180 (÷ 16)	11 (× 8)	88 (× 7)	616	2,640
40 (400 × .40)	160 (÷ 16)	10 (× 8)	80 (× 7)	560	2,400
35 (400 × .35)	140 (÷ 16)	9 (× 8)	72 (× 7)	504	2,160
30 (400 × .30)	120 (÷ 16)	8 (× 8)	64 (× 7)	448	1,920
25 (400 × .25)	100 (÷ 16)	6 (× 8)	48 (× 7)	336	1,440
20 (400 × .20)	80 (÷ 16)	5 (×8)	40 (× 7)	280	1,200

[a]For a 400-room property with a workload criterion of 16 rooms cleaned by each room attendant in one 8-hour shift.

Executive housekeepers should compile a **section housekeeper need table** establishing the number of room attendants required for each level of occupancy. The table can also be extended to include the number of hours that section housekeepers generate per day, per week, and per month. This information may be valuable to anticipate the **cost of labor** in any specific period of time. The cost of labor can be worked out by multiplying the number of hours by the average hourly wage paid to section housekeepers. The accounting office provides the **average hourly wage** to the housekeeping department on a regular base. Table 3.1 shows the number of room attendants needed per day at different levels of occupancy considering a workload of 16 rooms per section housekeeper in one 8-hour shift. The table also provides the hours of work generated per day, per week, and per month. As an example, let us consider an 80 percent level of occupancy. In this case, the number of rooms to be cleaned is 320 (400 × .80); the number of section housekeepers needed to clean the rooms is 20 (320 ÷ 16); the number of hours worked for the day is 160 (20 × 8); if the same occupancy were to be considered for one week, the hours generated would be 1,120 (160 × 7); if the occupancy were 80 percent for one month, the hours would be 4,800 (160 × 30). An estimated cost for section housekeepers can be anticipated by multiplying the forecasted hours by the average dollars per hour paid to these employees. For instance, if the average hourly wage paid to section housekeepers in this example were $8, the cost to clean guestrooms, at 80 percent occupancy would be $1,280 per day (160 × 8), $8,960 per week (1,120 × 8), and $38,400 per month (4,800 × 8).

STANDING SCHEDULES

The function of scheduling workers in the housekeeping department is of great importance. The manager must juggle several factors in order to protect the interests of the company, fulfill the individual needs of the workers, and provide guest satisfaction. To protect the company's interests, the manager must schedule the minimum number of workers to achieve an optimum labor cost percentage, because the more employees called to work, the greater the payroll cost will be. At the same time, employees have all types of individual requests: some of them may prefer to have weekends off; others may insist that they will not settle for less than rotating days off; others will need fixed days off every week to match those of their spouse. In any case, scheduling must be always done with the ultimate goal in mind of providing efficient service to the property's guests.

The first step in housekeeping scheduling is to prepare a matrix showing the scheduled consecutive days off for the **guestroom-cleaning teams**, **laundry teams**, and **relief teams**. Figure 3.5 shows the scheduled days off for a 400-room hotel that needs a total of five regular teams for guestroom cleaning, one team to operate the laundry, and two relief teams. The relief teams cover the days off of the regular and laundry teams and have two consecutive days off themselves. In this sample case the largest occupancy occurs Monday through Thursday, while the weakest days are Friday through Sunday (common in most business properties). If occupancy were consistently high seven days a week, a third relief team might be necessary to cover five additional days of work. In the example shown in Figure 3.5, Team One is off Saturday and Sunday and Team Two Monday and Tuesday, covered by Relief Team One. Relief Team One also covers one of the days off of Team Three (Wednesday) and is off itself on Thursday and Friday.

After the standing team schedule is done, a similar matrix should be prepared for the two consecutive days off of the fixed and evening teams. Figure 3.6 shows a sample **standing schedule** for these teams. In this example, the days off of the Linen Room Supervisor and the Evening Team Supervisor are covered by the Housekeeping Manager (Assistant Executive Housekeeper). An alternative to this would be to hire a relief supervisor to cover these shifts.

ROTATIONAL SCHEDULES

An alternative to standing schedules is rotating forward the teams' days off by one day each week. This means that if Team One is off Monday and Tuesday this week, next week the team will be off Tuesday and Wednesday. The only advantage of **rotational schedules** is to ensure that all teams will eventually have a weekend off. On the other hand, the disadvantages are substantial; workers will not be able to commit themselves to activities outside the workplace, they will not be able to secure stable babysitting help, or it will be impossible for them to have the same day off as their spouses. For example, a student who has to attend classes on Tuesdays and Wednesdays will not appreciate rotating days off at work. A working mother who relies on sending her child to a nursery Monday through Friday might not be able to find childcare on weekends. A worker who needs Wednesday and Thursday off to match her husband's days off will not be willing to work these days.

ADJUSTED DAILY SCHEDULE

The purpose of standing schedules, as described above, is to designate which days the working teams are off and which days they are scheduled to work. However, guestroom occupancy in the lodging industry is in most cases never constant. For this reason, whenever occupancies are below 100 percent, the number of section housekeepers must be adjusted down accordingly. For example, the sample team standing schedule described in Figure 3.5 indicates that on Mondays teams One, Three, Four, Relief One and Relief Two are scheduled to work. If each

FIGURE 3.5 Sample Team Standing Schedule

TEAM	MONDAY	TUESDAY	WEDNESDAY	THURSDAY	FRIDAY	SATURDAY	SUNDAY
One	ON	ON	ON	ON	ON	OFF / R-1	OFF / R-1
Two	OFF / R-1	ON	ON	ON	ON	ON	ON
Three	ON	OFF / R-1	OFF / R-1	OFF / R-2	ON	ON	ON
Four	ON	ON	ON	ON	OFF / R-2	OFF	ON
Five	OFF / R-2	ON	ON	ON	ON	ON	OFF / R-2
Laundry	ON	ON	ON	ON	ON	ON	OFF / R-2
Relief 1	ON	ON	ON	OFF	OFF	ON	ON
Relief 2	ON	OFF	OFF	ON	ON	ON	ON

FIGURE 3.6 Sample Fixed and Evening Team Schedule

POSITION	MONDAY	TUESDAY	WEDNESDAY	THURSDAY	FRIDAY	SATURDAY	SUNDAY
Linen Room Supervisor	OFF / HM	OFF / HM	ON	ON	ON	ON	ON
Janitor Supervisor	ON	ON	ON	ON	ON	OFF	OFF
Janitor 1	ON	ON	OFF	OFF	ON	ON	ON
Janitor 2	OFF	OFF	ON	ON	ON	ON	ON
Janitor 3	ON	ON	ON	ON	OFF	OFF	ON
Janitor 4	OFF	ON	ON	ON	ON	ON	OFF
Evening Supervisor	ON	ON	ON	ON	OFF	OFF / HM	OFF / HM
Section Housekeeper 1	OFF	OFF	ON	ON	ON	ON	ON
Section Housekeeper 2	ON	ON	OFF	OFF	ON	ON	ON
Houseperson	ON	ON	ON	ON	ON	OFF	OFF
Evening Janitor 1	OFF	OFF	ON	ON	ON	ON	ON
Evening Janitor 2	ON	ON	ON	ON	ON	OFF	OFF

Ocean Pool, The St. Regis Monarch Beach
Courtesy of Starwood Hotels & Resorts Worldwide, Inc.

team consists of five section housekeepers and each one cleans 16 rooms, the number of guestrooms that can be cleaned on Mondays is 400 (5 × 5 × 16). But what is it to do if the occupancy for Sunday night is just 80 percent? In this case the number of rooms that need to be cleaned Monday is only 320 (400 × .80) and the number of section housekeepers needed to do the job would be just 20 (320 ÷ 16). The standing schedule must, therefore, be adjusted to reflect only the number of section housekeepers needed to clean the rooms occupied. Figure 3.7 is a sample **adjusted daily schedule** showing the section housekeepers per team that are scheduled to work at 80 percent occupancy and those who are given an extra day off as there are not enough rooms to be cleaned by the entire crew. In this particular example, the adjusted schedule indicates that one section housekeeper of each team is given an extra day off on this

FIGURE 3.7   Sample Adjusted Schedule

Date: _____ Monday, September 3rd _____

Estimated Occupancy: _____ 80 percent _____

Rooms Occupied: _____ 320 _____

TEAM	HOUSEKEEPING NEEDED	SCHEDULED TO WORK	EXTRA DAY OFF
ONE	4	Erika Kate Melanie Jennifer	Maria
R-1	4	Onida Angela Atsuko Kellie	Lupita
THREE	4	Pat Dawn Amie Teri	Fernanda
FOUR	4	Deliah Ana Isabel June	Marjorie
R-2	4	Patty Mariann Romilly Kelly	Rachelle
LAUNDRY	4	Ramsey Meagan Char Sara	Bethany

particular day. The decision of who stays home when the occupancy is below 100 percent is generally made by the team supervisor by asking for volunteers among the team members or by following a sequential order. In Figure 3.7, Maria, Lupita, Fernanda, Marjorie, and Rachelle of the guestroom-cleaning teams, and Bethany of the laundry team, have either volunteered to have an extra day off or have been asked to stay out because it was their turn to do so.

The adjusted schedule includes the laundry team whose workers are also scheduled according to the property's occupancy. The standing schedule must be posted the day before, prior to the end of the morning shift, so that the workers know whether they are scheduled to work the following day. The estimated occupancy for the day is obtained from the front office, which usually is able to provide an accurate forecast based on reservations on hand, weather conditions, events taking place in town, and historical data from the same day in previous years. On some occasions, however, upon opening the department early in the morning, it may be found that the actual occupancy of the hotel differs substantially from the estimated forecast posted on the adjusted schedule the previous day. In this case, the opening supervisor should attempt to adjust the number of workers required to clean the number of rooms actually sold. This is usually done by calling the workers by phone. When the actual occupancy is above the forecasted estimate, the supervisor needs to ask those section housekeepers who were given a day off to come to work; when the actual occupancy is below the forecasted estimate, the supervisor needs to ask some of the scheduled section housekeepers to stay home. If, after all attempts are made, the number of workers is above the maximum needed, they can be assigned to extra work in the department, for instance deep cleaning of rooms or public areas. If the number of workers is below the maximum needed, the supervisor can assign public area attendants, housepersons, or laundry or linen room personnel to clean guestrooms. As a last resort, the department may have to incur overtime.

When the employees of lodging properties are unionized, daily scheduling must comply with the specifications of the contract in force. For instance, the contract may stipulate that workers are guaranteed 40-hour work weeks or that employees are not allowed to do any type of work different from that which they were hired to do.

Presidential Suite, Sheraton Hotel Ankara, Turkey
Courtesy of Starwood Hotels & Resorts Worldwide, Inc.

ALTERNATIVE SCHEDULING METHODS

Four-Day Work Week

Some large lodging properties have adopted a **four-day work week** system consisting of 10-hour shifts each working day. This type of schedule enables housekeeping employees to have more leisure time, to reduce time and expenses commuting back and forth to work, and to decrease childcare by one day per week. Companies can benefit, too, by decreasing employee meals and uniform cleaning costs. However, this approach raises the question of whether workers, particularly older employees, can endure 10-hour shifts without decreasing their normal productivity and quality of work. A section housekeeper who must clean 16 rooms in eight hours (30 minutes per room on the average) would have to clean 20 rooms with the 10-hour shift system, and this could affect the morale of the employees in the long run. Some properties have found that using the four-day work week system has not decreased guest satisfaction, while showing positive responses from their staff and substantial payroll savings.

Part-time Workers

Lodging properties may resort to hiring employees who are willing to work less than 40 hours per week, such as semi-retired people or students. In this case, the company will profit by reducing costs such as employee benefits and overtime. On the other hand, **part-time workers** are usually less reliable because their stake in the job is less substantial than that of full-time workers, which may create scheduling difficulties.

Flexible Work Hours

In smaller properties employees may be allowed to begin and end their shifts at times convenient to them. Needless to say, this system will appeal to workers and increase their morale. On the other hand, the coordination of tasks in the department can become a nightmare if the employees are allowed too much flexibility. The system of **flexible work hours** could be adopted in properties where the arrival and departure of guests is predictable, such as small highway motels where most check outs take place early in the morning and most check-ins occur late in the day.

Job Sharing

The purpose of **job sharing** is to allow two or more employees to accomplish a job regardless of who does it at any particular time. Although this system may be quite appealing to workers, the loss of supervisory control is very obvious. Job sharing could be adopted in small properties when the employees are well known to the manager and have proven to be reliable.

Guestroom Team Cleaning

Some recent surveys of housekeepers have shown that pairing room attendants for guestroom cleaning may improve productivity and enhance morale. On the other hand, **guestroom team cleaning** may have the risk of collusion and lower productivity by having two largely unsupervised workers in each other's company. An advantage of team cleaning could be improved security, as having two housekeepers working together may deter assaults by other employees or guests. In cases where the two workers are a good complement to each other, team cleaning might achieve higher levels of productivity and increased levels of morale, while in instances where the personalities of the team members are incompatible the results would be the opposite.

Extended Time Off

Some properties experience intense occupancy fluctuations during the year. While all workers are needed during peak season, during off-season there might be sufficient occupancy for just a skeleton crew. One way to solve this problem is to schedule workers on the basis of seniority, but this would necessarily result in losing those employees being laid off. A better arrangement is to have the staff agree on sharing the work. This can be done by asking all employees to work two weeks and take two weeks off during low season. When on layoff periods, employees are eligible to collect unemployment insurance in most cases.

TECHNOLOGY ASSOCIATED WITH THE HOUSEKEEPING DEPARTMENT

There are several housekeeping management systems being used by lodging companies that will be encountered by graduates when joining the industry. These push-button systems differ in their operation but they are easy to learn for those who have a basic knowledge of computers. Navis Housekeeping Management System (HMS), for instance, allows management to instantly track when section housekeepers begin the cleaning process and when the process is complete, while activating reports automatically alerting supervisors that the guestroom is ready for inspection. Guests waiting because their rooms are not ready can be notified, by entering their cell phone number in the system, with a prerecorded message that their rooms are available (marketingtechnologies.com). The GuestWare 3.0 system uses interactive voice response to link the housekeeping staff with the property engineers, allowing a housekeeper to pick up the room phone and follow an easy protocol to identify a specific maintenance problem. The report immediately alerts the engineer via his/her wireless phone (www.guestware.com). MTech offers its Rex workflow program, which operates on the Apple iPhone/iPod Touch platform. Rather than receiving a board with rooms to clean, section housekeepers can use an iPod Touch that can deliver information in the room attendant's own language. In the manufacturer's words, "Rex changes the paradigm of cleaning rooms by dramatically facilitating the workflow by significant system integration." (www.mtech.com)

KEY TERMS

Adjusted daily schedule	Laundry team
Average hourly wage	Management team
Cost of labor	On-premise laundry
Deep cleaning	Part-time worker
Evening team	Public areas attendant
Fixed team	Relief team
Flexible work hours	Rotational schedule
Four-day work week	Section housekeeper
Guestroom cleaning team	Section housekeeper need table
Guestroom team cleaning	Standard operating procedures
Housekeeping teams	Standing schedule
Houseperson	Team supervisor
Job sharing	

DISCUSSION AND REVIEW QUESTIONS

1. What areas are generally assigned to the housekeeping department for daily upkeep in large lodging properties?

2. Why should executive housekeepers avoid the responsibility of having to clean food and beverage and engineering areas?

3. What is the purpose of area cleaning inventories?

4. Why should cleaning frequency schedules be established for all areas?

5. What are cleaning performance standards?

6. What are the reasons why the formation of cleaning teams is recommended in house-keeping operations?

7. In a 450-room property with a workload criterion of 16 rooms to be cleaned by one section housekeeper per shift, how many section housekeepers are needed when the property is 75 percent full?

8. Why are all public areas attendants who are not off duty generally scheduled to work regardless of the property's occupancy?

9. What factors determine the workload criterion for cleaning rooms?

10. If the workload criterion for cleaning rooms in a lodging property is set at 15 rooms per eight-hour shift and each section housekeeper is allowed one half-hour for lunch, one 20-minute break per shift, and 30 minutes for cart setup, what would be the average number of minutes that each housekeeper should take to clean one guestroom?

11. How can an executive housekeeper determine the cost of labor for section housekeepers in one particular week of work?

12. Why must standing schedules be adjusted for occupancy on a daily basis?

MINICASES

SITUATION 1

How many teams (including relief) of five section housekeepers each would you need to form in the housekeeping department of a 576-room hotel if:

   a. Each section housekeeper cleans 16 guestrooms.

   b. The hotel has an on-premise laundry that takes one team to operate.

   c. The hotel is open seven days a week.

   d. The employees work 40 hours per week maximum.

   e. You need to have enough teams to cover days off.

SITUATION 2

You have just been hired as assistant executive housekeeper of the 600-room Cactus Resort in the Southwest. The section housekeeper workload per shift is 14 rooms and the average number of hours worked is eight hours. Your immediate boss, Mr. Brown, has been asked by the G.M. to provide the cost of labor for the housekeeping department for the upcoming month of June. The occupancy percent for the hotel has been estimated at 88 percent. Mr. Brown entrusts you with the job of working out the cost for the section housekeepers needed to clean the guestrooms in June, informing you that the average section house-keeper hourly wage next month is $9.50 per hour worked. What would your response be?

SITUATION 3

On Wednesday, June 5, you are asked to prepare the adjusted daily schedule for Thursday, June 6 for the same property as in **Situation 1**. The forecast received from the front desk indicates that the resort will have 519 rooms occupied Wednesday night. How many section housekeepers will you need to show up for work on Thursday morning to service the estimated occupied rooms?

SITUATION 4

As an assistant to the executive housekeeper of an all-suite resort in the Virgin Islands, you have been asked to set up a Section Housekeeper Needs Table for the 450-room property for 100 percent, 90 percent, and 75 percent occupancy levels. The workload per section housekeeper is 12 suites per one 8-hour shift.

Having taken this class, you are fully prepared to do so. Specify the number of section housekeepers to be scheduled each day at the three levels of occupancy given, the number of section housekeeper hours/day, the number of hours/week, and the total number of housekeeper hours in a 30-day period.

CASE STUDY

John Evans has been working as assistant to the executive housekeeper at a 624-room resort in Boca Raton, Florida, for six months. John has been left in charge of the department for the two weeks while his boss is on vacation. On May 15, he receives a call from Carol Collins, the property's controller, requesting a labor cost forecast for the month of June. John is told that the budgeted occupancy for the month has been downgraded because of the cancellation of three large conventions that had been previously booked. Carol provides John with the following information:

Budgeted occupancy in June	90 percent
New occupancy forecast for June	75 percent
Average **section housekeeper** hourly wage	$10.50
Budgeted monthly **team supervisors** and **Housepersons** total labor cost	$24,100
Budgeted monthly **laundry** labor cost	$19,760
Budgeted monthly **fixed team** labor cost	$11,800
Budgeted **evening team** labor cost	$7,100
Budgeted monthly **management team** salaries	$10,400

John knows that the **section housekeeper workload** for one 8-hour shift is 15 rooms. He decides not to change the labor cost for the fixed **and** management teams but to reduce the laundry budgeted labor cost by 15 percent, the supervisor/houseperson's by 8 percent and the evening team's by 5 percent.

Assignment

1. Calculate the new total departmental labor cost for the month of June and compare it with the budgeted labor cost. What is the difference between the budgeted and new labor cost in dollars?

Technical Skills Management

PART

3

King Room, Intercontinental New York Times Square
Courtesy of Six Continents Hotels, Inc.

Management of Inventory and Equipment

CHAPTER OBJECTIVES

- Learn how housekeeping material is classified.
- Define the concepts of fixed and operating assets.
- Explain the difference between capital expenditure and operating budgets.
- Discuss the function of purchasing material in the housekeeping department.
- Explain how housekeeping inventories are conducted.
- Describe the purpose of conducting inventories.

OVERVIEW

The amount of material used in the housekeeping department is considerable, ranging from guestroom furniture and accessories to departmental equipment and supplies. An important function of executive housekeepers is to classify all items into categories and subcategories as a first step in controlling cost, procurement, and usage. Costs are controlled by using budgets, which are yearly plans of operation used for the allocation of resources that itemize estimates of expense and income. This chapter includes a format for housekeeping budgets.

This section also explains the importance of the purchasing function in housekeeping, how to ascertain the value of goods, and how to assign purchasing specifications to products. The control of inventories, involving buying, receiving, storing, issuing, and cost accountability, is also discussed.

CLASSIFICATION OF MATERIAL

The administration of housekeeping material is an important component of the overall responsibilities assigned to executive housekeepers. This administrative function refers to the adequate selection and purchasing of supplies and equipment, their proper use, and suitable control of the amount of money invested while ensuring the presence of a sufficient amount of goods to supply the needs of the property. The classification of material is a prerequisite to the process of controlling the large number of items used in the housekeeping department.

Housekeeping material is divided into two major categories: **fixed assets** and **operating assets**. Fixed assets comprise housekeeping items that have a long-term life span, generally over one year. Fixed assets usually cost over $100 and are depreciated at the end of the fiscal year. Depreciation means that the company reduces the value of assets during the period of the assets' estimated useful life. For tax purposes, depreciation is a tax allowance that can be set aside by the company year after year for replacing the items once they can no longer be used. Table 4.1 lists material that is commonly categorized under fixed assets in housekeeping operations. Fixed assets are subcategorized into **FF&E** (furniture, fixtures, and equipment), **software**, and **department equipment**. Items that have a five- to seven-year life span are categorized under FF&E, such as beds, chairs, paintings, mattresses, and television sets that are used in guestrooms, public areas, and staff areas. Software items usually comprise guestroom fixtures of a textile nature that are not bed linens or bath linens, such as curtains, bedspreads, pillows, and blankets. The life span of software items is usually three to five years. Heavier, mobile equipment used in the housekeeping department for cleaning or transportation purposes is generally classified under department equipment. The life span of these items is between three and seven years. Included under this subcategory are items such as vacuum cleaners, shampoo machines, glass washers, and so on.

Operating assets include items under the control of the executive housekeeper that are generally used in the day-to-day operations of the department. They are considered cost items whose monetary outlay is charged to operating expenses. An important characteristic of operating assets is that they must be regularly inventoried. Operating assets are usually categorized into **cleaning supplies**, **linens**, **uniforms**, and **guest supplies**. The category of cleaning supplies includes every one of the items used for cleaning purposes, for example,

TABLE 4.1 Sample Classification of Housekeeping Fixed Assets

FF&E (Guestroom, Public and Staff Areas)	Software (Guestroom)	Department Equipment (Housekeeping Department)
Furniture	Accent curtains	Glass washers
Armoires	Blackout curtains	Hampers
Boxsprings	Bedspreads	Laundry equipment
Beds	Blankets	Maids' carts
Chairs	Comforters	Rotary floor scrubbers
Chests of drawers	Pillows	Pile lifters
Couches	Sheers	Sewing machines
Desks		Shampooers
Dressers		Vacuum cleaners
Employee lockers		Wheelchairs
Hutches		
Nightstands		
Sofa beds		
Tables		
Fixtures		
Accessories		
Ceramic ornaments		
Lamps		
Lighting fittings		
Mirrors		
Paintings		
Equipment		
Clock radios		
In-room safes		
Minibars		
Telephone sets		
Television sets		

cleaning solutions, disinfectants, polishers, brooms, mops, and rags. The classification of linens encompasses the subcategories of **bed linen** and **bathroom linen**. The subcategory of bed linen includes sheets and pillowcases and that of bathroom linen comprises towels, washcloths, bath mats, and washable shower curtains. The category of uniforms is self-explanatory, including apparel used in the housekeeping department by supervisors, section housekeepers, housepersons, laundry, and linen room personnel. Operating assets items used by guests are listed under guest supplies. This category is usually subdivided into two classifications: **nonreusable** and **reusable items**. Non reusable guest supplies include soaps, pens, paper items, mints, etc. Items that can be used again, such as ashtrays, clothes hangers, and wastebaskets, fall under the reusable subdivision. Table 4.2 is a sample list of items generally classified as operating assets.

The executive housekeeper is ultimately responsible for the control of assets in the housekeeping department. The control of expenses of fixed and operating assets is achieved maintaining budgets, sound purchasing procedures, and inventories.

TABLE 4.2 Sample Classification of Housekeeping Operating Assets

Cleaning Supplies	Guest Supplies	Linens	Uniforms
All-purpose cleaner	*Non-Reusable*	*Bed*	All housekeeping
Bowl cleaner	Bath soap	Pillowcases	department personnel
Brooms	Candy mints	Sheets	
Buckets	Coffee/Tea		
Cleaning rags	Facial tissue	*Bathroom*	
Disinfectants	Hand soap	Bath mats	
Furniture polish	Laundry bags	Bath towels	
Germicidals	Matches	Hand towels	
Laundry chemicals	Notepads	Shower textile curtains	
Metal polishers	Pens	Washcloths	
Mops	Postcards		
Rubber globes	Sanibags		
Scrubbing pads	Stationery		
Spray bottles	Toilet seat bands		
Window cleaners	Toilet tissue		
Wringers			
	Reusable		
	Ashtrays		
	Bibles		
	Coat hangers		
	Do-not-disturb signs		
	Glasses		
	Ice buckets		
	Loan items		
	Shower rubber mats		
	Shower plastic curtains		
	Trays		
	Waste baskets		
	Water pitchers		

CAPITAL EXPENDITURE AND OPERATING BUDGETS

Every lodging property is allocated with the necessary fixed and operating assets prior to its opening to the public. The costs of the initial allocation of material are itemized on a **pre-opening budget** that includes all inventory requirements to open the property and commence operations. Once operations begin, budgets for fixed and operating material items necessary for operating the property during the next twelve months must be prepared. The budget used to record the fixed assets needed for the upcoming fiscal year is called the **capital expenditure budget**. This budget is relatively easy to compile; it consists of a list of the number of fixed assets (FF&E, software, and department equipment) required by the housekeeping department, their individual prices, and the sum total for all items listed. Table 4.3 is a sample capital expenditure budget for a lodging property.

   Operating budgets are also prepared annually for the property's fiscal year operation. In large properties, the housekeeping operating budget is part of the **rooms division operating**

TABLE 4.3 Sample Yearly Capital Expenditure Budget**

15 armchairs at $405 each[a]	$ 6,075
1 oak bookcase[b]	790
25 extra firm, queen-size mattresses at $380 each[c]	9,500
10 metal employee lockers at $325 each[d]	3,250
1 wet vacuum[e]	490
400 guestroom coffee makers at $33 each[f]	13,200
Total	$33,305

**Description and specifications of all items is enclosed.
[a]Addition of one armchair to all suite rooms.
[b]Bookcase to be installed in lobby.
[c]Replacement of mattresses in third-floor queen rooms.
[d]Addition of 10 lockers in employee locker room.
[e]Needed by laundry room.
[f]Addition of one coffee maker to all guestrooms.

budget, which includes both the front desk and the housekeeping departments. Unlike capital expenditure budgets, operating budgets have a direct relationship to the day-to-day revenue resulting from the sale of guestrooms. The rationale behind this approach is to limit operating costs to a predetermined percentage of the generated revenue. For example, assuming that the housekeeping department is expected to expend 1.2 percent of sales on guest supplies, if the daily room revenue is, say, $20,000, the cost of guest supplies should be $240 (20,000 × 1.2%). If the revenue is $18,000, the cost should be $216 (18,000 × 1.2%), and so on. The cost percentage assigned to each operating budget expense category is based on the cost history of the property, the quality of the products used, and the pay scale and types of benefits that employees receive.

The housekeeping categories used by the housekeeping department usually include: housekeeping **salaries and wages**, **payroll taxes and benefits**, and **other expenses**. Salaries and wages include those of the entire housekeeping department; payroll taxes and benefits include the operator's share of additional costs related to payroll; the category of other expenses encompasses any other cost incurred by the housekeeping department that is not payroll-related. Table 4.4 is a sample rooms division operating budget for one month for a large hotel where the items related to housekeeping have been listed in bold. Under Other Expenses, the cost of outside services, telephone, postage, printing and stationery supplies, uniforms, and incentive plan is usually shared by the housekeeping and front-office departments.

PURCHASING HOUSEKEEPING MATERIAL

Buying goods in lodging institutions is a highly specialized job. Buyers must be knowledgeable about the items they purchase, be familiar with the market, and know how the materials are produced and marketed. The process of buying material for the housekeeping department involves finding the best sources of supply at the most satisfactory prices and obtaining the quality and quantity that the property requires. Although cost is always an important consideration, it should not take precedence over the quality of the product and the service of the company that sells it. Buyers should understand how to conduct **value analyses**.

TABLE 4.4 Sample Rooms Division Operating Budget

Rooms Division Department Month of March 201.		
	$	%
Revenue		
Total rooms sales	544,509	100.5
Allowances and rebates	2,709-	.5-
Net room sales	541,800	100.0
Salaries and wages		
Front office	24,925	4.6
Housekeeping	43,890	8.1
Payroll taxes and benefits		
Payroll taxes and employee relations	19,393	3.6
Employee meals	2,680	.5
Total payroll taxes and benefits	22,073	4.1
Total payroll and related	112,961	20.8
Other expenses		
Travel commissions	11,110	2.1
Outside services	160	
Cleaning supplies	1,085	.2
Linen replacements	3,795	.7
Guest supplies	6,550	1.2
Glassware	200	
Window washing		
Telephone	2,650	.5
Postage	50	
Printing and stationery supplies	1,625	.3
Uniforms	180	
Laundry supplies	1,630	.3
Incentive plan	1,600	.3
Shuttle van expense	3,026	.6
Total other expenses	33,661	6.2
Total expenses	146,622	27.1
Departmental profit	395,178	72.9

First, the performance of the products' components is evaluated by identifying their essential, desirable, useful, and unnecessary characteristics. Then, the buyer must find the products with the most essential and desirable quality factors. The value function can be quantified by the ratio Q/P, where Q = quality and P = price. Although not always possible, the goal of the buyer should be to keep the value of products as high as possible by increasing Q while keeping P down.

The buying function in lodging chains is often centralized. Items like soap, linen, mattresses, pillows, furniture, and fixtures are procured by the company's purchasing department and shipped to the different units on request. Purchasing in large independent properties is done by the **purchasing agent**, who is a specialized buyer in charge of procuring products for all departments in the property. Smaller properties often allow the department heads to purchase goods for their respective areas of responsibility. In any case, it should be the job of the executive housekeeper always to pre-test and approve all items used in the housekeeping department and decide the quantities and the specifications of the products to be bought. It should not be the job of the purchasing agent, or any other person for that matter, to purchase material and supplies without the consent of the executive housekeeper. It is also important to solicit the input of public area attendants, section housekeepers, housepersons, and laundry personnel on the appropriate characteristics of the items that in the end are to be used by them.

The St. Regis Monarch Beach
Courtesy of Starwood Hotels & Resorts Worldwide, Inc.

All merchandise purchased should have precise specifications, which are descriptions of the products' quality and factors that should reflect precisely the performance needs for each particular institution. Specifications should be stated clearly, giving the information needed to assure proper identification. A specification should include:

1. the name of the product: *bed sheets.*
2. the amount to be purchased: *12 dozen.*
3. the grade or brand desired: *180 threads per square inch.*
4. container size: *3 dozen cartons.*
5. the unit on which prices are to be quoted: *dozen.*
6. the specific factors needed to obtain the exact item: *made in USA, sanforized, 50/50 blend, queen size, etc.*

FIGURE 4.1 Sample Shopping Form

Item:_____

	PRICE	QUALITY	SERVICE
VENDOR 1			
VENDOR 2			
VENDOR 3			

Some specifications are generally the same for several properties. For example, a good detergent should be used in all laundry operations. Other specifications are different, depending on the type of property where they are to be used. For instance, a luxury resort does probably require the best bed linen money can buy, while a small, inexpensive motel may just need bed linen of fair quality.

Before buying a product, prices should be obtained from at least three different vendors. Figure 4.1 is a sample **shopping form** that can be used for every product before it is purchased. Product price and vendor dependability and service should be reviewed once or twice every three months. Purchasing decisions should be made based not only on price but on quality, suitability, and storage availability as well.

There may be three types of entities involved in the purchasing function: producers, middlemen, and consumers. Producers manufacture the items to be sold and sometimes sell the products directly to the consumers. Middlemen may bring the different commodities to their

Oceanfront Pool, Los Suenos Marriott, Costa Rica
Courtesy of Marriott International, Inc.

own warehouses from which they distribute them to consumers or act as order takers and have the goods shipped directly from the manufacturer. Middlemen always add a charge to the product's price. Usually, the fewer middlemen through which a product passes, the lower the price. However, although purchasing directly from the manufacturer may be less expensive, very often lodging properties benefit from buying through brokers (middlemen) because these can provide better service and in some cases employee training at no cost. Another disadvantage from buying directly from manufacturers is that they often require the purchase of large quantities of goods. In this case, the money saved because of lower price is offset by the cost of having assets tied down for long periods of time.

There is great competition among purveyors of cleaning and guest supplies. Some will lower their prices initially to obtain the property's account. Others may offer prizes or kickbacks to get their foot in the door. Executive housekeepers should be aware of these often unethical tactics and decline any "free" personal gifts.

If the executive housekeeper needs to order products directly from a manufacturer, filling out a formal purchase order may be necessary. The **purchase order** is, in essence, a sales contract stating the specifications of the product to be delivered and the conditions involving payment. Most lodging properties have adopted computerized purchasing systems allowing most purchases to be made on line. When the merchandise has been previously bought by the property's buyer and stored in the main storeroom, the housekeeping department usually needs to fill out a **requisition form** before the products can be obtained.

Executive housekeepers should always be on the lookout for new items on the market. Testing for new, better, or less expensive products often leads to improving the department's bottom line. The salespersons who visit the property on a regular basis may be a reliable source of product information and often have considerable experience in solving most cleaning or laundry problems encountered during operations.

INVENTORY CONTROL

The functions of purchasing, receiving, storing, issuing, and accounting for housekeeping material must be managed efficiently. The range of inventory used in the rooms division of lodging operations is quite large, varying from textiles, guestroom furnishings, and amenities to sophisticated department equipment and supplies.

The executive housekeeper must control the function of purchasing by defining clearly what is to be procured, who will be in charge of the buying, what specifications are to be considered, and what quantities will be needed. The person in charge of purchasing must consistently provide the needed quantities of products in housekeeping inventories. Although in some cases purchasing is done by the corporate office or by the property's purchasing agent, the executive housekeeper is ultimately responsible for the cost and results of what is purchased. For some products, linen for instance, **pars** need to be established; for others, for example soaps and paper products, **maximum and minimum quantities** are set up. Pars can be defined as the number of required on-hand items to perform housekeeping operations. In the case of linens, for instance, the optimum number of pars is four. This means that ideally the property should have on hand one set of sheets and pillowcases set up in the guestroom beds at any given time, another set being laundered, an additional set ready to go in floor closets and room-attendant carts, and one final set on reserve. For guest and cleaning supplies, the maximum quantity is the greatest number of units that should be in stock at any given time, while the minimum quantity refers to the smallest number of units. For example, the maximum and minimum number of cases of soap could be 35 and 25 respectively. That means that if at any given time the soap inventory is above 35, the product is overstocked. On the other hand, if the number of cases falls below 25, additional supplies must be ordered. This system eliminates the risk of overstocking or of running out of products.

The receiving function of goods ordered must also be controlled. Unless adequate inspection and receiving procedures are used, the best purchasing system may fail because it is at this point that determination must be made of whether or not the products meet the specifications and quantities of the order previously placed. Failing to inspect the merchandise adequately may result in higher costs, lower quality, theft, and fraud. On receiving a shipment, the goods should be compared with those listed on the receiving sheet or purchase order to verify the correctness of the delivery. If the goods meet the prearranged requirements, they are accepted by signing the invoice or delivery memo. If the products do not meet inspection requirements, they should be refused and a notation indicating the reasons for refusing the delivery made.

The function of storing merchandise must also be controlled adequately. Access to storerooms must be limited to authorized personnel only. The storeroom should be locked off-hours and a record should be kept of the person entering it and of the merchandise taken. Valuable items like towels and some guest supplies should be stored in an area that remains locked at all times. The storage area should be designed to hold the specific products stored in it; bottom shelving levels should be at least 10 inches off the floor to ensure adequate ventilation and to allow cleaning underneath. A rotation system should be established by which oldest stock is placed in front and issued first.

In large properties, housekeeping items may be stored in the main storeroom. In this case, the housekeeping department will need to fill in a requisition form to request products. Every requisition should bear the signature of a person designated by the executive housekeeper to sign it. Nothing should be requested without an approved signature. When products are stored in the housekeeping department, issuing controls must also be established so that the merchandise is handed out to authorized personnel only. Floor closet storage should also be locked at all times and access limited to the section housekeepers, housepersons, or supervisors in charge of the area.

To account for the cost of housekeeping operating assets used, physical inventories are conducted regularly, in most cases monthly. Linens, uniforms, and cleaning and guest supplies inventories are taken by counting all items on hand and listing them on a physical inventory form (Figure 4.2).

Laundry chemicals may be included in the cleaning supplies category or counted separately for better control. The purpose of taking physical inventories is to find out what amount of items for each category is on hand and to work out its current market value. Once the value of items used is ascertained, the costs are expensed against the revenue produced for the same period and the percentages obtained compared to the amounts budgeted for the different categories. For example, let us assume that the projected percentage of laundry chemical supplies for the month of March 201. had been set at 1.2 percent of room sales and that the cost of laundry chemicals used in that month, according to the physical inventory, was $6,960. If the guestroom revenue was $600,000, the control performance of the housekeeping department would have been good (600,000 × .012 = 7,200), the department having actually spent $240 less than projected (7,200 − 6,960 = 240). The cost of items used is determined by adding the total purchases

FIGURE 4.2 Sample Physical Inventory Form

Type of Product: *Laundry Chemicals*				(Month: *March*)
Product	Unit	Amount in Storage	Market Price	Total
Detergent	case	75	$90	$6,750
Neutralizer	case	31	65	2,015
Softener	case	15	12	180
Bleach	case	15	12	180
Starch	pail	5	126	630

during the month to the opening inventory and subtracting the merchandise on hand as per the physical inventory for every category. For instance, in the case of laundry chemicals:

Beginning inventory on 3/1	$15,800
Purchases for the month	2,900+
Total	**18,700**
Physical inventory on 3/31	11,740−
Cost of inventory used in March	**6,960**

The property's controller will then divide the cost of inventory used ($6,960) by the rooms revenue ($600,000) to find out the percentage cost of laundry chemicals used during the month ($6,960 ÷ $600,000 = 0.012, or 1.2%). The controller will then compare the result to the percentage budgeted for the month to find out whether the expense has been controlled effectively by the housekeeping department, in this case below budget.

Physical inventories are difficult to conduct as all items that need to be accounted for must be counted one by one. In the case of linens, for instance, linens are found in guestrooms, laundry room, linen room, floor closets, room-attendant carts, etc. Figure 4.3 is a sample linen inventory sheet that provides information about loss of items and total inventory value. The first section indicates the items on hand at the time of the last physical inventory, to which new purchases made during the month are added. The new total, minus the items discarded during the same month, indicates the items that should be on hand. The second section reflects the actual items on hand at the time of the physical inventory. The third section indicates the losses for the month and the current market price of the different items. The next step consists of finding out the value of the inventory on hand and the number of items of each category that need to be ordered to bring the inventory to the preestablished par.

To keep tight control on valuable items, for example imported chocolates for special guests, a **perpetual inventory** system may be implemented. A perpetual inventory is a form where items received and issued are recorded every time a transaction occurs. The form shows the quantity that should be on hand at all times. If the number of items on the balance does not correspond with the number of items on the shelf, the possibility of pilfering exists.

There are several software programs on the market that can be used to track inventory supplies and generate reports detailing consumption of supplies. Software packages can also provide order patterns, delivery schedules, and supply quantity levels by vendor.

FIGURE 4.3 Sample Inventory Form

Housekeeping Linen Inventory									

Inventory Date: _____

Prepared By: _____

PREDICTED INVENTORY (should have)	WHITE SHEET	PILLOCASES	BATH TOWELS	HAND TOWELS	WASHCLOTHS	BATHMATS	POOL TOWELS	CREAM SHEETS	MATTRESS PADS
1. Last Inventory (Date)									
2. New Received									
3. Subtotal (1. + 2.)									
4. Discards									
5. Total (3. – 4.)									
TODAY'S INVENTORY (have)									
6. In Guestrooms (1 par)									
7. In Laundry									
8. In Storage (Floor Closets)									
9. In Storage (Reserve)									
10. In Storage (Carts)									
11.									
12. Total on Hand (add 6. Through 11.)									
13. Losses (5. – 12.)									
14. $ Value per Item									

COST OF SUPPLIES PER OCCUPIED ROOM

An alternative method of controlling the cost of housekeeping department supplies is to use the **cost per occupied room** method. The cost is obtained by dividing each expense category for a certain period of time by the number of rooms sold during that period of time. The figure obtained is compared with that projected in the budget to find information on whether or not too much money has been spent. For example, if the budgeted cost of guest supplies per occupied room was $4.25 and the actual cost is $4.76, the department is spending $0.51 more for guest supplies each time the room is occupied. The executive housekeeper must investigate the

Guestroom, Hotel Indigo London, IHG
Courtesy of Six Continents Hotels, Inc.

probable causes for the difference in this case. The reasons could be: higher prices paid for guest supplies than forecasted at the time the budget was prepared, upgrade of the quality of guest supplies, placing a larger number of items in the guestrooms by section housekeepers, or pilfering.

KEY TERMS

Bathroom linen

Bed linen

Capital expenditure budget

Cleaning supplies

Cost per occupied room

Department equipment

FF&E

Fixed assets

Guest supplies

Linens

Maximum quantity

Minimum quantity

Nonreusable items

Operating assets

Operating budget

Other expenses

Par

Payroll taxes and benefits

Perpetual inventory
Preopening budget
Purchase order
Purchasing agent
Requisition form
Reusable guest supplies

Rooms division operating budget
Salaries and wages
Shopping form
Software
Uniforms
Value analysis

DISCUSSION AND REVIEW QUESTIONS

1. Explain the difference between housekeeping fixed assets and operating assets.

2. Why are fixed assets depreciated while operating assets are not?

3. Which are the three categories into which fixed assets are generally subdivided?

4. Executive housekeepers need to request expenditure allocations each fiscal year to run the housekeeping department. What are the two budgets used to request those allocations?

5. What is the difference between nonreusable and reusable housekeeping items?

6. In which subcategory would you classify a case of hand soap? Would a case of hand soap fall under a fixed or an operating budget? Why?

7. In large lodging properties, which two departments are included in the rooms division operating budget?

8. Buyers of housekeeping equipment and supplies need to be aware of the equation $V = Q/P$. Explain what the equation represents.

9. In a 150-room lodging property with two queen-size beds in each room and two sheets per bed, how many sheets do you need to have in stock for a four par?

10. As executive housekeeper of a lodging property, how much should you spend on cleaning supplies in a fiscal year period if the projected yearly revenue is $6,150,000 and the expenditure percentage for this category had been set at 0.3 percent of the revenue?

11. What was the cost of the linen expenditure in May if the beginning inventory on May 1 was $13,000, the purchases for the month were $2,500, and the physical inventory taken on May 31 was $12,900?

12. Prepare a sketch of a perpetual inventory showing the following transactions and the inventory balance on May 31:

   May 1: 112 bottles of French perfume on hand

   May 7: 6 bottles issued

   May 13: 15 bottles issued

   May 18: one bottle was found broken (unusable)

   May 20: 1 case with 25 bottles purchased

   May 25: 20 bottles issued

MINICASES

SITUATION 1

As a new housekeeping manager of a large lodging property, you are asked to classify the material in your department to facilitate inventory-taking and budgeting procedures. As a first step, you check out the storeroom, and find the following items:

bedspreads, rubber gloves, mattresses, towels, bath mats, brooms, pillows, candy mints, one minibar, vacuum cleaners, houseperson coveralls, furniture polish, all-purpose cleaner, washcloths, cleaning rags, one sewing machine, ashtrays, waste baskets, bed sheets, clock-radios, blankets, toilet tissue, facial tissue, television sets, ice buckets, pillowcases, stainless steel cleaner, various laundry chemicals, window cleaner, curtains, plastic shower curtains, two boxes of guest stationery, and three boxes of company letterheads

Classify the above items into fixed assets or operating assets. Within these two categories, subcategorize the items into FF&E, software, department equipment, cleaning supplies, guest supplies, linens, or uniforms. Furthermore, classify the guest supplies found into reusable and nonreusable.

SITUATION 2

After taking a monthly physical inventory in a housekeeping department, it was found that the cost of merchandise used during the month was as follows:

Cleaning supplies	$4,050
Linen replacements	3,125
Guest supplies	5,900
Laundry supplies	1,975

The preestablished percentages of revenue for the four categories were: cleaning supplies 0.6%, linen replacements 0.7%, guest supplies 1.2%, and laundry supplies 0.3%. If the rooms revenue for the month was $580,000, by how many dollars were each of the categories under or over budget?

SITUATION 3

On May 31, you have been assigned to conduct the following tasks:

a. Take a physical inventory of linens in the housekeeping department.
b. Ascertain the losses of each linen category for the month.
c. Prepare a list of items needed to bring the numbers up to par. The preestablished par for all items is 3.5.

One par consists of:

800 bed sheets
800 pillowcases
800 bath towels
1,600 hand towels
1,600 washcloths
400 bath mats
200 pool towels

The beginning inventory for all items at the beginning of May was:

2,700 bed sheets
2,850 pillowcases
2,550 bath towels

5,650 hand towels

5,490 washcloths

1,385 bath mats

660 pool towels

No items were discarded in May. The physical inventory showed the following amounts:

2,700 bed sheets

2,825 pillowcases

2,390 bath towels

5,585 hand towels

5,310 washcloths

1,370 bath mats

620 pool towels

CHAPTER EXERCISES

BUDGETING EXERCISE

You are the executive housekeeper of the Royal Hotel, London. It is September and the rooms division director asks you to submit a budget draft (rough estimate) for the coming fiscal year. The projected total rooms revenue has been set at $3,500,000.

Prepare the draft of your operating budget using the following list of items that you think you will need for the year. Show dollars and percentages for the projected revenue, costs, and income (departmental profit).

Estimated salaries and wages for the year:	280,000
Estimated cleaning supplies cost:	5% of total revenue
Estimated guest supplies cost:	35,000
Estimated linen replacement cost:	70,000

INVENTORY EXERCISE

As executive housekeeper of an Omni hotel in Orlando, Florida, you have been made aware by the hotel controller that the use of guest supplies has been unusually high for the past three months. To investigate the issue, you decide to take inventory on May 31. These are your findings:

Value of guest supplies on beginning inventory May 1st:	$4,500
Value of purchases of guest supplies for the month of May:	800
Value of physical inventory taken on May 31st:	2,800
The rooms division revenue for the month of May was:	$190,000
The budget percentage (expense:revenue) target for guest supplies was:	0.5%

Find:

a. Cost of guest supplies used in May

b. Difference between cost percentage results in May and budgeted cost percentage

c. Which are the probable causes for the difference?

COST PER OCCUPIED ROOM EXERCISE

Tyler Sachse is the executive housekeeper of a five-star hotel in San Francisco. The general manager has asked Tyler to upgrade the quality of the chocolates placed on the guests' pillows when the turndown service is conducted each day. The G.M. notified Tyler that he could increase last year's $3.75 cost of guest supplies per occupied room by 0.70 percent and invest the difference in upgrading the quality of the chocolates the hotel now used. The hotel projected selling 146,000 rooms next year,

Find: What would be the surplus amount in dollars that Tyler can now count on to purchase Godiva chocolates for the hotel next year?

Hotel Indigo San Diego, Intercontinental Hotels Group
Courtesy of Six Continents Hotels, Inc.

Characteristics of Housekeeping Equipment and Supplies

CHAPTER OBJECTIVES

- Define the basic characteristics of housekeeping fixed assets.
- Emphasize the importance of maintaining interior design consistency throughout the property.
- Describe the cleaning supplies most commonly used in lodging properties.
- Discuss strategies to be followed in purchasing housekeeping chemicals.
- Explain how to handle and store chemicals.
- Learn about nonreusable and reusable guest supplies.
- Discuss issues regarding uniforms.
- Describe the characteristics of linens, linen pars, and linen inventories.

OVERVIEW

One of the responsibilities of the executive housekeeper is to administer and maintain all assets allocated to the rooms division of lodging properties. In order to accomplish this task, executive housekeepers must know the characteristics of all items under their control as well as their cleaning peculiarities.

It is also important for executive housekeepers to understand the purpose of cleaning chemicals and to be aware of the dangers that they pose to employees who have not been effectively trained to use them properly. Federal regulations must be adhered to when handling and storing housekeeping chemicals.

This chapter also deals with the topics of guest supplies and uniforms, explaining the main characteristics of bathroom and guestroom amenities and nonreusable items, and how to deal with employee uniform procedures.

The management of linens in lodging properties is also an important component of the regular duties of executive housekeepers. There are several characteristics inherent in linens that must be understood when purchasing them, such as their composition and construction. For instance, buying durable-press, chemically treated fabrics that require no ironing will allow substantial labor savings in the department. Once the characteristics are understood, purchasing specifications within budget parameters may be established.

The establishment of pars for each linen item on the property is critical. Not enough sheets, for example, would cause the section housekeepers to be idle waiting for laundered linen to make the beds. Too large of a linen inventory, on the other hand, would mean tying down resources for long periods of time. Because of the common losses of linens due to pilfering and misuse, inventories must be taken regularly in lodging properties. This chapter shows how to conduct physical counts of bed and bath linens and recommends issuing and storage procedures to control the shrinkage of these products.

HOUSEKEEPING FURNITURES, FIXTURES, AND EQUIPMENT (FF&E), SOFTWARE, AND DEPARTMENT EQUIPMENT

Executive housekeepers must administer and maintain their properties' fixed assets classified as Furniture, Fixtures, and Equipment (FF&E), Software, and Department Equipment. Although new establishments are usually handed over to the management team already equipped with all items needed for operation, the executive housekeeper is directly involved in the replacement, refurbishing, and upkeep of most fixed asset items in the property. For this reason, executive housekeepers must have appropriate knowledge of the assets that are under their control.

DESIGN

Regardless of their type of service, lodging properties must maintain interior design consistency standards throughout the building. Whether a property has been classified as economy, mid-market, or luxury, its guestroom and public area design, color patterns, fabric and upholstery quality, and overall appearance must befit the category it represents. Doing piecemeal refurbishing or renovating must always be avoided. Colors, for instance, must be **complementary**. In general, blue is a complement of orange, green of red, and yellow of violet. Using several light tints and shades of the same color makes rooms seem larger, while full-intensity hues tend to make rooms seem compact. Adjoining walls should be painted the same color to provide a sense of continuity. When covering walls, smaller prints should be used in small rooms and in all cases, color patterns should be complementary in fabrics, wall coverings, and carpets. Earth-tone colors, often used in **art deco** design, such as ocher, mauve, and burgundy, are quite popular in guestroom and lobby outlines. These soothing colors, when combined with terracotta vases, lamp bases, and statuettes, are often found in classic settings and are generally pleasing to most guests. Lodging properties' design must comply with the Americans with Disabilities Act (ADA) regulations, revised in July 2010 to include new standards for accessible design of guests.

Surfaces look better and last longer when finished with durable materials like marble, granite, and corian. Public areas should be attractively decorated and furnished with special touches to please guests. For instance, lobbies may be fitted with fireplaces, bookcases, and live plants to make them seem more homey and inviting to travelers.

Guestroom, Waikaloa Beach Marriott Resort & Spa
Courtesy of Marriott International, Inc.

FURNITURE

Executive housekeepers are generally responsible for the refurbishing and upkeep of the furniture in guestroom, public, and employee areas. Furniture should be solidly built, easy to maintain, functional, and attractive. It is not advisable to purchase pieces of furniture directly from a catalogue or online; instead, the executive housekeeper should carefully examine samples to ensure that the products have been built to withstand repeated rough use. All furniture tops should be plastic-laminated or finished with water-repellent polyurethane to avoid scratches, rings, and stains caused by abusive treatment and spilled liquids. Desk chairs should have padded backs to provide comfort to guests and prevent wood from hitting desktops. Furniture dotted with glides or casters will prevent carpet damage when pushed or pulled around the room.

Luggage racks are better if built in and fitted with wall-protecting panels, as there is a greater likelihood that the luggage will bump against and deteriorate walls when detached racks are used. Desks should be large enough to accommodate a desktop computer and a fax machine. TV/VCR units should be an actual piece of furniture, rather than simply a conventional metal stand, and should be fitted with 180-degree swivels so that guests can see the screen from anywhere in the room. **Case furniture** such as chests of drawers, credenzas, armoires, desks, and bureaus also should be purchased with durability in mind. Drawers should be equipped with nylon ball bearings and slide glides so that they don't jam when opening and closing. In general, guestrooms should provide a warm residential look; for instance, love seats and armchairs can replace the standard chairs so often found in hotel rooms.

Upholstery

Upholstery fibers may be natural, synthetic, or plastic. Natural fabrics, such as cotton, linen, silk, and wool, are rich looking and long wearing but expensive and delicate to maintain because they stain easily. Synthetic fibers are less expensive and easy to clean, but they are less elegant and more likely to generate static electricity. Often, upholstered materials are a blend of natural and synthetic fabrics. The greatest advantage of upholstery plastic materials, such as vinyl, is that they can be easily cleaned by just wiping with a soapy cloth; however, they generally have a duller appearance than natural or blended materials.

Upholstery fabrics should be strong enough to withstand repeated shampooing. Treating fabrics with soil-retardant sprays can decrease the need for dry-cleaning the material. It is also important that upholstery fabrics be treated with flame-retardant finishes.

Before putting upholstered furniture fabrics into use, they should be pretested to ascertain the best way to clean the pieces without causing shrinkage or discoloration. Some fabrics can be cleaned with solvent, others can be cleaned with water and detergent, and some only allow for vacuuming. In general, synthetic fabrics such as nylon and plastics such as vinyl are the most stain-resistant and easy-to-clean upholstery materials.

Beds

Beds are the central attraction in guestrooms and often a big selling point for travelers when choosing a lodging property. When asked to pay an average of $100 per night per room, guests expect to receive a clean, well-maintained sleeping area and a comfortable bed.

In commercial operations, beds consist of a frame to support the springs and mattresses and unattached headboards. Bed frames usually consist of metal bars with legs attached to each corner or of a metal or wood platform. The main advantage of platform frames is that room attendants don't have to vacuum underneath the box frame, thus saving time when cleaning the room. Headboards are mounted on the wall and should match the general design of the room's furniture.

It is important to know the composition of the **bed structure** of each property in order to figure out the maximum number of people that the property can house. Knowing the different types of beds and how many guests can stay in the rooms will help executive housekeepers plan for bed and bathroom linen and supplies. Table 5.1 shows the different types of beds normally found in lodging properties.

Another type of sleeping equipment is the **mobile bed**. Families on vacation and traveling high school or college groups often require additional sleeping accommodations in guestrooms. The rollaway, or bed on wheels, consists of a folding frame with an attached bedspring body. The

TABLE 5.1 Sample Bed Structure in Lodging Properties

Type	Standard Size (inches)	Number of People per Bed
Single	38 × 74	One
Twin	42 × 76	One
Double	54 × 76	Two
Queen	60 × 80	Two
King	76 × 84	Two

mattress in rollaways must be made of latex foam or have very light, flexible innersprings so that they too can fold with the frame. Because rollaways are unable to provide a comfortable surface to hold the weight of an adult person, they should be recommended only for children or young people to avoid legitimate complaints about the property's not providing adequate accommodation. **Cribs** are also essential in order to accommodate infants or young children. While cribs should be collapsible to save storage space, their extension mechanisms should be kept in good working order to prevent the crib from collapsing when being used.

Dual-purpose sleeping equipment is common in guestrooms. These pieces of furniture provide both seating space and extra sleeping capacity, eliminating the need to roll in a mobile bed on short notice. Sofas, couches, chair-beds, and in-wall beds are the most common dual-purpose pieces of furniture found in lodging properties. Sofas, couches and chair-beds convert into beds by removing the cushions and pulling out the folding frame and mattress or by dropping the back to the level of the seat. In-wall beds, also called **Murphy beds**, are concealed in the wall behind a panel, giving the room the appearance of a studio or parlor rather than a bedroom. The wall is balanced in such a way that it can be swung open with a gentle pull on a handle. The advantage of having wall beds is that the room can be used as a living room when the bed is up.

Box Springs

The main purpose of bed box springs is to act as shock absorbers between the mattress and the bed frame itself. Box-spring coils are more rigid than those of mattresses to provide a firm base for the mattress to rest on. Besides cushioning the mattress, box springs increase the height of beds, giving them a more elegant look.

Mattresses

Surveys of favorite guest amenities conducted regularly by hospitality magazines consistently show that guests put comfortable mattresses at the top of the list, second only to cleanliness. Most mattresses used in lodging operations are of the **innerspring** type; they have metal coils that support the weight of the sleepers while conforming to their body contours. The strength and number of coils determine the mattress firmness, which may range from medium to super-firm. Heavy-gauge steel wire coils are best, allowing weights to flex down a specific area without disturbing the space surrounding the pressure points. This allows two persons of different weights to lie side by side and each get different levels of buoyancy. The firmness of the mattress is determined by the gauge of steel used, the number of turns of each coil, and the way the coils are attached to the mattress frame. Preferably, the springs should be encased in fabric pockets to provide independent coil action, rather than being attached to each other with wire or hooks. Good mattresses have sufficient padding to cushion the springs beneath and provide a smooth surface. The padding should be nonallergenic and comply with the government flame-spread regulation, which states that a lighted cigarette should not be able to ignite the insulation. The recommended way to purchase mattresses is to inspect a cutaway section to make sure that the padding is sufficiently dense, that the coils are of fine quality and closely spaced, and that the covering fabric is well attached to the main body. New, sophisticated mattresses are built using air chamber systems, which allow two people sleeping in the same bed to choose the firmness they prefer by using a number on a scale of 0 to 100. To avoid contours in mattresses, the housekeeping staff must turn and rotate them regularly.

Lodging properties may also use foam mattresses, especially for their rollaway beds. The synthetic material used in this type of mattress is usually latex foam or urethane. Although less expensive, rubber mattresses do not provide the adequate firmness expected by an adult guest, nor do they last nearly as long as those built with innersprings.

Water-filled mattresses (waterbeds) became quite popular with the public when they were first used in the 1960s, but they soon proved to be inconvenient for lodging operators because they often leaked and because the water had to be heated, which became costly. Although today's waterbeds are efficiently built with individually filled cells that need not be heated because of an insulating foam layer, there doesn't seem to be a great demand for them from lodging guests. Lodging properties, however, should have a few waterbeds to fulfill the request of interested travelers.

FIXTURES

Guestrooms and lodging property lobbies are also furnished with accessories such as mirrors, decorations, pictures, and lights, to complement the furniture. The color and style of fixtures should be balanced with the overall room décor; a vermilion vase, for instance, will probably not match a surrounding of pale yellow hues. The amount, style, and quality of furnishings will dramatically affect the appearance of rooms. For instance, strategically placed mirrors can give small rooms an illusion of depth; serene motifs in paintings will provide a feeling of tranquility; triple-magnification makeup mirrors and wall-mounted hair dryers in bathrooms are a welcome amenity; a well-stocked mahogany bookcase in the lobby will provide a homey feeling to guests who enjoy reading.

Carpets

Beautiful carpeting can enhance the appearance of lodging properties and make a lasting impression on guests. On the other hand, discolored, worn, or dirty carpets are usually sources of guest complaints. The first step in selecting the right carpet is to match its color, texture, and pattern with the design of the area where it is to be installed. Then, other factors need to be considered, such as the anticipated level of wear and tear caused by the intensity of traffic, the location of the carpet, and the budget allocated for it. When heavy traffic is expected, carpets should feature strong resistance to abrasion, as well as texture retention and anti-soiling and staining characteristics. The location of the carpet should determine specifications such as enhanced colorfastness, antimicrobial protection, resistance to snags, and resilience under rolling loads. Besides durability and stain resistance, carpets in lodging properties should be capable of withstanding repeated cleaning.

Before purchasing carpet, be sure you fully understand the warranty coverage offered by the manufacturer or installer. Warranties for commercial carpets should include protection for wear and tear, colorfastness (fading from sunlight and atmospheric contaminants), tuft bind deterioration, static charges, backing strength, raveling of seams and edges, and any other manufacturing defects.

Carpets must be professionally installed in order to comply with the manufacturer's instructions. If carpeting is not installed properly, it will buckle and wear out fast. One important component of the installation process is to use a quality carpet cushion or pad that will prolong the life of the carpet. In general, denser, thicker pads yield better results than thinner, softer ones by holding their shapes longer and being more resistant to dirt and stains. In back-of-the-house areas that are subject to traffic of heavy carts and where an impression of luxury and coziness is not necessary, carpets may be glued directly to the floor.

Carpets should be dense to the point of not showing the backing when bending a piece with both hands with the pile facing up. In woven carpets the density of the pile is measured by the number of lengthwise yarns in a 27-inch width of carpet. In tufted carpets, the density (gauge) is measured by the number of tufts per widthwise inch expressed in fractions where the numerator of the fraction indicates the number of inches and the denominator the number of tufts. A gauge of 3/40, for instance, indicates that there should be 40 tufts in every 3 inches of carpet. Another way of ascertaining the quality of a carpet, all else being equal, is by its **face weight**, or its number of ounces of yarn per square yard. The greater the face weight, the better the quality.

Two types of fibers are used in carpet construction: natural and synthetic, each one having peculiar characteristics and a number of usage advantages and disadvantages. Wool is a soft-to-the-touch, durable, resilient but expensive natural fiber that has been used in carpet making for centuries. Because of its absorbent fibers, wool is susceptible to damage from strong chemicals and has poor abrasion resistance. Most fibers used in carpets today are made of nylon, which has a high crush resistance and, therefore, long life.

Nylon also has a high melting point, which prevents marks caused by objects dragged across the carpet. Nylon fibers can be treated with chemicals to effectively prevent their soiling and staining. Carpets made with a blend of wool and nylon offer an excellent combination of the best qualities inherent in these fabrics.

The best characteristic of **polypropylene (olefin)** is that it doesn't absorb moisture, thus it resists stains and eliminate the need for much of the otherwise required maintenance. Because of its resistance to sun fading, olefin is recommended for outdoor carpeting. In general, solid colors in all carpets, especially light colors, show more dirt, which requires frequent vacuuming.

Executive housekeepers should have sufficient knowledge of carpet construction to ensure that the right carpet is selected for each area in the property. There are three main elements in the composition of carpets: the **pile**, or face; the **backing**, or material to which the pile is secured; and the **padding**, or cushion on which the carpet rests. Most commercial carpets are **tufted**, that is, the yarn is threaded through the backing material to form loops. The backing material usually is woven **jute** or polypropylene with a layer of adhesive latex extended over the material to anchor the tufts. Knitted carpets are made by interlacing together the pile yarn and the backing. The process of embedding the pile fibers electrostatically into a layer of adhesive material applied to the backing is called **flocking**. Weaving is the old-fashioned way of making carpets using conventional looms. The yarns are interlaced together to form the pile and the backing. As in linen, the yarns woven lengthwise are called the **warp** and the yarns going across are the **wefts**. The process of making carpets by compacting the fibers and the backing by mechanically punching them together is called **needle punching**.

Lighting

Improper lighting in rooms may discourage guests from staying in a particular establishment. Guests, particularly business travelers, expect to find adequate lighting to be able to work over flat surfaces such as tables and desks, or to read in bed or sitting on a couch or armchair. Lights of adjustable intensity should be placed strategically so that guests can arrange their preferences to suit their needs; for example, subdued lighting for relaxation or bright lighting for working or entertaining friends. Three-way lamps or lights activated by rheostats give guests the option to set the mood of the room to their liking. Floor lamps are not recommended in guestrooms because they can be easily knocked over and they create tripping hazards. Desk lamps should have the on-off switches at the base to reduce the risk of guests burning their fingers on the light bulb or upsetting the shade's balance when reaching around to locate the switch. Lampshades should be made of plastic rather than paper or fabric for longer life. When choosing fluorescent lighting, warm rather than cool light-giving units should be installed to avoid harsh tones of light. Pink incandescent light bulbs provide tones that enhance the appearance of guests when they look at themselves in the mirror. One advantage of fluorescent lights is that they use less energy and last longer than regular bulbs. In all cases, sufficient wattage must be provided in lamps that guests will use for reading or working purposes.

Health Club, Sheraton Hotel Ankara, Turkey
Courtesy of Starwood Hotels & Resorts Worldwide, Inc.

EQUIPMENT

Long gone are the days when hoteliers could sell rooms equipped with a minimum of basic features. Today's business traveler is putting a new spin on the concept of guestroom equipment. Examples of guestroom technology equipment are:

- High-speed wireless Ethernet offering isolation between users (private VLAN).
- TV with access to movies on demand and video games for kids.
- TV with Internet access for guests who have not brought their own laptop but would like to browse from their rooms.
- Rooms should be equipped with sufficient outlets for charging cell phones, cameras, and laptops.

Guestrooms are often equipped with multi-line telephones; some hotels even provide cellular phones and 24-hour access to translators and information in other languages. Office centers are fitted with high-tech office support equipment, such as computers with desktop publishing, a printer, a fax machine, a scanner, a video room, and a drafting center.

Refrigerators and microwave ovens are quite common in suite hotels, and coffee makers, together with selections of coffee and tea blends, are now available in the rooms of most properties. Wide-screen television sets and high-quality clock radios are a must in four- and five-diamond properties, as are in-room safes.

In-room strongboxes are seen as a last-ditch defense for the guests' personal belongings, including items as large as laptop computers. The locking systems of in-room safes range from ordinary keys to digital programmable push buttons, magnetic-lock devices, and the guest's credit card. Some microprocessor safes automatically lock for 30 minutes after four false attempts to open them. Besides being a great convenience for guests who don't want to line up for safety deposit boxes, in-room safes are effective against thieves and even employees who may use stolen keys to burglarize rooms. Valuables can be stored by guests themselves and remain secure during trips to the pool, jogging around the block, or going out to dinner. Some safes have built-in memory, which enables the front office personnel to read the date and time of the most recent safe openings and closings. This can provide convincing evidence in case of a loss claim against the property.

Some upscale lodging properties, particularly resorts and first-class hotels, offer minibars in their guestrooms and suites. Stocked with beverages and snacks, minibars can be profitable because guests are often tempted to have a last drink before going to bed or first thing in the morning. Fully automated minibars can electronically sense when an item is removed, sending the corresponding charge to the guest's room account. Nonautomated units must rely on the honesty of the guest to notify the front desk just before checking out if goods have been consumed. New technology allows minibar attendants to use a hand-held device to display and refill requirements electronically. This system helps to speed up replenishments and reduce labor costs.

SOFTWARE

Depreciable fixed assets that are not furniture or equipment, such as bedspreads, mattress covers, blankets, pillows, and window coverings, may be categorized as software.

Bedspreads

Like mattresses, bedspreads should be purchased with the qualities of durability, comfort, maintenance, and fire safety in mind. Bedspreads are an important component in the décor of guestrooms and should complement the motif, color, and design of the room. Fabrics made of 100 percent polyester offer excellent resistance to fading, staining, shrinking, and wrinkling. Woven fabrics perform better than knitted ones, which can make pattern colors appear faded if the knit loosens. **Polycottons**, a blend of polyester cotton (usually 50/50 or 70/30), are less expensive than fabrics made of 100 percent polyester, but their life span is shorter, they have fewer fire-retardant qualities, and they fade more easily. While the normal recycling life span of a good bedspread should be at least five years, polycotton bedspreads only last from two to three years.

Other factors to consider when specifying bedspreads are their fill and seaming. Fill is one of the key elements that determines the appearance of bedspreads. The number of ounces of fill per square yard should be seven or more. Noncompressed fills are better than mechanically packed fills because their ability to spring back to their original loft is greater.

Wide, seamless bedspreads are preferred to those constructed with seams because they don't come apart as easily. Bedspreads can be large enough to reach to the floor or just to cover the mattress. In the latter case, a pleated cloth skirting called a **dust ruffle** may be placed between the mattress and the box spring to extend around the sides and foot of the bed. Washable bedspreads should be purchased with the guarantee that they will not shrink, fade, or wrinkle. Par levels for bedspreads should be one plus 10 percent to allow for washing and replacement.

Blankets

The purpose of blankets is to act as insulators. A heavy blanket does not necessarily keep the warmth of the body from escaping through it. On the other hand, a material (even if it is light) that is tightly woven will retain body heat. However, all blankets should be porous enough to allow any moisture buildup under them to escape to the surrounding air. Wool is a delicate natural fiber that is very warm but requires extreme care when laundered. Cotton, on the other hand, washes easily but is a poor insulator and shrinks up to 15 percent if not purchased preshrunk. Blankets made of synthetic fibers such as acrylics and **polyester**, if properly constructed, are suitable for commercial operations. Vellux, a material that contains nylon fibers and foam, is commonly found in the composition of commercial blankets. Acrylic fibers cause fewer allergic reactions in guests and are warmer than polyester but not as strong.

Because guests may fall asleep while smoking in bed, blankets should be fire retardant. The size of the blanket should be large enough to cover the length and width of the mattress and have some additional inches for tucking. Blankets that are too short will wear out from constant tugging by the guests.

Mattress Covers

All mattresses should be fitted with moisture-proof covers at all times to prevent staining. Vinyl plastic covers are impermeable and can be washed like any other fabric. Their use is recommended for cribs or small cots for young children and hospital beds. Felt pads made of moisture-proof, flame-retardant, 100 percent polyester resist shrinkage and are quite durable. Quilted all-cotton pads are very comfortable but have a tendency to shrink and pucker after a few washings.

Pillows

Comfortable pillows are a necessary complement to comfortable mattresses. It is advisable to provide two pillows per person, for most guests like to prop them up high to watch television in bed. Most commercial pillows are filled with synthetic fiber, mainly polyester. Synthetic pillows are quite common in commercial properties because they are inexpensive, easy to launder, and nonallergenic. When purchasing pillows, it is important to make sure that the fill is of good quality so that it springs back into shape easily; lumpy, heavier fills are an indication of inferior grade. The synthetic covering of the pillow must be fire retardant, stain proof, and able to withstand frequent washings.

Pillows with natural fills such as down and feathers are very expensive, particularly goose down. Lodging properties should stock a few natural-fill pillows to meet the occasional request for them. Because of the price, down and feather pillows should be provided to guests on a loan basis in non-luxury properties, that is, a record should be kept in the housekeeping department of the room number where the pillows were delivered and then should be recovered after the guest's checkout.

Wall Coverings

The first consideration for selecting wall coverings is that they match the general décor of the room; the second, and just as important, consideration is their durability and ease of maintenance. The two most common forms of wall coverings are paint and vinyl. The paint used to finish walls should be easy to wash with soapy water and of very good quality so that the surface doesn't require repainting after a short period of time. Vinyl wall coverings are available in several thicknesses to suit the area to be covered; for instance, walls covered with thin layers are vulnerable to bumps from baggage and carts and should be used only to cover no-traffic areas. Heavier vinyl can withstand heavy impacts and can be used over surfaces susceptible to abrasion. Although far more expensive than paint, vinyl wall coverings generally pay for themselves because they require very little maintenance. Vinyl coverings are made by laminating the material to cotton or polycotton backings and are glued to walls using an adhesive paste. To prevent mildew from loosening the vinyl from the adhesive, the glue should contain a mildewcide. Fabric wall coverings can provide rooms and hallways with a luxurious, elegant look but they should be avoided in commercial operations because of the difficulty of cleaning or replacing them when soiled. Wallpaper should be used only if it is stain- and-water-resistant and allows for damp cleaning with soap and sponge.

Service areas, busy hallways, and elevators where carts and dollies may gouge the walls should be protected with rubber or heavy vinyl cove base and wall guards. Corner salients should be reinforced with thick plastic corner guards.

Window Coverings

Most windows in guestrooms are covered with curtains and sheers. Windows in offices, lobbies, and employee areas are usually fitted with vinyl blinds.

Because of their susceptibility to fading, fabrics used for curtains must be resistant to direct sunlight. As curtains attract dust and odors, they require frequent washings and dry cleaning; for this reason, it is advisable to purchase good-quality, vinyl-coated fabrics that can retain their shape and color for long periods of time. Curtains should be flame retardant to comply with local fire departments specifications.

Drapery can be simple or quite ornate. Valances and shirred or pinch-pleated fabrics can add elegance and warmth to rooms, although they will require more cleaning time to keep them dust free. In all cases, the curtain rods and cords must be sturdy to avoid damage; having batons instead of cords may reduce the chance of breakage.

DEPARTMENT EQUIPMENT

Besides FF&E and software material, the housekeeping department needs major pieces of equipment to clean guest, public, and employee areas and to transport clean and soiled linen, trash, and supplies. In all cases, the department equipment used in housekeeping should be of heavy-duty quality, able to withstand rough and continuous use. Often, purveyors of chemical supplies also carry a complete line of equipment. In some cases, manufacturers have their own representatives who will describe the machines and demonstrate their performance.

Perhaps the most significant piece of housekeeping equipment is the housekeeping cart. Usually, one cart is assigned to the cleaner of each section of guestrooms (the section housekeeper) and one to each public areas attendant. The cart should be large enough and have enough shelves to carry a full complement of supplies needed in each working shift in order to avoid unnecessary trips to the linen room for additional supplies. Although sturdy, the cart must be light and maneuverable enough to be pushed by one person from door to door and from floor to floor, including into and out of service elevators. The cart should be contoured with rubber bumpers to protect walls and wall corners and have casters with brakes of superior quality. Some carts can be purchased with side panels that can be locked in order to prevent linen and guest amenities from being exposed to whoever walks past them, thus eliminating theft. If fitted with laundry and trash bags, these should be made of heavy-duty material to withstand hard use. Plastic baskets or **caddies** containing guest amenities and cleaning supplies are generally placed on the top shelf of carts.

Vacuums

Several types of vacuum cleaners are used by housekeeping. One requirement common to all of them is that they be heavy-duty and powerful enough to provide efficient, one-pass cleaning. The typical vacuum cleaner used in guestroom carpet cleaning is upright, with one or two motors. The dual-motor type has one motor to drive the beater brush and another to provide the suction. Some useful characteristics of commercial vacuums are as follows: having collector cups or zipper receptacles instead of paper bags (some models can be messy and difficult to empty, in which case it is better to use disposable bags), long electric cable, wraparound bumpers, secondary filters to protect the vacuum motor, adjustable brush settings, three-position handles, and self-lubricating brushes. Some vacuums are incorporated into the housekeeping cart. This arrangement, however, may cause some difficulties. Because the hoses must be long enough to reach all corners of the room, suction power may be reduced. Also, because the machine is attached to the cart, repairs and maintenance are more difficult to perform on site than in the engineering shop.

Large-area vacuums are used in hallways and lobbies that contain extensive areas of carpeting. In very large ballrooms and meeting rooms, vacuums with 30-inch brushes should be used. These high-power machines can operate at 1,200 rpm and are able to service 14,000 square feet of surface per hour. **Wet/dry vacuums** are designed for wet pickup on any type of hard flooring surface. Equipped with a wide squeegee, they can be used to remove liquids when hard floors are stripped or for any kind of liquid absorption. **Back vacuums** worn by the housekeeper are convenient for dusting and cleaning vertical or high surfaces and fixtures, especially curtains, drapes, and wall coverings. Back vacuums are light, quiet machines equipped with adjustable straps and hoses that can be expanded to three times their normal length.

Floor Machines

Floor machines are designed to mechanically polish, buff, strip, scrub, grind, sand, burnish, and shampoo surfaces. Usually one multipurpose machine can be used for several tasks by changing the pad as needed to accomplish the task at hand. **Burnishers** are used when the property has large areas of terrazzo or tile floor. These machines are capable of burnishing up to 30,000 square feet per hour. **Polishers** are heavily weighted machines used to grind, sand, and polish marble and other stone floors. **Scrubbers** are used to automatically scrub hard or resilient surfaces by applying a stripping solution and recovering the liquid as the machine is pushed along the surface. Large scrubbers feature 40-gallon stripping solution and recovery tanks, a 34-inch self-propelled scrubber, and a 37-inch squeegee assembly, and can service 44,000 square feet per hour. **Extractors** are used to clean carpets and rugs. The simplest and least expensive consists of a machine with two tanks—one that holds the cleaning solution and one that collects the suctioned liquid. A better version has a beater brush attached to the wand to deepen the penetration of the cleaning solution into the carpet fabric. **Self-contained extractors** are very convenient to operate as they don't require a wand or hoses. The best models have four-phase cleaning action (spray, scrub, rinse, and extract in one pass) with a spray power of 100 psi. Self-contained carpet extractors are also available with dry foam instead of liquid solution.

OTHER DEPARTMENT EQUIPMENT

When large lodging properties use drinking glasses made of glass (rather than plastic), glass washers are necessary. The practice of washing housekeeping glasses in the kitchen's dishwashers is not an effective one as it is usually seen as an "encroachment" by the food and beverage department personnel. When operating a glass washer, the right type of detergent and the correct water temperature as determined by the local health department must be provided.

Rather than transporting trash, soiled linen, and supplies in plastic bags, lodging properties should use light trucks or **hoppers**. This is preferable to hauling material in bags carried over the shoulder, especially along public hallways.

CLEANING SUPPLIES

Cleaning supplies are categorized under operating assets and are included in the property's operating budget. Cleaning supplies comprise the chemicals necessary to perform the myriad cleaning jobs throughout the property and the nonchemical utensils needed to apply, scrub, rub, cleanse, wipe, etc. the chemicals onto all types of surfaces. There are several hundred manufacturers of cleaning chemicals, each of which markets and sells countless products. The responsibility of selecting and using the right chemicals rests with the executive housekeeper.

PURCHASING SUPPLIES

In large properties, the purchasing function, including housekeeping products, is performed by the **purchasing agent**. However, it should be up to the executive housekeeper to determine what products to use in the department, and to inform the purchasing agent of the specifications and characteristics required for the supplies to be bought. Because marked differences exist among products, before choosing cleaning supplies they should be tested by the employees who will use them regularly. Public areas attendants, housepersons, and section housekeepers must agree that the products chosen will be effective. An agreement should be made between the department and the vendor to train workers, at no cost, on how to use the cleaning supplies properly.

As with many other products, price should be only one of the factors regarding the purchasing decision, the others being availability, service, and quality. For instance, if a product is difficult to obtain, if the purveyor doesn't provide training and technical support, and if much larger quantities than a more expensive one have to be used, you might not obtain the expected value from it. Shopping for cleaning supplies must be done competitively, that is, trying to obtain the best price for the same or comparable product. When asking for a product quotation, the executive housekeeper must be very specific regarding its packaging, composition, and concentration. Figure 5.1 is a **competitive shopping form** on which the price, service, and other remarks are kept for cleaning supplies of similar quality from at least two different vendors. Product prices should be obtained once every two or three months. In practice, it is common to select one vendor for most cleaning supplies needs, while keeping abreast of new products and prices offered by competitors.

FIGURE 5.1   Sample Competitive Shopping Form

	UNIT	VENDOR 1	VENDOR 2	REMARKS
All-purpose cleaner	gallon			
Liquid degreaser	gallon			
Disinfectant spray	6-ounce can			
Deodorant spray	8-ounce can			

It is important to designate specific days and times to receive salespeople. Placing orders by phone can help save time, although direct contact with vendors is essential as they generally are specialists in their fields and, therefore, are able to suggest the solution to severe cleaning problems. Periodic shipments of supplies may be arranged for those products used in large quantities; however, in no case should vendors be allowed to place an order without the direct approval of the person in charge of purchasing.

Because the cleaning supplies market is quite competitive, it is common for vendors to offer free items and personal prizes to the person in charge of buying. It is only ethical to assume that any discount or give-away should benefit the property and not the buying individual. Accepting gifts or kickbacks should be prohibited, so for example if a vendor gives the purchasing agent tickets for an upcoming football game, the tickets should be rejected or, if accepted, raffled off among all employees.

Bulk purchasing of chemicals generally allows for great savings in price to the house-keeping department. There are, however, serious disadvantages with buying chemicals in large quantities. For instance, overbuying products may mean having to store them for long periods of time, tying up resources and space. Chemicals may also deteriorate while in storage and actually be more labor intensive. For example, decanting a liquid from a 55-gallon drum into smaller containers may take a considerable amount of time. Human error when mixing concentrates and water or causing spills may also be a considerable disadvantage. Although **pre-measured chemicals** are ready to be used as purchased, thus not requiring much handling, their higher cost is a disadvantage. The fact that they generate a lot of trash as they are used is also an inconvenience. In-house **chemical dispensers** or mixing stations can be a good alternative to both bulk and pre-measured products. The dispensers, plumbed to hot or cold water, can automatically mix bulk chemicals, eliminating human error and labor cost from the process.

HOUSEKEEPING CHEMICALS

The three major purposes of chemicals used in the housekeeping department are to remove dirt, to destroy harmful microorganisms, and to preserve and beautify furniture, fixtures, and surfaces. Chemical cleaners are manufactured to remove soils from surfaces through chemical action. The stronger the chemical is, the better it will get the job done. The strength of cleaning chemicals is measured on the **pH scale**. In chemistry, pH is a measure of the acidity and basicity of a solution; a low pH indicates a high concentration of hydronium ions, while a high pH denotes a low concentration. The scale goes from 1 to 14, 1 indicating a very acidic solution, 14 a very alkaline solution, and 7 a neutral solution. For example, a very acidic solution should be near pH 1; pure water is neutral, giving a pH of 7; and a solution highly alkaline should be close to pH 14. Cleaning chemicals that have been enhanced with alkalis or acids to strengthen their cleaning powers can be dangerous to humans and often cannot be used on certain surfaces. A neutral cleaner can be used for all types of jobs, but its cleaning power is limited.

The executive housekeeper should have adequate knowledge of the department's needs to select cleaning chemicals appropriate for each type of cleaning job performed regularly in the housekeeping department. Generally speaking, high-alkaline cleaners are effective degreasers while acidic cleaners are good for fighting lime and rust, which are always found in urinals and toilets. Another name for cleaners is **detergents**. Detergents act chemically to emulsify dirt, holding it in suspension so it can be removed away from the surface. Synthetic detergents are easy to rinse off and often have excellent cleaning, deodorizing, and germicidal characteristics. Most cleaning detergents are made from mineral oils. **All-purpose cleaners** have close to neutral pH-balanced formulas for general-purpose cleaning jobs. They usually are synthetic detergents, often vegetable-oil-based, of which pine oil is very popular because of its pleasant scent and strong deodorizing power. All-purpose cleaners may have corrosion inhibitors to protect metal surfaces. **Single-purpose cleaners** are heavy-duty cleaners used for specific cleaning jobs. Abrasive cleaners are cleaning powders or pastes combined with silica for tough cleaning jobs. These cleaners will scratch soft surfaces like fiberglass or porcelain. Gentler cleansers made with nonscratching calcite instead of silica greatly reduce their abrasive action. Degreasers are highly effective cleaners, often biodegradable, that remove grease, tar, ink, food deposits, smoke film, fats and other grimy soils. Degreasers can be highly effective on concrete floors. It is important to remember that some products advertised as degreasers may be toxic and, therefore, not suitable for use on kitchen surfaces.

Although most all-purpose cleaners can be used as deodorizers, stronger chemicals are needed to counteract stale odors. Deodorizers, or air fresheners, should neutralize odors without adding strong perfume scents in the space to be deodorized. Deodorizers can be purchased as mists, wall and urinal blocks, cup and wick, and aerosols. Glass cleaners are ammonia- and alcohol-based products that clean and provide a protective coating to glass surfaces. Glass treated with good-quality glass cleaners resists fogging caused by moisture and temperature changes and to some extent repels dust, dirt, fingerprints, and smudges. Most glass cleaners can also be used as multipurpose cleaners on chrome, stainless steel, enamel, formica, ceramic tile, and other washable surfaces. Metal cleaners are nonscratching products that remove rust, tarnish, corrosion, and grime from metal surfaces and fixtures. These products can be used on brass, stainless steel, copper, chrome, and aluminum materials. Metal cleaners can be purchased as liquids, aerosols, pastes, and cotton wadding.

Another purpose of housekeeping supplies is to beautify surfaces and fixtures. Furniture polishes are liquid waxes or oils or silicone-based sprays designed to protect and give shine to wood, leather, vinyl, metal, and plastic surfaces. When pigments are added to liquid furniture polish, the product helps cover nicks and scratches in wood furniture, paneling, and floors. Most metal surfaces can be dusted, cleaned, and polished with metal polishes. Strong liquid metal polishes can remove rust, corrosion, tarnish, and grime from brass, stainless steel, copper, chrome, and aluminum. Cream polishes are quite effective in cleaning sterling silver, silver-plated utensils, nickel, and pewter.

Restroom and Bathroom Cleaners

Strong acidic cleaners are needed to clean away lime and rust deposits in restroom and bathroom fixtures. Bowl cleaners may contain hydrochloric or phosphoric acid to cut scale and calcium deposits with little or no scrubbing. Milder bowl cleaners are nonacid and nonabrasive, designed not to etch or pit porcelain fixtures, but their cleaning power is lower. Most toilet cleaners kill bacteria and viruses, including the HIV-1 virus, on contact. Public areas attendants and section housekeepers should be trained well in how to handle these powerful products. Acidic bowl cleaners, for example, should not come in contact with metal attachments, stone, or tile surfaces. Public and employee urinals are usually deodorized and disinfected with paradichlorobenzene blocks that neutralize offensive odors.

Graffiti removers consist of a gel formula that effectively effaces ink, crayon, lipstick, some spray paints, magic marker, and bumper stickers from most hard surfaces. These powerful products should not be used, however, on rubber, vinyl, plastic, or painted surfaces.

Besides cleaning, housekeeping chemicals can be used to control and kill pathogenic bacteria by sanitizing and disinfecting surfaces and utensils. Disinfectants are germicidal chemicals that kill microorganisms and prevent them from multiplying. Often, germicides are combined with chlorinated liquid detergents to act as both germ killer and cleanser, making them effective against many forms of microorganisms, including salmonella, fungi, and a broad range of viruses. Aerosol disinfectants are generally much stronger as they are able to eliminate most bacteria and viruses such as herpes simplex, influenza, and HIV-1. Hand soaps are also important in fighting contagious diseases. Liquid soaps used by employees in back-of-the-house areas should be antimicrobial and capable of reducing nosocomial infections caused by the fungal organism *Candida albicans*. Guest liquid soaps should be formulated with emollients to soften the skin, have a pleasant fragrance, and produce a rich lather.

Floor Care Chemicals

Hard and resilient floor cleaners must be pH neutral, that is, mild enough to clean dirt from surfaces without affecting polymer finishes, sealers, and shines. Floor cleaners are water- or vegetable-oil-based and can be applied to synthetic surfaces, marble, terrazzo, and other washable floors. Stronger solvent-based cleaners, capable of erasing heel marks, rubber burns, tar, and grease from concrete and hard wood surfaces, are very effective but will affect the floor finish when applied. **Strippers** are chemicals used to remove and clean old floor finishes prior to rewaxing, resealing, or refinishing them. These products penetrate and emulsify worn wax buildup, polymer and acrylic finishes, and surface dirt deposits. After the floor has been stripped, the alkaline residue should be neutralized with a **neutralizer rinse** prior to applying a new finish. Floor **sealers** are used to protect porous surfaces such as concrete, terrazzo, wood, and marble from staining. Stronger sealers have a substantial amount of solids and are formulated to fill scratches and provide a base for floor finishes. Some sealers can coat and polish surfaces at the same time. Resilient floor finishes usually contain detergent-resistant acrylic polymers. Good products are burnishable and resistant to scuffing and black marks, acting both as sealers and finishes.

Carpet Chemicals

Carpet shampoo is marketed under many commercial brands, and its composition can be different as well. Some shampoos are water-based and are a blend of polymers, biodegradable surfactants, and solvents. Soil-retarding carpet shampoos provide a fluorochemical barrier to protect against dirt, dust, spills, and stains. Defoamers are silicone foam suppressors used to eliminate foam from the recovery system of steam cleaners. Anti-static sprays are designed to eliminate static electricity buildup on wool and synthetic carpets caused by foot traffic or low humidity. Spot removers are concentrated formulas used to pre-spray carpets before shampooing to remove tar, grease, lipstick, graffiti, and food or beverage stains.

CLEANING ACCESSORIES

The number of nonchemical cleaning supplies in the housekeeping inventory can be substantial, ranging from broom to wringer. Upright brooms are sold under several denominations, such as warehouse, household, lobby, porter, and whisk brooms. In all cases, upright brooms should be heavy duty and have wire bands to help retain their shape. Push brooms usually consist of a combination of horse hair and synthetic fibers. For durability, the broom block should be attached to the handle by a sturdy metal brace. Wet mops also come in a variety of forms: four-ply cotton-synthetic fiber blend mops have good absorption; mops with looped ends are more durable than cut-ended. Some brands feature mildew- and bacteria-resistant mops with scrubber headbands and double banding. Tight-twisted string-style eight-ply mops are specially designed for floor finishing applications. Mop buckets/wringers come in different shapes and forms as well. Dual-bucket systems consist of two overlapping buckets mounted on a mobile platform with casters; one bucket holds the cleaning solution and the other carries the rinse water for better sanitation. Heavy-duty plastic buckets are preferable to zinc ones as they are quieter, have no corrosion, and will not dent.

Handling and Storing Chemicals

Hazardous materials are dangerous as they can harm both workers and property. Knowing how to safely handle, mix, and store them can protect employees, guests, and the company from explosions, fires, environmental contamination, higher insurance premiums, and costly litigation. Besides being dangerous, chemicals are expensive and strict guidelines should be followed to hold employees accountable for their proper dilution and use.

HAZARD COMMUNICATION (HAZCOMM)

Because chemical exposure may cause or contribute to serious health effects, the Occupational Safety and Health Administration (OSHA) requires, in order to protect workers from unsafe working conditions, that employees handling chemicals are informed of the risks that these chemicals pose and that the employer provides appropriate training on how to use them safely. Failure to comply with OSHA's HazComm regulations may result in fines if inspections of the property indicate that the directions have not been followed. HazComm requires that a list of all hazardous chemicals used in the housekeeping department be compiled and kept updated. The OSHA program lists the following employer responsibilities:

- Identify and list hazardous chemicals in the workplace.
- Display **Material Safety Data Sheets (MSDSs)** and labels for each hazardous chemical, if not provided by the manufacturer or distributor.
- Implement a written HazComm program, including an employee training plan.
- Communicate hazardous information to employees.

Each container of hazardous chemicals entering the workplace must be labeled or marked with the identification of the chemical, appropriate hazard warnings, and the name and address of the manufacturer of the product. The Material Safety Data Sheet is provided by the manufacturer or importer of the product and should describe the following:

- Physical hazards inherent in the product.
- Possible health hazards.
- Precaution for safe handling and use.
- Emergency and first-aid procedures.
- The information must be provided in English (plus other languages if desired).
- MSDSs for each hazardous product must be readily accessible to employees in the work area.

The executive housekeeper must then develop a program to let all employees be aware of and alert to the hazardous materials they will come in contact with, teaching them about their specific characteristics and dangers. The program may include lectures provided by distributors of chemical products, videos, discussions, and hands-on demonstrations. Because people who work in housekeeping maybe unable to understand English, labels with color codes or signs are strongly recommended.

Workers should wear the right personal protective equipment when handling certain chemicals—mainly gloves, face masks, and goggles. Mixing or combining hazardous materials must be done strictly following the manufacturer's guidelines. Acids and caustics, for instance, can cause violent reactions when combined. Transferring liquids from one container to another can produce flammable vapors that can ignite easily. Worker exposure to hazardous materials may cause allergies, such as eye, nose, and throat irritation, skin rashes, anxiety, and nausea. In severe cases, chemicals may cause dizziness, vomiting, blindness, and even death.

To comply with OSHA's regulations, the housekeeping department must display a list of all the chemicals used, specifying information about the manufacturer, the product's hazardous ingredients, its physical and chemical characteristics, flammability, recommended handling, health hazards, and what to do in case of ingestion, fire, or explosion. This information is obtained from the manufacturers' MSDS provided when the product is purchased. Employees working with chemicals should be required to read and understand product warning labels. The list must be updated and made available to employees at all times. Chemicals should never be stored near food products but in separate storage, preferably under lock and key. Flammable liquids and sprays should be stored in a cool, dry place away from heat and sunlight. Enclosing them in metal lockers is best, in order to avoid possible fires from spreading. Acid chemicals should be stored separately from each other. Detailed information on how to be in compliance with HazComm standards may be obtained from the Superintendent of Documents, Government Printing Office, Washington, D.C.

GUEST SUPPLIES

Lodging companies provide their guests with guestroom items intended to make their stay as convenient and comfortable as possible. These items also raise the guests' perceived value for the rate paid when occupying a room or rooms.

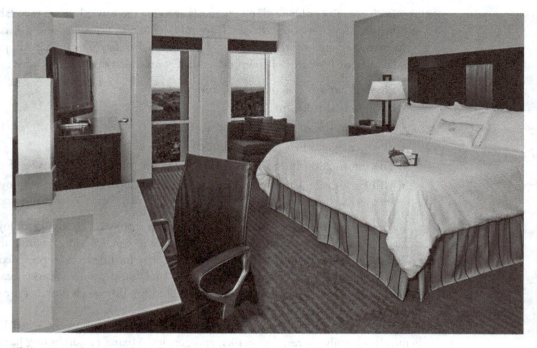

King room, Crowne Plaza Tampa, IHG
Courtesy of Six Continents Hotels, Inc.

NONREUSABLE SUPPLIES

Also called **amenities**, nonreusable supplies are items that guests are expected to use up or may take away with them when at the end of their stay. Tables 5.2 and 5.3 are limited lists of bathroom and guestroom amenities commonly supplied by lodging properties. Finding the right amenities for a property must be a calculated endeavor; the higher the room rate is, the more luxurious amenities should be. Conversely, rates paid by guests in economy properties do not allow providing them with extravagant supplies. But, in all cases, today's travelers have come to expect the best possible

TABLE 5.2 Sample Bathroom Amenity Items

After-shave lotion	Hand lotion
Bath gel	Hand soap
Bath salts	Mouthwash
Bath soap	Nail clippers
Body lotion	Perfume
Body powder	Razor
Cologne	Scissors
Cosmetics	Shampoo and conditioner
Deodorant	Shaving cream
Fabric wash	Shower cap
Facial tissue	Suntan lotion

TABLE 5.3 Sample Guestroom Amenity Items

Bathrobe	Mints
Candy	Notepads
Chocolates	Pens
Coffee and tea	Postcards
Cookies	Sewing kit
Corkscrew	Shoe horn
Flowers	Shoe mitt
Fruit	Slippers
Laundry bags	Stationery
	Matches

amenities for the type of establishment they patronize. For example, guest surveys indicate that about 75 percent of respondents rank bathroom amenities as "extremely" or "very desirable" attributes when traveling on business, second only to the property's full-scale services. Overall, a property's amenities figure very highly in the total sum of what a particular establishment represents to the traveler, who often equates the facility's image with the amenities provided.

Bathroom Amenities

Some lodging properties offer guests their own private-label products, stamped with the company's logo, because they can be customized to fit their clientele's needs or because in most cases the cost is less. Others opt for adopting brand names, arguing that guests instantly recognize and prefer the quality of national and international brand amenities. The basic bathroom amenities for most properties are deodorant and hand soaps, shampoo and conditioner (often provided combined in one container), shower caps, and paper products.

Soap bars should be of reasonable size, usually 1.5 ounces for bath and .75 ounce for facial. Shampoo and conditioner should be provided in easy-to-open bottles with large tops or snap caps, as packets are very difficult to tear open with soapy hands. Shower caps are a necessity for guests to shower or bathe without wetting their hair if they so desire. Luxury properties usually provide sophisticated products like almond oatmeal and glycerin soaps, fancy toiletries, all-inclusive lost-luggage kits, and ecologically sensitive, all-natural items, packaged in recycled paper printed with soybean inks and wrapped in parchment to emphasize minimal paper use.

Paper products must be of premium quality. The facial tissue must be soft, absorbent, and durable, preferably 2-ply rather than 1-ply. Bath tissue should have a large number of sheets per roll so that less time is spent refilling dispensers. Adequate thickness and strength, as well as softness, are also necessary.

Guestroom Amenities

Upscale lodging establishments outdo each other by offering a vast range of amenities aimed at pampering their guests while they relax in their rooms. Today's hoteliers view personal-care amenities as a positioning tool for their lodging properties, in that the more plentiful and novel they are, the higher value for the rate paid is perceived by guests.

Coffee makers, together with several blends of gourmet and decaffeinated coffee and a variety of teas, are common. Besides the typical candy placed on the pillow at turndown-service time, companies are adding specialty confections, such as Belgian and Italian chocolates or fancy fortune mints, described as "rectangles attractively wrapped with witty fortunes and/or proverbs inside the wrappers." Chocolate-chip and oatmeal cookies, cosmetics, and safe-for-all-fabric stain removers are just a few of the $300-million-a-year products that the industry invests in for indulging guests.

REUSABLE SUPPLIES

Depending also on the quality of lodging establishments, reusable supplies can range from the bare-essential items offered by economy properties to the highly sophisticated, state-of-the-art technology found in first-class establishments. Supplies provided by most lodging properties are coat hangers, ice buckets, wastebaskets, ashtrays, a Bible, and glasses.

Coat hangers should be made of wood or hard plastic instead of flexible wire. Hangers with ball tops rather than hooks are usually not taken by guests, although some travelers find it difficult to fasten them to the lip on the closet rod. Women's hangers with skirt clips are designed for garments that hang better clipped than on a bar. Hangers are also available with clamping trouser bars to assure guests that the clothing will stay in place. Ice buckets are preferably insulated with polyethylene liners and have a lid; stainless steel buckets are very durable and have a stylish look. Providing tongs with the ice bucket is a nice touch. Rather than plain-looking rectangular rubber wastebaskets, oval fireproof ones made of metal with simulated grain leather are more elegant. For smoking rooms, heavy crystal ashtrays with beveled edges are best. The Gideons, a nonprofit organization, provide free of charge guestroom Bibles on request. The appearance of all guest supplies is greatly enhanced by imprinting the property's or chain logo on them. The cost of logo items taken as souvenirs may be compensated by the advertising effect they will have when seen by members of the family and friends proudly displayed in the guests' own residences. Glasses made of real glass are classier than the ones made of plastic, but they must be sterilized in a glass-washing machine. If management decides to use plastic glasses, they should be made of hard (rather than soft) plastic and be individually wrapped.

UNIFORMS

Uniforms for section housekeepers, housepersons, and public areas attendants should be functional, good looking, and comfortable, with sleeves that allow ease of movement. Badly designed, unstylish uniforms can affect the workers' morale and lower the property's image. Because of turnover, smocks, shirts, and pants must be easily alterable and able to stand frequent washings. While 100 percent cotton uniforms are comfortable to wear, they usually shrink, wrinkle, and cost more. Polyester/cotton blends are wrinkle-, shrink-, and soil-resistant, less costly, and easier to wash.

It is important to establish an adequate par of employee uniforms so that each worker is provided with a clean, fresh-looking outfit each day. The executive housekeeper should have on hand enough sizes of uniforms to fit all employees at any given time. The sight of large-framed employees clad in small-sized clothing and small-framed workers wearing large-sized uniforms should be avoided. In large properties, when the housekeeping department is in charge of keeping and maintaining uniforms for other departments, it is advisable to assign a specific employee to this particular task. In this case, a large, secure storage space and a commercial-size sewing machine for repairs and alterations should be provided. Uniformed departments, such as front desk and porters, often require outfits that need dry cleaning. Having uniforms dry cleaned outside of the property can be quite expensive, so the purchase of a dry-cleaning machine for employee and guest clothing should be considered.

In order to save space, capital investments, and labor costs, some properties may resort to having uniform services provided by companies that furnish a five-par of uniforms for each full-time employee on a weekly basis. Although quite convenient, this service may cost the property a considerable amount of money. The executive housekeeper must analyze the cost of purchasing, laundering, and maintaining uniforms in-house and that of having the service provided by an outside contractor. If the cost of the latter is substantially greater, the service should be conducted on the property.

One way to maintain adequate control of employee uniforms is to make each worker responsible for his or her outfit. A good procedure is not to issue a clean uniform unless the soiled one is returned. When employees are dismissed, their final checks should be retained until their uniforms are accounted for. If employees are required to clean their own uniforms, the law requires that they be compensated for the costs they incur.

LINEN CHARACTERISTICS

The category of linens encompasses bed sheets and pillowcases, described as bed linens, and towels and bath mats, described as bath linens. Other guestroom textiles (pillows, bedspreads, bed covers, mattress covers, etc.) have been described under the category of software). The management of linen inventories in lodging operations is always assigned to executive housekeepers. Expenses for linens in the rooms division budget is substantial, usually second only to the cost of salaries and wages. When the property has food and beverage outlets, such as banquets, restaurants, and coffee shops, the housekeeping department is usually in charge of laundering napkins and tablecloths. However, the expense of the **napery** (the name that describes these items) is not allocated to the housekeeping department budget but to that of the food and beverage department.

BED LINENS

The fabric for bed sheets and pillowcases is usually a blend of 50 percent of the natural fiber cotton and 50 percent of the synthetic fiber polyester. Fabrics made solely of cotton are not recommended for commercial use because they are not as durable as those blended with synthetic fibers; in some cases, a 50/50 blend cotton/polyester can last three times longer than full cotton. Usually, sheets made with blended fabrics can withstand over 500 washings, while all-cotton sheets begin to deteriorate after 200 washings.

Other disadvantages of cotton-only bed linen are that it absorbs more water, it shrinks, and it wrinkles in larger proportions than do the blends. Because full-cotton fabrics retain more water when being laundered, the drying time is greater, which means higher energy and labor costs. While fabric blends do not necessarily need to be ironed after washing, 100 percent cotton material must be pressed.

Quality

All other factors being equal, bed linen fabrics are better when their **thread count** is higher. Thread count is the number of threads per square inch of material. Commercial linen should have at least 180 thread count per square inch, represented as T = 180, in order to withstand multiple washings. Obviously, materials with a T count higher than 180 are preferable to those with a lower T count. Another method of ascertaining quality is to compare the amount of weight it takes to tear a 1 inch by 3 inch piece of fabric. All other factors being equal, the fabric that has a higher **tensile strength** is of better quality.

The way in which the cotton fibers have been prepared before spinning also determines fabric quality. Carded fibers are rougher to the touch and less durable than combed fabrics. Bed linen textiles made with carded fibers are called **muslin**; fabrics manufactured with combed fibers are called **percale**. Sheets and pillowcases made of percale fibers are of better quality, and therefore more expensive, than those made of muslin.

The way fabrics are woven is also an indicator of quality. **Plain-weave** textiles are made by interlacing the vertical thread (**warp**) with the horizontal yarn (**weft**). When the weft threads are woven by crossing the warp to produce an effect of parallel diagonal lines, the fabric is called **twill**. Because of the extra diagonal pattern, twill fabrics are denser, more durable, and therefore more expensive than plain-weave fabrics. Before linens are sold to commercial and residential buyers, the fabric is washed and treated with chemicals to give the cloth a shiny look. Linen is usually shipped in cartons containing lots of 12 units.

Size

Sheets and pillowcases must fit the mattresses and pillows they are to cover. Although several sizes of mattresses are used by lodging operations, executive housekeepers should limit the number of sizes in order to minimize the cost of sorting, counting, and storing them. The standard sheet sizes usually used in lodging properties are twin, double, queen, and king. The sizes for pillowcases are standard and large (see Table 5.4). The size (in inches) of the sheets should not include the top and bottom hems.

BATH LINENS

Towels, washcloths, and bath mats are made of a pile fabric with loops on both sides called **terrycloth**. The **ground warp**, or main body of the item, usually consists of a blend of two parts polyester and one part cotton. The **pile warp**, or yarn making the loops on both sides of the material, is made of 100 percent cotton fibers for full absorbency. The four narrow, flat side edges of the item with no pile warp are called the **selvage**. The selvage prevents unraveling.

TABLE 5.4 Sample Guestroom Linen Sizes

	Size (inches)
Sheets	
Twin	66 × 104
Double	81 × 104
Queen	90 × 108
King	108 × 110
Pillowcases	
Standard	20 × 30
Large	20 × 40
Bath Linen	
Bath towel (standard)	20 × 40
Bath towel (large)	24 × 50

Quality

All other factors being equal, the quality of terrycloth is determined by the weight of the item. The heavier the item, the thicker it will be. Good terry has double-thread loops for extra absorbency. Bath mats are made with extra heavy terry and are, therefore, more expensive.

Size

Terrycloth items come in several sizes, depending on the type of lodging property. Standard sizes in inches may be: 24 by 50 for bath towels, 16 by 26 for hand towels, 12 by 12 for washcloths, and 20 by 30 for bath mats. Luxury, oversize towels, sometimes called bath sheets, may be as large as 36 by 70 inches (see Table 5.4).

NAPERY

Because executive housekeepers are in charge of laundering table linens, they are often involved in selecting and purchasing napery. In properties offering restaurant, coffee shop, room service, and banquet services, the number of napkins and tablecloths used every day can be substantial.

Quality

Like bed linens, blended fabrics last longer than full-cotton materials. The least expensive material used in napery is **momie cloth**. This fabric is usually a plain weave 50/50 cotton/polyester blend that wears well. More high-end restaurants may use **damask**, a twill-woven fabric blend with a glossy, silky appearance. While momie cloth is made of carded cotton, damask is made of combed fiber that is more elegant and lasts longer than momie cloth. As for bed linen, napery should be ordered preshrunk and nonfading.

Size

The drape of a tablecloth should be level with the chair's seat or fall at least 12 inches below the table's edge (Table 5.5 provides some common tablecloth and napkin sizes).

SHOWER CURTAINS

Some lodging properties use shower curtains made of natural fibers. The advantage of this type of shower curtain is that they can be laundered at every guest's checkout, but on the downside, because they are light, they flap when the shower is turned on and don't contain the water within

TABLE 5.5 Sample Napery Sizes

	Size (inches)
Tablecloths	
Table for 2	54 × 54
Table for 4	64 × 64
Table for 6	72 × 72
Table for 8	90 × 90
Napkins	
Regular	17 × 17
Large	22 × 22

the tub. Most shower curtains are made of synthetic fibers such as vinyl or nylon. Nylon shower curtains are resistant to mildew and don't become brittle over time. Often, shower curtains consist of a nylon curtain on the outside and a vinyl liner on the inside for better protection against soap stains. In this case, the linen liner must be washed after each use.

LINEN PURCHASING

Linens can be purchased directly from the mill or through a linen broker. Orders placed with the mill must be for large quantities and may take considerable time to be delivered. For smaller orders, fast delivery, and dependable service, lodging properties usually purchase linens from local or regional brokers, who will make frequent scheduled calls on the property.

As with many other products, minimum standards for linens have been established by the federal government. The American Standards Association can provide the Minimum Performance Requirements for Institutional Textiles on request. The standards provide information about desirable characteristics of linen products regarding shrinkage, strength, and so on.

The main factors to consider when purchasing linen are, in this order: durability, laundry costs, and purchase price. These three factors can be used to ascertain the **cost per use** of an item. The cost per use of an article refers to the true cost of using an item. Although this method is quantifiable, its practicality is doubtful due to the difficulty of determining exactly the durability and laundry costs of linens. For example, although the life expectancy of a towel can be pre-established by the manufacturer, the final results are generally a direct cause of factors such as the chemicals used to launder the item, the number of times the item has been presoaked for stains, the temperature of the water, and so forth. Students, however, should be instructed how to ascertain the cost per use of articles so they understand that the purchase price is not the most important factor to be considered when buying linens.

The cost per use of an item is arrived at by multiplying the total number of washings expected of the item (its life expectancy) by its weight in pounds, times its preestablished laundry cost per pound, plus the purchase price of the article, divided by the same life expectancy. Thus, cost per use =

$$\frac{\text{Weight in pounds} \times \text{laundry cost} \times \text{life expectancy} + \text{purchase cost}}{\text{Life expectancy}}$$

For example, the laundry cost of a towel weighing 1.7 pounds has been determined at $0.15 per pound. The towel's life expectancy is 240 washings and its purchase price $6.50. The cost per use of the towel is $ 0.282 [(1.7) × (.15) × (240) + (6.50) = 67.7; 67.7 ÷ 240 = 0.282].

It is evident from the application of this formula that the purchase price should not be the most important consideration when purchasing linen; rather, the life expectancy and the laundry cost are the critical factors to be kept in mind.

Linens should be purchased **sanforized**, meaning that the fabric has been preshrunk at the source and, therefore, will not shrink considerably after the first washing. In order to minimize labor costs, the material should be purchased as "durable press" or chemically treated to require no ironing after laundering. White is the most common color choice for bed linens because they don't fade after several washings as dyed fabrics usually do.

Linens that have minor imperfections, hardly detectable by guests, are sold as **seconds**. It is common for lodging properties to save considerable costs by purchasing items marked as seconds. For instance, towels with an uneven selvage sold as seconds do not lose absorbency in any way and can be perfectly well used as firsts.

Whether or not to use towels with the property's or chain's monogram or logo woven on them should be decided by upper management. Logoed items are often taken by guests as souvenirs, which may cost the company a considerable amount of money over time. On the other hand, management may consider the loss a matter of marketing and may be willing to incur extra expenses for the sake of advertising the property or chain.

Dyed linens must be of very good quality to ensure that the colors do not fade after repeated washings. Improper laundering procedures also contribute to color fading; too much bleach used to remove stains, for instance, can make a dyed item look lighter than items that have not been pretreated before washing.

Smaller properties that don't have on-premise laundry may rent linens from companies that deliver on a daily basis. Most establishments, however, own their own bed linen and napery, in order to minimize costs and control quality. Companies or very large properties that order linen products directly from mills to minimize linen cost should plan ahead as much as possible to allow for possible long delays in production. Keeping track of linen usage in low and high occupancies during the year can help implement annual reordering plans on a regular basis. For example, a large property in Phoenix, Arizona, with a full occupancy from October through April and a lower occupancy thereafter, may have two large standing orders for bath towels to be delivered in November and February and two smaller orders in May and August. In all cases, any linen order should be equal to the par stock level minus the linen on hand at any given time:

$$\text{Order} = \text{Par Stock} - \text{Linen on Hand}$$

It is important to check carefully shipments of linen to verify that the goods received match the goods originally ordered. The executive housekeeper is usually in charge of placing new linen orders when items are below par, as revealed by physical inventories or when linens are discarded because of unsalvageable stains, damage, or excessive wear. New linens not in use should be under lock and key and their quantities recorded on a perpetual inventory where new deliveries are added on and issues subtracted.

PAR LEVELS

Lodging establishments must carry enough linen inventory to ensure that sheets, pillowcases, towels, bath mats, napkins, and tablecloths are available when needed. In properties where the linen stock is under par, the labor cost is usually high. This may occur if section housekeepers have to wait until linen is available to make up the beds and fit the bathrooms with clean towels and bath mats. It may also be the case that the laundry room needs to work around the clock to launder the soiled linen, which will require overtime pay and cause faster deterioration of linen and equipment. On the other hand, too large a linen inventory will mean tying down resources that might be needed elsewhere.

The amount of linen needed to outfit the property at 100 percent occupancy is defined as one **par**. The number of pars that lodging establishments require differs from property to property, depending on such factors as the output capacity of the laundry, the overall occupancy percentage of the establishment, the rate of replacement of worn, damaged, or stolen linen, and so forth. Another factor is the number of times the sheets are changed in guestrooms. First-class hotels insist in changing the bed linen daily, whether the guest stays over or not; others will change sheets every other day if the guest stays on. Other properties may follow the environmental protection trend to limit the use of water and laundry chemicals and place cards asking stay-over guests to notify housekeeping if they want sheets changed daily. In normal circumstances, the "ideal" number of pars for bed linen and terry items is four, distributed as follows: one par in the guestrooms, one in the floor service stations and carts ready to be used, one in the laundry room being washed, and one in reserve. A property operating with a par of four will need to stock four pieces of every item needed to set up one guestroom times every guestroom in the property.

Most lodging properties use two sheets per bed and provide two bath towels, two hand towels, and two washcloths per guest. Sometimes, a third sheet—often called snooze sheet—is set over the blanket to protect it from overuse. One bath mat is needed per bathroom. Figure 5.2 shows how to ascertain the linen requirements for a 500-room property that has 200 rooms with

FIGURE 5.2 Sample Linen Calculation Work Sheet

500-room property with:	200 king rooms				
	200 Q/Q rooms				
	100 Twin-bedded rooms				
Linen distribution per room:	2 sheets per bed				
	2 pillows per guest				
	2 hand towels per guest				
	2 washcloths per guest				
	1 bath mat per room				
Maximum houseguests: 1,400 (400 + 800 + 200)					
3.5 par for all items					

SHEETS

Room type	# of beds	× 2 sheets	total	× par	total sheets
King	200	2	400	3.5	1,400 king-size
Queen	400	2	800	3.5	2,800 queen-size
Twin	200	2	400	3.5	1,400 twin-size

PILLOWCASES

Maximum House guests	× 2 pillows	total	× par	total pillowcases
1,400	2	2,800	3.5	9,800 pillowcases

BATH TOWELS

Maximum House guests	× item per guest	total	× par	total towels
1,400	2	2,800	3.5	9,800 bath towels
1,400	2	2,800	3.5	9,800 hand towels
1,400	2	2,800	3.5	9,800 washcloths

BATH MATS

Number of bathrooms	× 1 bath mat	total	× par	total bath mats
500	1	500	3.5	1,750 bath mats

one king bed, 200 rooms with two queen beds each, and 100 twin-bedded rooms. Each guest is provided with two pillows, two bath towels, two hand towels, and two washcloths. All rooms have one bathroom. The predetermined par for this property was set at 3.5.

The par for table linen depends mainly on the number of covers served at each meal period and the output frequency of the laundry. For tablecloths, a par of four per each table in the restaurant is usually sufficient. For napkins, a par of four per number of covers served is also recommended. For instance, a restaurant with 70 seats and a diner turnover of 2.3 for lunch and 1.75 for dinner will need to establish a par of 1,134 napkins:

Type of service	Number of seats		Diner turnover		par	Total napkins needed
Lunch	70	(×)	2.3	(×)	4	= 644
Dinner	70	(×)	1.75	(×)	4	= 490

LINEN CONTROL

The loss (shrinkage) of linen in lodging properties can be staggering. Wear and tear, permanent stains, theft by guests and employees, and the use of towels, washcloths, and napkins for cleaning purposes are the main causes of linen loss. Employees and guests are fond of stealing the property's linen, especially if marked with the company's monogram. Misuse is also widespread; for example, polishing shoes, wiping all kinds of stains, and handling kitchen utensils with washcloths and napkins are common. Two basic steps to help minimize linen pilfering and misuse are providing the kitchen and cleaning staff with sufficient cleaning rags and establishing effective security measures. Cleaning cloths can be purchased directly from vendors or made on-premise from discarded linen. One way for employees to distinguish the difference between cleaning cloths and usable linen is to permanently dye the rags so that workers can be easily spotted when using the wrong items. Linen theft can be prevented by establishing security controls and by adopting a system of communication between housekeeping and the front desk by which the desk is rapidly notified of items missing from checkout rooms. The cost of the missing linen can be added to the guests' folio before checkout or charged to their credit card if they have already departed. However, being overzealous about controlling linens can be counterproductive and result in excessive labor costs. For instance, keeping track of linen in large properties by requiring section housekeepers to exchange soiled items removed from guest-rooms for clean ones can be exceedingly time-consuming. A more efficient method of linen control consists in spot-counting the linen issued and received in the laundry to and from a particular section or floor. This may show a difference large enough to be worth investigating.

Control of damaged linen should also be in place. Careful records of discarded linen are necessary for inventory purposes as well as to ascertain if the number of damaged items is too high. In this case, the quality of the linen purchased and the laundering procedures should be closely investigated. Laundering fabrics improperly or overusing potent chemicals will wear linen quickly. Damaged linens can be repaired only in very few cases; for instance, a torn sheet should be sewn only if the seam can be hidden by tucking it under the mattress. The cost of having a seamstress in the housekeeping department is in most cases prohibitive, so it is usually less expensive to buy new linen than to have the old item repaired. Figure 5.3 is a sample form for discarded linens.

FIGURE 5.3 Sample Linen Discard Form

Discarded Items From ____ to ____

DATE	Bath Towels	Hand Towels	Wash-cloths	Bath Mats	King Sheets	Queen Sheets	Twin Sheets	Standard Pillowcases	Large Pillowcases	Crib Sheets
Total Discarded										

STORAGE

Soiled and clean linens should be secured at all times, in dry, well-ventilated spaces. After hours, the laundry and linen rooms must be kept locked. Likewise, the floor closets where linen is stored and the service carts carrying linen should also be under lock and key. After laundering, linens should be moved out of the laundry room where the humidity is usually high. If possible, sheets should be left to rest overnight from the time they have been washed until they are used again. This "breathing time" before putting it back into use is necessary to smooth out wrinkles.

ISSUING

In order to exert control, clean linens should be stored in a central area, usually the housekeeping **linen room**. Here, section housekeepers are provided with clean linens according to the room occupancy of their respective sections. At the end of their shifts, their service carts are returned to the linen room, where they are restocked. In properties where the use of floor closets is necessary, a par for each closet should be established to keep the right amount of linen in every floor. At the end of the regular shifts, the evening crew will restock the floor closets for the next day's work. Overstocking floor closets or food and beverage outlets for the convenience of housepersons, section housekeepers, and food service personnel should be avoided.

INVENTORIES

Once proper control of linens has been established, physical inventories must be regularly conducted. The two main purposes of physical inventories are to ascertain linen losses (shrinkage) and to determine the amounts of items needed to bring the stocks to their original pars. Lodging properties usually conduct linen inventories semiannually or quarterly. If the losses are severe, inventories are taken monthly to determine where and how the losses are taking place.

Physical inventories are time-consuming and difficult to take because the procedure involves counting all items in the house, one at a time. In addition, the counting must be done off-hours, at the end of the normal workday when all guestrooms are made up and no laundering is taking place. Usually, two-person teams are formed in which one person calls out the items and the other writes down the amounts. Often, a representative of the controller's office is present to guarantee that the results are accurate. When counting bed and bath linen, distinctions must be made for all sizes. Obviously, all items in all locations of the property must be counted. These, generally include

- Guestrooms
- Laundry room
- Linen room
- Floor linen closets
- Section housekeeper carts
- Soiled linen ready to be laundered
- Made-up mobile bedding

Count forms or a digital device should be used at every location and all totals transferred to a master inventory list or entered in the appropriate computer program whose totals will indicate the existing inventory of all items, the losses for the month, and the amounts needed to restock the property. Figure 5.4 is a sample master inventory form that can be summarized as follows:

FIGURE 5.4 Sample Linen Discard Form

INVENTORY DATE: _____

1. ITEM	Bath Towels	Hand Towels	Wash Cloths	Bath Mats	King Sheets	Queen Sheets	Twin Sheets	Standard Pillowcases	Large Pillowcases	Crib Sheets
2. BEGINNING INVENTORY										
3. PURCHASES										
4. SUBTOTAL 2 + 3										
5. RECORDED DISCARDS										
6. TOTAL 4–5										
7. GUESTROOMS										
8. LAUNDRY ROOM										
9. LINEN ROOM										
10. FLOOR LINEN CLOSETS										
11. CARTS										
12. SOILED LINEN										
13. ON ROLLAWAYS, CRIBS, ETC.										
TOTAL ON HAND 14. ADD 7 THROUGH 13										
15. LOSSES 6–14										
16. PAR STOCK _____ TURNS										
17. AMOUNT NEEDED 16–14										
18. ON ORDER										
19. NEED TO ORDER 17–18										

> beginning inventory (of each item counted)
> + purchases for the month
> − documented discards for the month
> = amounts that should exist
> − current physical inventory (total on hand)
> = losses (shrinkage)
> par stock (of each item counted)
> − total on hand
> = amounts needed
> − amounts on order
> = need to order

The controller will multiply the number of items on the "losses" line by price to find out the total loss of linens for the month in dollars. Most properties assign full market price to new linen in stock but not yet used and half-price to linen in use. The total value of all linens in stock is determined as follows:

(Linen in use × its original price ÷ 2) + (new linen × market price) = linen valuation

The items calculated on the "need to order" line will be the number of items that need to be procured to bring the property to its original par. If the losses for the month are abnormally large, an investigation of the causes will be in order. In this case, an inquiry into possible pilfering, theft, quality of the products purchased, laundry chemical quality, laundering procedures, and improper use of the linen must be conducted. In any case, if the linen monthly percentage cost calculated by the controller is above the budget target, efforts must be made to bring the percentage down in subsequent months.

KEY TERMS

All-purpose cleaner	Crib
Amenities	Damask
Art Deco	Detergent
Backing (carpet)	Dual-purpose sleeping equipment
Back vacuum	Dust ruffle
Bed structure	Extractor (carpet)
Burnisher	Face weight (carpet)
Caddie	Flocking
Case furniture	Ground warp
Chemical dispenser	HazComm
Competitive shopping form	Hopper
Complementary colors	Innerspring
Cost per use	Jute

Large-area vacuum
Linen room
Master inventory list
Mobile bed
Momie cloth
MSDS
Murphy bed
Muslin
Napery
Needle punching
Neutralizer rinse
Padding (carpet)
Par
Percale
pH scale
Pile (carpet)
Pile warp
Plain weave
Polisher
Polycotton

Polyester
Polypropylene
Pre-measured chemicals
Purchasing agent
Sanforized fabric
Scrubber
Sealer
Seconds
Self-contained extractor
Selvage
Single-purpose cleaner
Stripper
Tensile strength
Terry cloth
Thread count
Tufted
Twill
Warp
Weft
Wet/dry vacuum

DISCUSSION AND REVIEW QUESTIONS

1. Why is it important for executive housekeepers to maintain a consistent interior design pattern in lodging properties?

2. What are the advantages of using synthetic fibers in furniture upholstery?

3. What is the number of guests that a property with the following bed structure can lodge (see Table 5.1): 80 rooms with one king-size bed in each room; 75 rooms with two double-size beds in each room; 50 twin-bedded rooms; 150 rooms with one queen-size bed in each room?

4. What are the advantages of selecting a carpet made of olefin fiber?

5. What par level would you establish for bedspreads in your lodging property?

6. What are the advantages and disadvantages of purchasing cleaning supplies in bulk quantities versus pre-measured products?

7. (a) What is the purpose of HazComm?
   (b) How would you, as an executive housekeeper, comply with HazComm in your housekeeping department?

8. Which are the advantages and disadvantages of having a property's uniforms furnished by an outside contractor?

9. What would be the cost per use of a linen item that weighs 3 pounds, has a laundry cost of two cents per pound washed, has a life expectancy of 300 washings, and costs $7.25?

10. What is one par of king sheets in a property that has 100 rooms with one king-size bed each and 300 rooms with two queen-size beds each? All beds are set with two sheets.

11. What is (are) the purpose(s) of conducting physical inventories in lodging properties?

12. Two methods of ascertaining quality of bed linen fabrics are: the thread count per square inch and the tensile strength of the material. Describe both.

MINICASES

SITUATION 1

Having been appointed assistant to the executive housekeeper of a new property in Denver, Colorado, you have been instructed to present the initial opening inventory for bed linen (sheets and pillowcases). The bed structure of the property is:

- 25 suites with one king-size bed and a double-size couch each.
- 200 rooms with two queen-size beds each.
- 100 twin-bedded rooms with twin-size beds.

Each bed is using two sheets. Two large pillows will be placed on each king-size bed, one large pillow on each twin bed and couch, and two standard-size pillows on each queen-size bed. The par for all items is 3.5.

SITUATION 2

After graduating from a hotel administration program, you have been hired by a lodging company and sent to open a 300-room mid-market property located by a major highway near Houston, Texas. The marketing plan focuses on attracting transient travelers on their way into and out of Houston, families, and some corporate business from three nearby office buildings. Upon your arrival at the property you are asked to list and describe the specifications of the reusable guest supplies needed for each guestroom. Do so.

SITUATION 3

On August 31, as the executive housekeeper of the Royal Hotel in San Antonio, Texas, you have taken the monthly inventory for sheets, finding that the total number on hand is 5,715. The Royal has 400 rooms with two queen-size beds. Each bed is set with two sheets. The pre-established par for sheets is four. The beginning inventory on August 1 was 5,500. The hotel purchased 40 dozen sheets on August 18. Twenty-eight damaged sheets were discarded during the month. There are 12 dozen sheets on order.
Find:

a. Shrinkage for the month
a. Number of sheets that you need to order to bring the stock to par

CASE STUDY

Linen Pars

As the executive housekeeper of a new resort opening by Marriott in San Diego, Joe Ramirez has been asked to present a proposal for bed linens and terrycloth six months prior to the grand opening. What will be his proposal after considering the following information?

- The par stock for all items has been approved to be 3.5.
- The room structure of the property is:
  - 25 suites with one king-size bed each
  - 110 rooms with one king-size bed each

- 110 rooms with one queen-size bed each
- 150 twin-bedded rooms with twin-size beds
- The bed linen and terry cloth distribution is:
  - 2 sheets per bed
  - 1 pillowcase per pillow
  - 1 bath towel per person
  - 2 hand towels per person
  - 3 washcloths per person
  - 1 bath mat per room
  - 1 pillow per person

Assignment

1. Work out the number of pieces of each item that you need to order before opening the resort.

CHAPTER EXERCISES

INVENTORY EXERCISE

As the assistant to the executive housekeeper of a Hilton hotel in Austin, Texas, you have been asked to compile the linen inventory for the month of May, ascertain the loss (shrinkage) for the month, and figure out the number of pieces to be ordered from the broker to bring up the par to four for each category.

	Sheets	Pillowcases	Bath towels	Hand towels
Beginning inventory	750	780	1500	1450
Purchased in May	100	200	50	75
Physical inventory on 5/30				
In guestrooms	180	180	360	360
In laundry room	300	325	525	480
In floor closets	50	75	140	225
Under lock and key	80	50	180	190
Discarded	0	10	15	12

The hotel has 102 rooms with one king-size bed each. You supply two bath towels per person, two pillowcases per bed, and four hand towels per room.

NAPERY DETERMINATION EXERCISE

Maya Poepel has been asked to determine the napery needs for the food and beverage division of the same Austin hotel. The food and beverage director has provided Maya with the following information:

Atrium Restaurant

- Breakfast: 95 seats and a daily turnover of 4.25 per seat. (Small red-and-yellow napkins used.)
- Lunch: 95 seats and a turnover of 2.50 per seat. (Regular-size copper-color napkins used.)
- Dinner: 70 seats and a turnover of 1.75 per seat. (Same napkins as for lunch.)

Banquets Department

- Maximum function capacity of 900 seated guests. (Rust-color napkins used.)

Based on the results of previous inventories, Maya decides to establish the following pars for the different types of napkins:

Breakfast napkins :   5.50 — Lunch and dinner napkins :   4.50 — Banquet :   3.50

ASSIGNMENT: Determine the number of dozens of napkins of each of the three types (red and yellow, copper, and rust) that Ms. Poepel needs to carry on hand.

LAUNDRY COST PER USE EXERCISE

As the executive housekeeper of a resort in Colorado Springs, you are presented with two types of bath towel similar in quality offered by two companies: Valiant Industries and H.W. Baker Linen Co.

- The Valiant Industries towel weighs 4 pounds, its cost per wash is $0.20, its guaranteed life is 200 washings, and it sells for $72.00 per dozen.
- The towel sold by H.W. Baker Linen Co. weighs 4.5 pounds, its cost per wash is $0.25, its guaranteed life is 180 washings, and its price is $6.25 each.
- The resort has 500 rooms, each one furnished with one king bed. The projected room occupancy for one year is 80 percent. The forecasted person per room average occupancy is 1.5. It is estimated that each guest uses an average of 1.5 bath towel per day.

Find:

1. The cost per use of the Valiant towel.
2. The cost per use of the Baker towel.
3. The savings per year if you purchase the towel with the lowest cost per use.

CHAPTER
6

Laundry room, Drury Inn & Suites Phoenix, Arizona
Courtesy of Drury Hotels

Laundry Room Management

CHAPTER OBJECTIVES

- Describe the process of planning on-premise laundries.
- Discuss the main characteristics of laundry equipment.
- Explain the operation of laundries, from the collection to the finishing of linens.
- Provide benchmarks for linen cost controls.
- Learn about staffing the laundry room.

OVERVIEW

The operative success of on-premise laundries depends on the adequate planning of the facilities based on a detailed analysis of the property's needs. Planning a laundry includes its design and space allocation, the selection and layout of equipment, and the initial staffing and training of workers. This chapter describes the main characteristics of washers, dryers, and ironers, and lists the chemicals used in the washing process. Laundry operation, from the collection to the finishing of linens, is also explained.

Students are provided with percentages based on national averages to approximate laundry costs in five categories: labor, linen replacement, energy, laundry chemicals, and other costs. Some considerations are provided for smaller companies that contract out their laundry services, emphasizing that executive housekeepers should be closely involved in the contract closing as they will have to live with the agreement once it is signed. Consideration is also given to staffing and training of laundry personnel.

PLANNING THE LAUNDRY

Most large lodging properties process their linens in on-premise laundries (OPL). There are some compelling reasons why laundries are built within the property rather than having the products processed by an outside company. Some of the advantages are substantial reduction of costs, control over linen quality, and better product availability. The annual savings of an on-premise laundry versus a linen service company can be as high as 50 percent. By having an OPL, operators can also eliminate pick-up and delivery times and lengthy turnaround cycles. In cases where laundry companies do not deliver on time, the housekeeping department personnel must wait until the products are delivered in order to finish the daily tasks of making beds, fitting the bathrooms with towels, or providing the food and beverage division with napkins, tablecloths, and uniforms. Other advantages of on-premise laundries are having control of the laundering and handling of linens to conform with recommended hygienic standards and increasing the life of the linen by adopting efficient processing procedures.

Setting up a laundry room requires a detailed analysis of the property's needs. Poor planning may result in inadequate space to perform daily operations, insufficient equipment to keep up with the volume of linen to be washed, too small drains to funnel away the discharged water, poor working conditions caused by inadequate ventilation, and so on.

DESIGN OF THE LAUNDRY ROOM

The first step in designing the laundry consists of building a facility with enough capacity to process the maximum amount of linen that the property can generate per day. Ample space should be allocated to install all equipment required and to provide an area large enough for clean and dirty linen to be easily separated. The space allocated varies with the size of the property and can range from 1,000 square feet in small properties to over 20,000 square feet in larger operations. The laundry room should be equipped with enough washers and dryers to process all items that the rooms and food and beverage divisions will require at 100 percent occupancy without incurring overtime or running the laundry operation around the clock.

The design should anticipate all mechanical, electrical, and ventilation installation connections for the equipment as well as identify the optimal location of drains for washers and soak sinks. If water restriction in the area is severe or if the water costs are high, a system for recycling washer rinse water can be installed. These water recovery systems route rinse water from the washer's dump valve into a recovery tank to be reused in the wash cycles. Over 25 percent of water usage can thus be saved.

The selection and specifications of the equipment depend on the type of linens to be laundered. For instance, a lodging property with restaurants and banquet department should have extra washers to process food and beverage napkins and tablecloths; a property offering in-house dry cleaning service will need to install dry cleaning equipment; an establishment that uses no-iron sheets may not require a **mangle** to iron these items. Choosing the right linens will result in substantial savings of equipment and labor costs. Most nylon and polyester/cotton blend fabrics require less washing and drying time, and do not need to be ironed. One negative aspect, however, of synthetic fibers is their sensitivity to high washing and drying temperatures.

Once the equipment has been selected, it should be installed to allow for the best possible layout. An adequate work-flow pattern should be designed to provide an efficient distribution of space and avoid worker cross-traffic. Ideally, the work flow should follow a circular pattern in the following order: laundry room entrance → soak sinks → washers → dryers → mangle(s) → sheet folder stand → folding table → shelves and mobile racks → laundry room exit. Figure 6.1 provides a typical floor layout for a laundry room using three washers, six dryers, one mangle,

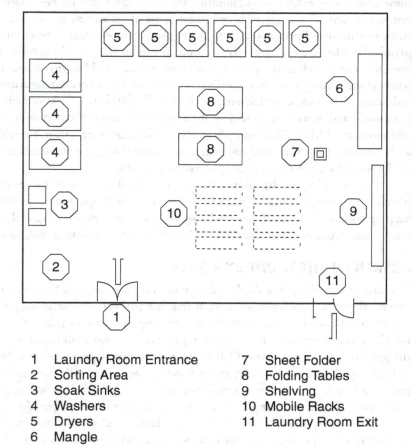

1	Laundry Room Entrance	7	Sheet Folder
2	Sorting Area	8	Folding Tables
3	Soak Sinks	9	Shelving
4	Washers	10	Mobile Racks
5	Dryers	11	Laundry Room Exit
6	Mangle		

FIGURE 6.1 Sample Laundry Room Layout

and other additional equipment. The soiled linen can be sorted out, presoaked if necessary, washed, dried, ironed, folded, and stored for immediate use without workers bumping into each other because of a cross-traffic pattern.

Because laundry operations are conducted in a hot, humid environment, sufficient exhaust capacity should be provided to draw out the moist air. Because of frequent liquid spills, the floor of laundry rooms should be waterproofed and consist of a nonslippery material. Adequate drainage should be provided to dispose of runoffs caused by water-soaked linen and possible washer overflows.

Laundry rooms must be well lighted so stains, spots, and shades in linens can be easily detected. A minimum of 2 feet of space between all machines and walls should be allowed to facilitate cleaning and repairs.

WASHERS

With the introduction of microprocessor-controlled machines, washing linens has been greatly simplified. Gone are the days when loading detergent in the machine and setting water temperatures and time cycles were done by hand. Instead, these functions are done automatically by programmed processors that regulate the amount of soap injected in the machine, activate thermostats, and control the machines' timers. Smaller washers, for instance 18-pounders, operate on the same principles as conventional residential machines; that is, the soiled linen is placed in the machine's receptacle and agitated through washing and rinsing cycles. The washer finally spins the moisture out and the load is ready to be transferred to a dryer. Larger washers, however, are built with high efficiency and productivity in mind in order to maximize laundry outputs. Some washer-extractors, for instance, feature single-pivot tilts to facilitate loading and unloading, high-speed extract to reduce drying and ironing time, and thermal cool-down to eliminate wrinkles. The tilt feature minimizes operators' fatigue and back stress, helping the establishment keep its people by making the job easier.

The incorporation of microprocessors to washer-extractors has also simplified operations and ensured consistent, reliable results. Some machines offer over 20 preset wash programs that can be activated at the touch of a button or by simply using a hand-held digital device. These machines can be preprogrammed with washing formulas specifically designed for hospitality linen; thus, a lodging property can have different preprogrammed formulas for bed linen, terrycloth, napery, and greasy kitchen aprons and rags. Large washer-extractors may comprise two or more separate pocket cylinders that allow different loads to be processed at the same time. Some lodging chains that operate a central laundry serving several establishments and, therefore, process over 2,000 pounds of linen per hour, use **tunnel washers**. Tunnel washers have several chambers that enable the machine to process multiple loads simultaneously. Some models incorporate unrestricted counterflow, enabling the machine to be water and energy efficient by continuous water recovery and reuse.

Investing in washer-extractors with high G-force (spinning power) can result in as much as 30 percent savings in time and energy. The lower the water retention of the fabrics is, the less time and energy consumption will be needed during drying and ironing. For example, machines with greater than 200 G-force will reduce substantially the gas or electricity used during the drying process over 90 G-force washer-extractors. Operators of lodging facilities should install washing equipment with extraction flexibility, as all fabrics do not have the same extract G-force requirements. For instance, an extraction force of 90 is ideal for permanent press and blends, while a 140 G-force range is necessary for hard-to-dry items such as blankets, spreads, and mattress pads. Because of the high gravitational force exerted by these powerful machines, large washer-extractors must be professionally anchored onto the laundry floor. When located near guestrooms, washer-extractors should be suspended to cushion vibration and avoid excessive noise.

The use of ozone in commercial washers allows for shorter wash cycles and can result in substantial energy and water savings. Manufacturers of ozone systems claim that it can act as a powerful oxidizing, cleaning, and bleaching agent, effective with most organic soils while killing bacteria faster than chlorine bleach does. Being biodegradable, it doesn't leave any chemical residue behind. Ozone systems use a generator that forces compressed air through a high-voltage electrical arc; this process converts oxygen molecules into ozone gas. The ozone is then dissolved in cold laundry wash water where it exerts its powerful cleaning action attaching itself to fatty and other soils, destroying them effectively. Because it works well at ambient water temperature, instead of the conventional 140–160°F, it can drastically reduce water heating costs.

Estimating the number and size of washers to be installed in a property depends on the type of linen to be processed, the desired number of hours within which the linen must be finished, and the **linen poundage** of the establishment. A lodging property with food and beverage facilities should have at least three washers installed, one for bed linen, one for terrycloth, and one for tablecloths and napkins. These three different kinds of linen require different washing formulas because of the different composition of the fabrics and the type of soiling that must be laundered. For instance, napkins and tablecloths are usually soiled with fats and oils, while guestroom linen usually has different types of stains.

The number of hours allocated for daily laundering is also a key factor for sizing laundries. If it was originally determined that 1,500 pounds of linen should be processed in eight hours, it would be necessary to have twice as many washers if it is decided to launder the same amount of linen in four hours.

Drury Inn & Suites
Courtesy of Drury Hotels

The linen poundage is the weight of one par of linen: that is, the maximum output for peak business period or the weight of all items that need to be processed at 100 percent occupancy. Using the same example as before, a lodging property with three 50-pound washers and half-hour washing cycles would theoretically require five hours to process 1,500 pounds of linen (3 × 50 = 150; 150 × 2 = 300; 300 × 5 = 1,500). If the linen poundage to be washed in the same period of time had been 3,000, twice the number of washers would have been required. Table 6.1 shows how to calculate the linen poundage of a 400-room hotel that has 100 rooms with one king-size bed in each room, 200 rooms with two queen-size beds in each room, and 100 twin-bedded rooms, each bed using two sheets. The poundage is calculated by multiplying one par of linen by the respective weight of each piece of bed and bath linens used in the property.

Assuming that this lodging property has no food and beverage outlets, theoretically only two washers would be needed to process bed and bath linens separately. However, having a small commercial top-load washer as a backup unit for smaller or emergency loads would be a wise step to take. Washers can be purchased from 50-pound to over 500-pound capacity. Choosing the right capacity washers is also important; using too many small machines would require more loading time and, therefore, more labor cost. On the other hand, using only large machines would require more energy to operate and would not offer the flexibility to separate washing loads by category (king sheets, queen sheets, twin sheets, pillowcases, etc.).

Using Table 6.1 as an example, if it is decided that the ideal washer setup for this property is three 100-pound and two 50-pound machines, each one using half-hour washing cycles, the processing of the 5,438 pounds would take about seven hours. Thus:

$$100 \times 3 = 300; \quad 300 \times 2 = 600$$

$$50 \times 2 = 100; \quad 100 \times 2 = 200$$

Theoretically, at full capacity, the five machines can process 800 pounds of linen in one hour. In seven hours:

$$800 \times 7 = 5,600 \text{ pounds}$$

DRYERS

Most commercial dryers are computer programmed so that cycle times and temperatures can be automatically controlled. As with washers, the number of dryers needed to process one par of linen in a given number of hours depends on the poundage and type of fabrics to be dried. Bed linen that is put through mangles for ironing, for instance, does not need to be passed through dryers. In general, because the drying cycle usually takes twice the time of the washing cycle, twice as many dryers of the same capacity are needed to get the job done.

In order to save energy, a battery of dryers should be enclosed on the top and sides so that heat is not lost around the equipment. This contained heat can, thus, be used as warm intake air. When using gas dryers, the outside air intake for combustion should not be larger than needed so that no extra cold outside air is absorbed into the dryer area. A damper closing the aperture when dryers are not in use can effectively block the outside air from coming into the laundry room. Dryer burners should be cleaned regularly to ensure that lint has not caused the burners to partially clog. The inefficient burning of gas can be identified by a flame that is yellowish, rather than blue.

TABLE 6.1 Linen Poundage Determination

Sheet Poundage

Room Structure	Beds per Room	Total Beds	Total Sheets	Weight per Item (lb)	Total Weight
100 King	1	100	200	2.05	410
200 Queen	2	400	800	1.55	1,240
100 Twin-bedded	2	200	400	1.10	440
400		700	1,400		**2,090**

Pillowcase Poundage

Type of Bed	Type of Pillow	Pillows per Bed	Total Pillows	Weight per Item (lb)	Total Weight
King	Large	4	400	0.40	160
Queen	Large	3	1,200	0.40	480
Twin	Standard	1	200	0.30	60
					700

Towel Poundage

Type of Room	People per Category*	Towels per Person	Weight per Item (lb)	Total Weight
King	200	2 BT; 2 HT; 2 WC	0.70; 0.25; 0.06	404
Queen	800	2 BT; 2 HT; 2 WC	0.70; 0.25; 0.06	1,616
Twin	200	2 BT; 2 HT; 2 WC	0.70; 0.25; 0.06	404
	1,200			**2,424**

Bath Mat Poundage

Number of Rooms	Mats per Room	Total Mats	Weight per Item(lb)	Total Weight
400	1	400	0.56	224

	Sheets	2,090
	Pillowcases	700
	Towels	2,424
	Bath Mats	224
	Poundage	5,438

*2 persons per king and queen bed; 1 person per twin bed.

Dryer lint must often be removed from the dryer ventilation system and the dryers' adjacent areas. Lint is not only a major fire hazard but may cause allergies and other respiratory ailments in laundry workers. Some manufacturers have designed dryers with a built-in sensor that activates a water jet to extinguish fires within the machine. In general, gas-heated dryers are more economical to operate and maintain than electric dryers.

MANGLES

Linen can be ironed by feeding it to rollers (mangles) or by placing it on presses. When done by hand, ironing linen is a labor-intensive, time-consuming process. Sophisticated tandem units on the market today can dry, iron, and fold linen automatically to the tune of over 2,000 pounds per hour. These flatwork finishers have a built-in folder assembly that can handle items from pillowcases to king-size sheets that require an ironed look. Most lodging properties use no-iron bed linen to avoid the high labor cost associated with pressing. However, they usually have small or medium-size mangles to iron napkins, tablecloths, and pillowcases to add to the facility's image. In this case, linens go directly from washer to finisher, reducing the amount of energy needed to dry them.

OTHER LAUNDRY EQUIPMENT

Besides washers and dryers, the laundry room must be fitted with additional equipment necessary for linen processing. **Soak sinks** are needed for spot and stain removal using strong chemical formulas. The soak sinks should be placed between the soiled-linen sorting area and the washers. **Folding tables** and **folder stands** should be placed by the dryers and mangles, close to storage shelving. The folding tables are used to fold terrycloth items and the folder stands to fold sheets, blankets, shower curtains, and bed pads. Only one worker is needed to fold items using the folder stand, while two attendants are necessary to fold them by hand. Plastic or vinyl-coated canvas laundry **hampers** can be very useful to transport linen to and from washers and dryers and to hold soiled and clean items while being processed. Stainless steel **mobile racks** are often necessary to hold the clean linen for later transport to the different floor closets on the property. Mobile racks are a must in laundry rooms where shelving space is limited.

LAUNDRY OPERATION

The linen laundering cycle begins with the collection of soiled items from guestrooms and the food and beverage outlets, and ends with the distribution of clean linen to all locations.

COLLECTION OF SOILED LINENS

Section housekeepers should be trained to sort bed and bathroom linens in order to facilitate the laundry department's work. If at all possible, the room attendants should separate bed from bathroom items, placing them in different containers. Heavily soiled items should be clearly set apart so laundry workers can initiate the necessary pretreatment as soon as they arrive in the laundry room. The use of hampers to transport linen, rather than plastic bags, gives a better impression to guests, causes no environmental waste, and saves bagging and unbagging time. When the property has **linen chutes**, all sorting is done in the linen room.

Good communication and cooperation are needed between the laundry manager and the food and beverage director to ensure that napery items are sorted and inspected for debris before they are brought to the laundry room. Napery mixed with silverware, pieces of bread, and food scraps should not be accepted by laundry personnel for processing. Items heavily stained with butter, ketchup, wine, or sauces should be delivered separately. Kitchen rags and chef's aprons must never be bundled together with napery items.

SORTING THE LINEN

Once in the laundry room, linen must be sorted out by category and readied for washing. Because each category requires a different water temperature and chemical formula, linens must be carefully separated before being loaded in the washers. For instance, greasy kitchen aprons require strong washing chemicals while wool needs milder detergents. Colored napery should not be processed with bleach, while white bed linens require bleach to kill bacteria and whiten the fabric. In general, bed linen, terrycloth, napery, blankets, and bedspreads should be washed separate from each other.

Besides being sorted by category, each laundry batch should be separated by degree of soiling. Items that are not soiled or very lightly soiled require weaker formulas and less agitation (and therefore less washing time) than heavily soiled items. Because the number of heavily stained items is usually smaller, having a couple of small-size washers to process small loads will prevent having to use larger machines for partial-load washings. Sorting personnel should be trained to detect unrecoverable items such as torn, burned, or heavily soiled articles, which should be made into cleaning rags.

PRETREATMENT OF STAINS

Before loading the linen into the washers, special care must be taken to presoak and pretreat heavily stained items. For example, blood, egg, fruit, and dark beverage stains should be soaked in cold water and spot-cleaned with detergent. Grass, paint, and grease stains should be spot-cleaned before washing. All fabrics, however, should be tested for colorfastness before chemicals are directly applied.

LOADING

Washers and dryers should be loaded with the maximum amount of linen that their capacity allows; thus, a 35-pound machine should hold about 35 pounds of dry soiled linen. If the soiled linen is damp, as may happen with bath items, fewer pieces will make up the recommended weight. Not using machines to full capacity will increase the operating cost of the laundry, as washers and dryers will use the same amounts of water, chemicals, and energy required for full loads. On the other hand, overloading will cause improper results, for the machines will not be able to properly wash or dry items if they cannot be turned and tossed freely.

WASHING/EXTRACTING

Most washing machines in the market today are equipped with several washing programs aimed at processing diverse types of fabrics and degrees of soiling. The programs consist of different washing times, water temperatures, levels of agitation, and amounts of chemicals to be used. These programs, used properly, can help conserve energy and lengthen the life of fabrics. For instance, a program for washing lightly soiled linen will be set to use less time, a lower temperature, and fewer chemicals than a program set to process greasy items. The lighter program will cost less to run and prolong the number of washings that the material can stand.

The water temperature needed to wash articles usually varies from 140°F to 160°F. For example, while greasy kitchen items require the hottest temperature, lightly soiled sheets can be washed at 140°F. Some programs, however, are preset to use cold water as

Ecolab stain treatment products
Courtesy of Ecolab USA Inc.

some types of stains do not require hot water for removal; on the contrary, warm water might imprint the stain permanently. In addition, no-iron fabrics better retain their wrinkle-free characteristics when washed in cold water. Laundry operators should use cold-water programs whenever possible to save the energy needed to heat the water.

A sufficient level of agitation is necessary for adequate washing action; not enough agitation due to insufficient washing time, improper water levels, or machine overloading will not provide adequate results. Washing linens with the wrong chemicals or with incorrect amounts of chemicals either will not produce good results or will ruin the articles by deteriorating their fabric composition. Using too much chemical can also damage linens as well as waste precious budget dollars.

Each washing program consists of several cycles, similar to those found in a residential machine. The **flush cycle** soaks the linen and dissolves the soils; the **wash cycle** uses alkaline soil-breaking products, detergents, and other chemicals such as bleach to clean and sterilize the items; the **rinse cycle** removes chemicals from the linen by injecting a sour compound that neutralizes any residual alkali, bringing the pH to a reading of 5.5 to 6.5; and the **extract cycle** spins the moisture from the load before it is moved on to the drying or ironing phase.

Water

Good water quality is necessary for washing linens. Hard water prevents detergents from releasing their sudsy action to remove soils, leaving a grayish shade and an "unclean" odor in finished linens. Often, lodging properties must install water softeners before they can obtain adequate results. Large quantities of water are used in washing linens; some programs may require one flush cycle, one break cycle, one washing cycle, one softener cycle, and three rinse cycles. In locations where water is expensive, special care must be taken to minimize the use of water whenever possible. Partial loads are a waste of water and can cause wear and tear on washing machines. Newer washer-extractors reduce the amount of water necessary to clean linens. Where old machines may use 4 to 5 gallons per pound of wash, newer ones need just two to 2–$2^{1}/_{2}$ gallons per pound.

Chemicals

Several factors determine the types of chemicals needed for commercial laundries: these include the water used, the different texture of fabrics to be washed, and the degree of soiling that must be removed. The chemicals commonly used in laundry operations are **alkalis** that help neutralize acids in the washing solution. Alkalis are often necessary because suds in detergents act better on soils and stains if the washing solution is lightly alkaline. **Antichlors** are added to rinses to ensure that chlorine bleach is totally removed from the washed fabrics. **Bleach** is a powerful chemical that is very effective in killing bacteria, whitening linens, and removing stains. Chlorine bleach, however, can destroy some fabrics, particularly certain synthetics. Oxygen bleach is milder and can be used with most washable fabrics, including colored ones, but it is ineffective on heavy stains. **Breaks** are heavy-duty alkaline compounds designed to break soils in the soak cycle. Breaks are used for heavily soiled loads. The washing agent used in the washing process is the detergent. Detergents containing suspending agents and alkaline builders are very effective in removing grease and oils. Some detergents have water-softening ingredients to increase their cleaning action; others contain enzymes that break down and liquify organic stains such as food, blood, urine, and fats. **Softeners** are added in the final wash cycle to eliminate static cling, smooth wrinkles, and make ironing easier. **Sours** are acidic chemicals used to neutralize any alkaline residues left after washing and rinsing linens. A single product that combines a fabric softener and an alkaline neutralizer may also be used. **Starches** are carbohydrate compounds that are added to give linens a stiff appearance. This procedure is commonly used to give a crisp look to cooks' uniforms and toques (chefs' hats). Today, there are products in the market that combine most of the chemicals needed in washing linens in one single solid compound.

DRYING

Although drying times vary with different types of fabric, generally it takes twice as long to dry linens as it takes to wash them. Drying temperatures also vary from item to item; for instance, fluffy all-cotton towels require higher temperatures than thin synthetic fibers. All linens should be loaded into dryers with the minimum moisture possible to reduce drying time. Modern washers are equipped with high-speed spins as a final cycle to remove excess moisture from washed items. Dryers should be loaded to capacity to minimize energy costs. No-iron linens and terrycloth should not be overdried, as they are better folded when very slightly damp.

IRONING

Items that need ironing are best processed when slightly damp; for this reason, they don't need to be dried. Ironing is a labor-intensive process that should be avoided whenever possible. On the other hand, pressed tablecloths, napkins, and pillowcases create a favorable impression for guests, as do ironed cooks' and serving-personnel uniforms.

FOLDING

Like ironing, folding is a time-consuming, labor-intensive process, particularly if it is done by hand. Linens should be folded immediately after drying or pressing to avoid wrinkling. Sheet-folding stands can save labor costs, as only one worker is needed to fold the items instead of two. Laundry folders should be trained to sort out linen items with imperfections such as tears, fading, stains, and loose seams before they are distributed for usage.

STORING

Once linens are folded, they should be handled as little as possible. Folded linen should be shelved in the linen room, placed on mobile racks for transportation to the floor closets, or placed directly onto the section housekeeper carts for ready use.

BEST RESULTS

The ultimate goal of a well-run laundry is to obtain optimum results in terms of appearance, odor, and feel. Regarding appearance, the linen must be snow white (for white items) and free of wrinkles and spots caused by staining. The odor must be fresh and clean, not stale or musty; the feel should be smooth and velvety, not coarse or rough.

Laundries can benefit from the expertise of nationwide chemical companies to obtain best results; in some cases, these companies guarantee that the quality of linens processed with their products will be optimum. In order to check quality, their service personnel conduct routine tests for water hardness, iron residue in finished linens, and the pH of washed items. Improper results in finished products include discoloration, stains, abraded fabric, lint specks, excessive wrinkling and shrinking, and fabric pilling.

VALET SERVICE

Most first-class lodging properties offer laundry and dry cleaning services to their guests. However, it is common to contract these services with an outside commercial laundry because of the specialization and time-consuming details that valet service entails. Properties that wash and dry clean employee uniforms and draperies usually process valet-service items in-house. In this case, smaller washing and drying machines and dry cleaning equipment need to be installed, as well as additional personnel to tag, process, and bag each guest's articles.

On-premise valet service can greatly encumber housekeeping operations and take up considerable laundry room space. In all cases, good communication between valet attendants and the laundry room must be established, and clear, specific procedures put in place to avoid misunderstandings and complaints. Some of these procedures include setting up times for laundry pick-up and delivery, billing guests promptly after each service, and having a quick response system to compensate guests for lost, misplaced, or damaged articles.

CONTRACTING OUT LAUNDRY SERVICES

Small lodging properties may decide to contract out laundering services rather than installing their own on-premise laundry. While the disadvantages are numerous, a few advantages of outside laundry contracts include not having to make a substantial initial investment and having

Pool at Dusk, Aruba Marriott Resort
Courtesy of Marriott International, Inc.

the additional space otherwise taken up by the laundry room. In all cases, contracts must be carefully set up between the lodging property and the commercial laundry company to ensure efficient, reliable service, for instance, requiring delivery seven days a week on peak occupancy period. The contract should specify details regarding delivery and quality, such as days of the week and time of day, emergency service, appearance of the linen, folding specifications, sorting procedures, billing method, and method of inventory.

Delivery bundles should be clearly marked with the date, time, number of items, and weight. The housekeeping department must check that all items are accounted for before signing the delivery slip.

LAUNDRY OPERATING COSTS

Typically, the cost of operating an on-premise laundry is broken down into the categories of labor, linen replacement, energy, chemicals, and other. Of these, the labor cost is always the highest. Although expenses can be strongly affected by exceptionally high energy or labor costs, depending upon the location of the property, national laundry cost percentages for a typical laundry operation may be averaged thus:

Labor	45%
Linen replacement	20%
Energy	15%
Laundry chemicals	10%
Other	10%

Under normal circumstances, executive housekeepers can work out rough estimates to monitor expenses using these averages as a benchmark. For example, a laundry operation that has had an annual total expense of $50,000 should have spent $22,500 in labor (50,000 × .45), $10,000 in linen replacement (50,000 × .20), $7,500 in energy (50,000 × .15), $5,000 in chemicals (50,000 × .10), and $5,000 in other costs (50,000 × .10).

STAFFING THE LAUNDRY ROOM

Laundry operations in large properties are usually coordinated by a **laundry manager** who reports directly to the executive housekeeper. Laundry shifts normally consist of one shift supervisor, several laundry attendants, and one utility helper (houseperson). Because of the different tasks to be carried out in the laundry room, job specifications must be clearly spelled out. For example, the job of wash persons may be to handle the loading and unloading of washers and dryers; the utility helper may presort, count, and shelf linen; others may fold and stack; and so on.

An ideal staffing scenario is to have enough equipment and personnel to process the property's poundage in eight hours, to avoid overtime. In this case, six hours could be spent on washing and drying and two hours in other laundry activities and breaks. When the property is not 100 percent full, the hours of operation should be reduced or the number of people called to work lowered. If establishments operate with insufficient linen pars, two shifts rather than one may be necessary to turn out enough finished items.

Training laundry workers is of paramount importance, as laundry room operations require the performance of specialized tasks and the handling of sophisticated equipment. Usually the equipment supplier and the company supplying laundry chemicals will provide training assistance. One important training consideration is compliance with OSHA's working standards for laundry workers. Some of these standards specify that all machinery must be equipped with guards to prevent injury to fingers, that steam pipes within employee reach are covered with heat-resistant material, and that power-driven machinery has easily accessible starting and stopping devices. When employing workers who do not read English, safety procedures should be made available in their native language and training workshops should be given by bilingual personnel.

Laundry employees should also be trained in preventive maintenance, energy saving, and expense-reduction procedures. Manufacturers always provide preventive maintenance routines in easy-to-follow manuals. Typically, maintenance personnel make sure that dump valves don't leak or are not stuck in their open positions, that water levels in washers are correctly set, and that lint is regularly removed from dryer traps and ducts. All machines should also be routinely lubricated and calibrated.

KEY TERMS

Alkalis	Linen chute
Antichlors	Linen poundage
Bleach	Mangle
Breaks	Mobile rack
Equipment layout	Rinse cycle
Extract cycle	Soak sinks
Flush cycle	Softeners
Folder stand	Sours
Folding table	Starch
Hamper	Tunnel washer
Laundry manager	Wash cycle

DISCUSSION AND REVIEW QUESTIONS

1. Give some reasons why having an on-premise laundry can be more advantageous than having the linens processed by an outside commercial company.

2. "Setting up a laundry room requires a detailed analysis of the property's needs." Explain the meaning of this statement.

3. Explain the steps needed to design a laundry room.

4. What are the benefits of installing washers featuring single-pivot tilts?

5. Why are washers with a high G-force preferable to washers with lower spinning power?

6. Define a property's poundage.

7. What is the purpose of adding softeners to the final washing cycle?

8. How should the training of laundry workers who do not read English be conducted?

9. What are some specifications that should be detailed in a contract for laundering services with an outside commercial company?

10. Based on the national averages given in the "Laundry Operating Costs" of this chapter, what should have been the breakdown for "labor," "linen replacement," "energy," "laundry chemicals," and "other expenses" if the total cost of operating the laundry department had been $47,600?

11. Draw an "ideal" floor plan of a laundry room that has four washers, seven dryers, and one mangle (include soak sinks, folding tables, and one sheet folder stand).

12. What are the advantages and disadvantages of offering valet service to guests in lodging properties?

MINICASES

SITUATION 1

Having been hired by a hospitality management company, you have been asked to join the team assigned to open a 500-room hotel in California. Your first task is to work out the "poundage" of the property for bed linen and bathroom linen as a first step to determine the number and capacity of washers to be installed in the laundry room. Do so from the information that follows:

Bed structure:

200 rooms with one king-size bed in each room

200 rooms with two queen-size beds in each room

100 twin-bedded rooms

Bed-linen distribution:

2 large-size pillows per king-size bed

2 medium-size pillows per queen-size bed

1 medium-size pillow per twin bed

2 sheets for all beds

Bathroom linen distribution:

king rooms are set with 2 bath towels, 2 hand towels, 2 washcloths, and 1 bath mat

queen rooms are set with 4 bath towels, 4 hand towels, 4 washcloths, and 1 bath mat

twin rooms are set with 2 bath towels, 2 hand towels, 2 washcloths, and 1 bath mat

The weight of each piece is as follows:

king sheet	2.10 pounds
queen sheet:	1.60 pounds
twin sheet:	1.10 pounds
large pillowcase:	0.70 pounds
medium pillowcase:	0.50 pounds
bath towel:	1.25 pounds
washcloth:	0.14 pounds
bath mat:	0.70 pounds

SITUATION 2

After one year in operation, you decide to compare the laundry costs of the hotel to national average percentages. Your property's costs for the year were:

labor:	$47,700
linen replacement:	15,300
energy:	18,900
laundry chemicals:	5,500
other costs:	4,200

The national average percentages are:

labor:	45%
linen replacement:	20%
energy:	15%
laundry chemicals:	10%
other costs:	10%

After comparing your costs to national average percentages, list the possible reasons that might have caused the existing discrepancies.

SITUATION 3

Your company has promoted you to general manager of a resort in Colorado. After analyzing the results for the first three months that the property has been under your control, you find that the labor cost in the laundry room of the resort is extremely high. Further investigation points to the fact that the washing capacity of your laundry is very low. For this reason, the laundry has to be operated round the clock, its employees often working overtime.

You decide to lower the labor cost by providing the resort with enough washers to wash one par of linen in six hours. The bed linen and terrycloth poundage of the resort is 6,700 pounds. The laundry room is currently equipped with one 50-pound washer to process food and beverage napery and kitchen items. This washer is sufficient to take care of the food and beverage department's needs with one shift, without going into overtime.

The laundry is also equipped with two 100-pound washers to process guestroom linens. Their washing cycles take 27 minutes (roughly one half-hour). How many 100-pound washers do you have to have installed (besides the two that you already have) to finish the 6,700 pounds in six hours?

CASE STUDY

Kathleen Boger has been appointed rooms division director of a Sheraton hotel soon to be opened in Victoria, Canada. She has been asked to organize the laundry of this 500-room property. The guestroom distribution of the hotel is as follows:

- 300 rooms with one king-size bed
- 100 rooms with one queen-size bed
- 100 rooms with two double-size beds

Kathleen decides to adopt the following bed linen and terrycloth:

- 3 pillows for each bed
- 2 bath towels per person
- 2 hand towels per person
- 2 washcloths per person
- 1 bath mat per room
- 2 sheets in each bed

Food and beverage will generate up to 3,400 pounds per day
The weight of each linen piece is:

- King sheets   4.00 pounds each
- Queen sheets   3.15 pounds
- Double sheets   2.85 pounds
- Pillowcases   0.75 pounds
- Bath towels   3.00 pounds
- Hand towels   2.50 pounds
- Washcloths   0.25 pounds
- Bath mats   1.75 pounds

Assignment

1. How many pounds will have to be washed at 100% occupancy?
2. How many 100-pound washers are needed to do the job in seven hours if each washing cycle takes about one-half hour?

Applying Ecolab floor products
Courtesy of Ecolab USA Inc.

The Cleaning Function

CHAPTER OBJECTIVES

- Explain the distribution of work at the beginning of the housekeeping day.
- Describe the daily sequence of functions performed by the housekeeping department.
- Explain guestroom and bathroom cleaning procedures.
- Discuss lost-and-found and guestroom inspection.
- Learn about public areas and back-of-the-house cleaning.
- Discuss cleaning and maintenance of surfaces.

OVERVIEW

The primary function of the housekeeping department is to keep its areas of responsibility clean and functional. Every cleaning function must be set down in detail in the department's **standard** operating procedures (SOPs). These procedures describe the routines associated with the daily functions of the department. Specifically, standards are determined to equalize employee workloads, to ensure that employees know what is expected of them, and to maintain high-quality services.

This chapter covers the cleaning of guestrooms, public and employee areas and surfaces, and describes procedures for inspections, quality assurance, and lost-and-found.

GUESTROOM CLEANING

The essence of the lodging industry is to provide guests with impeccably cleaned rooms and bathrooms. Students in hospitality programs must understand from the beginning that guests do not patronize establishments in which the cleaning function is not conducted effectively.

SEQUENCE OF HOUSEKEEPING FUNCTIONS

The section that follows is intended for students to understand the theoretical framework of how tasks are distributed daily in housekeeping departments. Although most lodging properties today have computer software programs to facilitate scheduling, it is important for students to learn the theory behind the procedures that take place routinely in a housekeeping setting. The series of reports that follow are commonly generated by computer programs.

Distribution of Work

The housekeeping department is usually opened very early in the morning by an assistant manager or senior supervisor who receives the front desk report (Figure 7.1) from the front office department. The front desk report, which is usually prepared by the night clerk or night auditor, consists of a computer printout specifying the status of each guestroom in the house, the number of rooms occupied the previous night, and the rooms that are expected to check out and stay over. This report is an exact copy of the guestroom status found in the front desk computer, or the **room rack** if the property is not computerized. A code beside the numbers of all rooms in the house describes whether the rooms are occupied, vacant, ready, out of order, expected to check out today, and so on. The example in Figure 7.1 is for a 400-room property consisting of five floors. Each floor has 80 guestrooms. On the night of June 3,320 rooms were occupied, 83 of which were scheduled to check out on June 4, while 237 rooms were to stay over.

The supervisor receiving the front desk report first verifies whether the number of department employees scheduled yesterday to work today is sufficient to service the number of rooms occupied. If not enough workers were scheduled, the supervisor will have to telephone around to ask people to come to work. On the other hand, if too many workers were scheduled for the occupancy reached, calls will be made to ask some employees to stay away that day, saving them an unnecessary trip to work. Having the right number of workers each day to service the rooms occupied prevents higher than necessary labor costs due to overstaffing or to overtime wages for not having enough employees to do the work in eight hours.

FIGURE 7.1 Sample Front Desk Report

Front Desk Report

Date: _____ June 3 _____

Room Occupied: _____ 320 _____
Expected Check-outs: _____ 83 _____
Expected Stay-overs: _____ 237 _____

101:	201:	301:	401:	501:
102:	202:	302:	402:	502:
103:	203:	303:	403:	503:
104:	204:	304:	404:	504:
105:	205:	305:	405:	505:
106:	206:	306:	406:	506:
107:	207:	307:	407:	507:
108:	208:	308:	408:	508:
109:	209:	309:	409:	509:
110:	210:	310:	410:	510:
111:	211:	311:	411:	511:
112:	212:	312:	412:	512:
113:	213:	313:	413:	513:
114:	214:	314:	414:	514:
115:	215:	315:	415:	515:
116:	216:	316:	416:	516:
177:	277:	377:	477:	577:
178:	278:	378:	478:	578:
179:	279:	379:	479:	579:
180:	280:	380:	480:	580:

The information received on the front desk report is then transferred on to the **team supervisor work report** (Figure 7.2) to inform all team supervisors of the status of all guestrooms in their respective sections.

Each team supervisor will then communicate the status of the rooms in each section to the team's section housekeepers using a **section housekeeper work report** (Figure 7.3), which is given to them at the beginning of the shift.

When the property is not at 100 percent occupancy and not all section housekeepers are called to work, the occupied rooms of the sections that are open are assigned to the section

FIGURE 7.2 Sample Team Supervisor Work Report

Team Supervisor Work Report

Date: June 3   Team: One

Section 1 HSK Erika	Section 2 HSK Kate	Section 3 HSK Melanie	Section 4 HSK Open	Section 5 HSK Jennifer
101: OCC	117:	133:	149: OCC	165:
102: C/O	118:	134:	150: OCC	166:
103: OCC	119:	135:	151: VR	167:
104: OCC	120:	136:	152: OCC	168:
105: VR	121:	137:	153: OCC	169:
106: VR	122:	138:	154: C/O	170:
107: OCC	123:	139:	155: OCC	171:
108: C/O	124:	140:	156: OOO	172:
109: OCC	125:	141:	157: VR	173:
110: VR	126:	142:	158: OCC	174:
111: OCC	127:	143:	159: C/O	175:
112: C/O	128:	144:	160: VR	176:
113: OCC	129:	145:	161: OCC	177:
114: VR	130:	146:	162: VR	178:
115: OCC	131:	147:	163: OCC	179:
116: OCC	132:	148:	164: C/O	180:

housekeepers who are working that day. Figure 7.2 shows that the section housekeeper of section 4 in team 1 (Maria) has been asked to stay away today. The 11 occupied rooms in section 4 are picked up by the remaining section housekeepers on duty that day—Erika (4) and the remaining 7 by Kate, Melanie, and Jennifer. Figure 7.3 shows Erika's work report with 12 occupied rooms in her section, plus four rooms that she will pick up from Maria's open section. The form has a "remarks" column to advise housekeepers of VIP arrivals, early check-ins, late checkouts, deep cleaning, and so forth.

Beginning Daily Activities

At the beginning of the working day, housekeeping personnel congregate in the linen room, where they clock in and receive a briefing on the day's activities. Generally, daily activities in the housekeeping department start at 8:00 A.M., although in some cases this time may be different depending on the type of establishment, day of the week, or special functions taking place at the property. For instance, most of the guests in business hotels get up early for meetings, to catch an

FIGURE 7.3   Sample Section Housekeeper Work Report

Team: _____One_____   Section: _____One_____

Date: _____June 3_____   Housekeeper: _____Erika_____

Room	Remarks	Pick-Ups	Remarks
101: OCC		149	E/A
102: C/O		150	
103: OCC	VIP	152	E/A
104: OCC		153	
105: VR			
106: VR			
107: OCC			
108: C/O	L C/O		
109: OCC			
110: VR			
111: OCC			
112: C/O	DEEP CLEAN		
113: OCC			
114: VR			
115: OCC			
116: OCC			

early flight, or attend a convention. On the other hand, on Saturdays and Sundays, guests traditionally get up late and like a late checkout. Also, if the guests of a large convention have been granted permission to check out late in the afternoon, most of the housekeeping work force will be needed to work late to prepare the rooms for the next day's arrivals.

The day's work begins with the section housekeepers collecting their fully equipped service cart and work report and signing for the passkey for their respective sections on a key control sheet. In high-rise buildings, all housekeeping personnel should use service elevators only. The work report indicates the status of all rooms in the respective housekeeper sections. Instead of knocking on doors at random, section housekeepers should follow a logical order so that guests are not awakened or disturbed while still in their rooms. Rooms that have already checked out should be serviced first, followed by rooms showing requests for early service, expected checkouts, stay-over rooms, and requests for late service. Last, usually after check-out time, the status of "do-not-disturb" (DND) rooms must be ascertained. It is important to verify what is behind a DND room lest a guest in need of help is unable to use the phone. This situation can occur if the guest is unconscious or in a coma. The first attempt to contact the guest should be done by phone; if the guest answers, the section housekeeper should ask if a cleaning of the room is required. If there is no answer, the section housekeeper should knock at the door and try to enter the room. If there is no answer and the room is double-locked, a manager should enter the room using a master key. In situations when the room is finally opened and the security chain is on, the chain must be cut with a chain cutter. It is important to remember that in connecting rooms, the guest could have left the DND sign on, double-locked the door, and set the chain in one of the rooms while exiting from the room next door.

Also at the beginning of the working day, hallways, stairwells, vending-machine areas, elevators, and floor closets and vestibules should be inspected by the houseperson of each team. Common problems found early in the morning are leftover room service trays, spills, overflowing wastebaskets, and signs of vandalism. After correcting these flaws, the housepersons proceed to help the section housekeepers in their respective teams by providing them with supplies, moving heavy pieces of furniture, taking soiled linen to the laundry room, and so on. The housepersons usually finish their shift by vacuuming the public areas assigned to each of their teams.

Room Status Verification

As the daily work progresses, section housekeepers should notify their team supervisors if any discrepancy is found between the status of rooms as shown in their work report and the real status of the rooms. For example, if the section housekeeper work report shows that room 105 is occupied and there is no sign of guests in the room, the front desk report might have been wrong. In this case, the front office must be immediately notified of the discrepancy.

Some lodging properties require that the housekeeping department file a status report for the accounting department as a cross-reference to the occupancy report submitted by the front office. If the front desk is selling rooms and pocketing the money, or if they let employees or friends stay in guestrooms for free, the problem is soon discovered. At about 10 o'clock, the A.M. room check is conducted by all teams entering the guestrooms at about the same time. All relevant differences found from the front desk report must be communicated to the front desk as quickly as possible.

As work progresses, the team supervisors coordinate the activities related to the rooms in their sections, such as communicating to the front desk the rooms that are vacant and ready to be sold, notifying section housekeepers of guests changing rooms, communicating the need to clean rooms for early arrivals, VIP treatment, and so forth. In most properties, team supervisors are also in charge of inspecting guestrooms.

Guestroom Cleaning Procedures

Section housekeepers should knock at the door with their knuckles, announcing themselves as "housekeeping," at least twice prior to entering the room. The door should remain open, with the service cart blocking the entrance for safety reasons. This way, if someone attempts to pull the cart to enter the room, the section housekeeper will be alerted.

All lodging properties have standard operating procedures for guestroom cleaning; however, these procedures differ from property to property. Usually, section housekeepers are asked to air out the room by opening windows and turn on all lights to make sure that they are in working order. The TV set and the heating/air-conditioning units are then checked, and the thermostat is reset to the lowest comfortable setting. The section housekeeper ascertains whether any items are missing, broken, or vandalized. If that is the case, the team supervisor should be notified immediately and, in turn will call the front desk so that the guest is charged accordingly. If out-of-order or nonworking equipment is found, a work order is generated and sent to the maintenance department. If the guests have checked out of the room, the section housekeeper should ascertain that no personal belongings have been left behind. If they have, the team supervisor is notified as soon as possible and, in turn, will notify the front desk and security department. If the guests have not checked out, all scattered clothing items, papers, documents, or magazines should be placed away neatly, making sure that nothing is thrown away that may be useful to the guest.

The first step in cleaning the bedroom is to empty out the trash in the refuse bag of the service cart, changing the wastebasket liners for new ones and cleaning the ashtrays. The bed is stripped, keeping items off the floor and handling the linen carefully lest guest items have been left there. Special care must be taken with sharps (needles) that may be in the sheets. At this time, the mattress, box spring, blanket, bedspread, pillows, and bed pads are carefully inspected for stains or torn spots and replaced as needed. The soiled bed and bathroom linen is placed in the service cart receptacle for fast delivery to the laundry room as soon as the bag is full. In most properties, the houseperson regularly empties the receptacles into a hamper for transportation.

Basic Bed-Making Procedures

The first step in making the bed is to place the bottom sheet smoothly on it, tucking it at the head and sides. The bottom and top sheets and blanket are then mitered at the foot of the bed and tucked along the sides. The bedspread is then placed over the blanket, turned about 15 inches back from the headboard, and the pillow(s) placed over it. Both bedspread and pillow(s) are then rolled back toward the headboard. The bedspread should be smoothed out so no lumps or creases show after the bed has been made. Section housekeepers should be trained to make beds moving around them only once in order to save time and energy.

Dusting and Wiping the Bedroom

Lamp shades are brushed with a dry cloth or feather duster. All furniture, fixtures, and doors are lightly sprayed with a cleaning solution or furniture polish and damp-wiped with a dust cloth. Air vents, windowsills, light bulbs, telephones, the tops of thermostats, and closet shelves are also wiped clean with a damp cloth. Drawers are wiped out and inspected for cleanliness and ease of operation. If the drawers are difficult to open (or close), a work order should be generated. All recycled items should be meticulously cleaned or replaced. The property or chain literature and phone books must be kept as new, without marks or creases. Missing clothes hangers should be replaced and those not belonging to the property removed. Mirrors and TV screen should be sprayed and wiped with a dry cloth. All drapes, lamp shades, and pictures must be centered and balanced.

The carpet is then vacuumed, including under the bed, starting at the far end of the room and ending at the door. Finally, deodorant spray is applied to curtains and carpet before leaving the room. This procedure is particularly necessary in "smoking rooms."

When the guestroom has a balcony or patio, the floor is swept and the door and furniture dusted. If the room is at floor level, the patio door should be properly secured by setting the security bar in place. Properties offering suites with kitchenettes require considerable labor to service the living, cooking, and dining areas. Dishes must be washed, cooking equipment and utensils scrubbed and polished, and refrigerators, cupboards, and drawers wiped clean.

Some lodging properties have experimented with guestroom team cleaning; that is, having two section housekeepers clean guestrooms at the same time. Although team cleaning may be preferred by housekeeping workers, it usually is not labor-cost effective. In practice, a room that is serviced in 30 minutes by one room attendant cannot be finished by two room attendants in 15 minutes.

Bathroom Cleaning

Section housekeepers should wear gloves when cleaning the bathroom for chemical and germ protection. After checking all lights, inspecting the faucets for leaks, and dumping the waste-basket, the commode is cleaned inside with bowl cleaner and a toilet brush and outside (including the tank) with a germicidal solution. The bath area should be cleaned by the section housekeeper standing inside the tub on a rubber mat placed at the bottom of the tub to keep from slipping. The bath walls, soap dishes, plumbing fixtures, and shower doors are cleaned with all-purpose cleaner and wiped dry with a cloth. The tub is cleaned, using mild scouring powder/liquid if necessary. The tub stopper should be pulled out, freed from hair, and wiped clean.

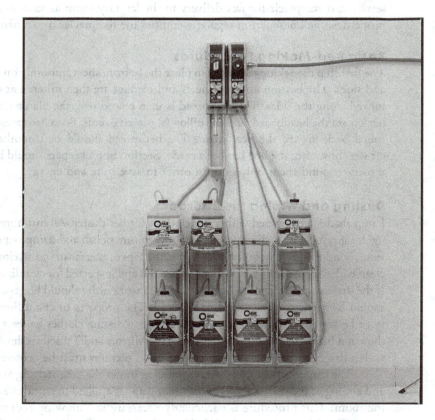

Ecolab liquid cleaner dispenser
Courtesy of Ecolab USA Inc.

The vanity and sink are cleaned with all-purpose cleaner and wiped dry. The sink stopper should also be pulled out and wiped clean. The mirror should be cleaned with a damp cloth or sprayed with a mirror-cleaning solution and wiped dry. The bathroom floor should be wiped with a cloth and germicidal, including behind the door. Any lint in the bathroom ventilation vent or fan grill should be removed. All supplies and guest amenities should be replaced as needed. Towels should be neatly folded in racks or hung properly from towel bars. Toilet and facial tissue should be replaced if less than one-quarter full. A second toilet tissue roll should be left in the bathroom as a reserve. It is a good idea to have section housekeepers place a card stating that the room was serviced by them; this increases pride and identifies the worker with the job performed; for example, "Hello, this room has been serviced by Erika. Have a pleasant stay with us."

After the room has been cleaned, the section housekeeper notifies the supervisor that the room is ready for inspection. In some properties, section housekeepers may use codes through the telephone or the television set to inform the housekeeping office that the rooms have been serviced.

Lost-and-Found Procedures

All items found in a lodging property are usually deposited in and controlled by the housekeeping department, given that most articles are left behind by guests in the property's guestrooms. Standard operating procedures for lost-and-found items must be in place and made clear to all employees. In all cases, when articles are found anywhere in the property they must be taken to the housekeeping department (usually to the linen room) and adequately tagged and logged for fast identification. The lost-and-found logbook or applicable software program must include the date on which the item was found, its description, the place where it was found, the person who found it, and the number assigned to the tagged item. At times when the housekeeping department is closed, the article will be securely kept at the front desk and brought to the linen room first thing in the morning. Items containing multiple articles, such as bags, wallets, or purses, should be inventoried and their content described and verified by two employees. All tagged items must be kept under lock and key for security reasons. All inquiries regarding lost-and-found items should be addressed to the housekeeping office. After proper identification, the items are returned to their owners. If the inquiry is made from out of town, the property should send the item free of charge to its owner by mail or UPS package. Valuable articles should be sent by registered mail or insured for their approximate cost. It is customary in the hospitality industry that items not claimed within a reasonable period of time, generally three months, are given either to the employee who found them or to a charitable organization.

The P.M. Housekeeping Report

Prior to the end of the morning shift, all section housekeepers conduct a check of all the rooms in the house simultaneously. Each room attendant records on a blank daily work report (Figure 7.3) the status of each guestroom in his or her section. The reports of all section housekeepers are recorded on a blank front desk report (Figure 7.1) and delivered to the front desk. The front desk will then compare the housekeeping room status with the status kept in the front desk's computer, or room rack if the property is not computerized. Any discrepancy between the room status provided by the housekeeping department and the room status at the front desk is quickly investigated and corrected. For example, if the housekeeping room report indicates that room 101 is occupied and the records at the front desk show that the room is vacant, the room is checked to see whether housekeeping or the front desk was in error.

At the end of the morning shift, the housekeepers of every team restock the floor closets assigned to them with clean linen and guest and cleaning supplies, vacuum hallways, tidy vending areas and stairwells, and dump all trash. If time allows, section housekeepers refit service carts for the following day and store them for the night.

Inspection of Guestrooms

The general rule in lodging properties is to have all guestrooms inspected by qualified staff before they are handed over to the front desk for renting them to guests. This control function is important for properties with quality assurance programs, as inspectors are the last employees to catch any errors made during cleaning before guests arrive. Small properties with no or very low turnover may decide to trust their section housekeepers and leave to them the job of inspecting the rooms just after they have been cleaned. Large properties, however, should have a rigorous system of inspecting guestrooms prior to rental to guests. Usually, the guestrooms are inspected by the supervisor of each team; some large hotels have designated inspectors whose only job is to check rooms.

In all cases, standards should be set to help section housekeepers and inspectors work toward the same goals of cleanliness and room appearance. Figure 7.4 is a sample **guestroom inspection form** for a suite hotel that can be used in room inspections. Often, inspectors give scores to the section housekeeper responsible for cleaning the room that determine, after a certain period of time, whether the room attendant qualifies for bonuses or rewards attached to superior performance. On the other hand, substandard scores will lead to retraining room attendants or disqualifying them for the job. Inspectors should be trained to do fair and accurate inspections. Some properties enter the data collected on a computer to show performance over the long term. The data may show that the performance of a particular team is low in a specific area, for example bathrooms. In this case, additional training in bathroom cleaning should be emphasized to bring the team up to bathroom-cleaning standards. Vacant-and-ready (VR) rooms should be inspected first so they can be turned over to front desk for assignment to early arrivals. The person who inspects rooms must be well trained to detect errors and make sure that everything in the room is in perfect order. Well-trained inspectors can perform this function very quickly and effectively without having to use checklists.

Some inspection programs include the preventive maintenance inspection of guestrooms in order to anticipate mechanical or functional breakdowns before they may occur. Figure 7.5 is a sample maintenance inspection checklist used for this purpose. When deficiencies are detected, a **maintenance work order** (Figure 7.6) is filed and sent to the engineering department for immediate attention. This procedure is done using computer programs that link the housekeeping and engineering departments for this purpose. If the deficiency is not corrected after a reasonable amount of time, a second work order request should be initiated. The request for emergency repairs, such as broken guestroom door locks, should be marked "urgent" and tracked closely until the job is completed.

The Evening Shift

The housekeeping evening activities in medium-size properties are usually conducted by a team consisting of a supervisor, a houseperson, a reduced number of section housekeepers, and one or two public areas attendants. In large and very large properties, a greater number of employees is necessary.

FIGURE 7.4 Sample Guestroom Inspection Form

Date: _____ Room: _____ Housekeeper: _____ Inspector: _____

1. Closet shelf clean	____	25. Notepad and pen	____
2. Laundry bag with ticket	____	26. Ashtrays clean with matches	____
3. 8 hangers properly placed	____	27. Wastebaskets empty and clean	____
4. Microwave and fridge clean	____	28. Drapes neat and working	____
5. Shower walls and soap dish clean	____	29. Window sills/inside windows clean	____
6. Shower curtain/liner clean/dry	____	30. Night stands clean/dusted	____
7. Sink and wet bar clean	____	31. Telephone books/Bible in drawer	____
8. Bathtub clean/no mildew	____	32. Pictures clean and dust free	____
9. Sink and vanity clean	____	33. Bed made neatly and properly	____
10. All chrome cleaned and shined	____	34. Headboard clean and dusted	____
11. Stoppers clean and free of hair	____	35. Carpet edges clean	____
12. Mirrors clean and spot free	____	36. All drawers and shelves clean/dusted	____
13. T.P./Kleenex folded and stocked	____	37. Vanity mirror clean and spot free	____
14. Entire toilet clean	____	38. Light switches clean	____
15. Bathroom floor clean/no hair	____	39. Baseboards clean and dusted	____
16. All linen placed properly folded	____	40. Thermostat properly set and dusted	____
17. All amenities in proper place	____	41. Door frames and doors clean	____
18. Glasses clean and spot free	____	42. DND sign clean/in good condition	____
19. Ice bucket in place/clean/dry	____	43. Safety lock in good condition	____
20. TVs and remote clean and in place	____	44. Entry mat/doorway clean/no cob webs	____
21. Table and chairs clean/dust free	____	45. All lights dusted and working	____
22. Table lamp clean and working	____	46. Carpet vacuumed and edged	____
23. All printed collateral placed neatly and properly	____	47. Clock radio clean/time and station properly set	____
24. Phones and receivers clean	____		

The evening team receives the housekeeping P.M. report showing the status of all the guestrooms at the end of the morning shift and continues with the task of cleaning late checkout and day-rate rooms so these can be rented to guests. If the property offers **turndown service**, the evening team will perform the tasks of unfolding the bed, drawing the drapes closed, and refreshing the room by emptying the trash and replacing used towels. The evening section housekeepers also fill guest requests, such as delivering extra pillows or blankets to rooms, providing cribs or roll-a-way beds, or bringing extra towels. The evening teams also wash drinking glasses, restock service carts and **caddies** (portable cleaning-supply containers with a handle), clean public restrooms and, if necessary, process soiled linen in the property's laundry. It is important to provide answering devices to members of the evening team so that the front desk or manager-on-duty can effectively communicate with housekeeping personnel.

The service carts are also stocked in the evening to facilitate operations and avoid confusion the following morning. Each service cart is supplied with bed and bathroom linens, paper supplies, guest amenities, and recycled items. The cleaning supplies commonly placed in caddies

FIGURE 7.5 Sample Maintenance Inspection Sheet

Date: _____ Room: _____ Housekeeper: _____ Inspector: _____

Bathroom
1. Bathtub safety strips ____
2. Tub and sink stoppers ____
3. Tub and sink plugs ____
4. Shower head clean ____
5. Bath tile/walls ____
6. Toilet drain/flush ____
7. Toilet—no leaks ____
8. Toilet seat, hinges, bumpers ____
9. Toilet seal—no leaks ____
10. Faucets—no leaks ____
11. Chrome fixtures ____
12. Shower rod—secure ____
13. Vanity and tub—no scratches ____
14. Toilet paper holder ____
15. Facial tissue holder ____
16. Soap dish—secure ____
17. Grab bars—secure ____
18. Towel racks—secure ____

Electrical
19. Lamp switches ____
20. Lamp sockets—tight ____
21. Lamp shades—tight ____
22. Plugs and cords ____
23. Light switches ____
24. Wall plates ____

Television/Radio
25. Audio—clear ____
26. Visual—in focus ____
27. Cable connections ____
28. Chassis—secured ____

Telephone
29. Audio—clear ____
30. Bell—ringer ____
32. Message light ____

Doors
33. Handles ____
34. Lock ____
35. Hinges ____
36. Door chain ____
37. Door bumpers ____
38. Door stoppers ____

Furniture
39. Drawer handles ____
40. All surfaces ____
41. Chair/tables ____
42. Headboard—secure ____
43. Nightstand—undamaged ____
44. Pictures—secure ____

Sliding Doors
45. Tracks—clean ____
46. Doorstops ____
47. Latches ____
48. Security bar ____

Windows/Mirrors
49. Window guides ____
50. Window latches ____
51. Window caulk ____
52. Drapery hardware ____
53. Mirrors—secure ____
54. Mirrors—no scratches ____

Room
55. Coat racks—secure ____
56. Baseboards—secure ____
57. Wall coverings ____
58. Ceiling-no cracks ____
59. Smoke detector ____
60. Insulation ____
61. Hot water—120°F ____

are cleaning solutions, brushes, scrubbers, sponges, and cleaning rags. The service cart is equipped with trash and soiled-linen bags.

Guestroom Deep Cleaning

Section housekeepers are usually allotted an average of 30 minutes to service a stay-over or check-out room. Periodically, room attendants are given extra time to clean guestrooms in depth, performing tasks such as brushing carpet edges, rotating mattresses, vacuuming drapes, and cleaning under the furniture. In order not to tie up guestrooms for long periods of time, deep cleaning should be combined with maintenance tasks conducted by the engineering department,

FIGURE 7.6   Sample Maintenance Work Order

Date: _____   Location: _____
Problem: _____
           _____
           _____
           _____
           _____
Completed by: _____
Date completed: _____
Remarks: _____
           _____
           _____
           _____
           _____

such as recaulking tubs, changing air-conditioning filters, or performing minor repairs. Deep cleaning of guestrooms should be intensified during low-occupancy periods. Generally, all rooms in the house should be deep cleaned at least once a year.

PUBLIC AREAS AND BACK-OF-THE-HOUSE CLEANING

The housekeeping department is also in charge of the cleaning and maintenance of offices, public and back-of-the-house areas. Potential guests and visitors have a first-hand opportunity to judge the cleanliness of the property from what they see in the "on-stage" public areas. Public and employee areas are cleaned by public areas attendants, who are scheduled to work regardless of the property's occupancy, because the front- and back-of-the-house areas must be kept clean, whether the property is full or not, 24 hours a day.

The cleaning of public areas is conducted following preestablished area cleaning inventories and frequency schedules (see Figure 3.1).

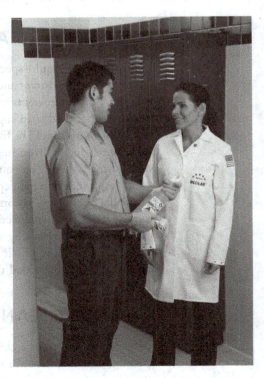

Ecolab Specialist Gives Advice to Hotel Worker
Courtesy of Ecolab USA Inc.

Thus, the public areas attendants will know exactly what and how often all their assigned areas must be cleaned. For instance, while the chandelier in the lobby of the property usually is dusted every two months, the carpet in the same area is vacuumed daily (or twice a day). Besides cleaning, public areas attendants should keep public areas in good order by straightening the furniture, emptying ashtrays, trash cans, and cigarette urns, and taking away empty glasses and used newspapers. The handset of public telephones should be wiped clean with a germicidal solution and the telephone book replaced if it has scribbled lines on it.

Special attention must be given to the foyer and lobby where guests will get a first impression of the property upon entering the establishment. Handprints and smudges on glass doors are common, as well as footprints and traces of mud on the carpet when the weather is inclement. Appropriate matting and runners must be placed strategically to protect the appearance of the lobby's floor. The presence of dust, cobwebs, smudges, dull-looking water fountains, or unpolished wood surfaces in the public areas is unacceptable. Elevators, including service elevators, require frequent attention as bell carts and heavy suitcases do often bump against walls and floor, scratching or marking their finish.

Just as important as cleaning public areas is the cleaning of employee areas and other sections at the back of the house. The employee locker room and restrooms are areas where vandalism and graffiti marks frequently occur. The upkeep of these areas, hallways, and the employee cafeteria is a reflection of the care and concern that the company bestows on its employees, which may positively or negatively affect the morale of the property's work force.

RESTROOM CLEANING

Public restrooms require special and dedicated attention, as they are used not only by guests, but also by visitors, restaurant and bar patrons, and people attending meetings or conventions in the property. Public restrooms must be constantly checked, cleaned, and stocked with high-quality sanitary, paper, and soap supplies.

Restrooms should be fitted with automatic air fresheners or other method of odor control. Battery-operated wall cabinets can automatically deliver fragrances using 30-day cartridges. Men's urinals should be equipped with screens and deodorizing blocks containing chelating agents to prevent mineral deposit buildups. Basins and counter tops should be sanitized with a germicidal cleaner. All chrome fixtures should be wiped clean and polished. Toilets should be brushed inside with an effective bowl cleaner and the tank cover (if any) and body of the bowl wiped clean with cleansing solution. Special attention must be given to graffiti and lipstick marks, so common in public spaces. Mops used in restrooms should be sanitized with a strong disinfectant solution added to the water in the bucket/wringer.

SURFACE CLEANING

Surface coverings may be classified into resilient and nonresilient according to their hardness. Cleaning and maintenance of floors and walls depend on the composition of the surface's material. Surfaces must be preserved from deterioration as much as possible by protecting them from wear and tear. Once the surface shows signs of wearing away, it must be redone to bring it back to its original state.

Worker Applies Ecolab All-purpose Cleaner
Courtesy of Ecolab USA Inc.

The first step to redo floors is to remove the worn-out finish. This process is called stripping. Commercial floors are stripped using a stripping solution mixed with water and scrubbing the surface with a rotary floor machine. The resulting mixture is picked up with a wet vacuum or mop and bucket and the floor rinsed with clean water. After the floor dries, porous surfaces are treated with a **sealer** to protect them from wear and tear and liquid spills. The last step is to apply a **finish** to the surface to make it slip resistant and give the floor a glossy, shiny look. Often, sealer and finish are combined into one product. Finished surfaces are maintained by polishing them with rotary floor machines that clean, buff, and burnish the floor using different types of pads.

The most common resilient surfaces found in lodging operations are made of synthetic rubber, vinyl, wood, and, of course, carpeting. The most common hard floors (nonresilient) are ceramic, marble/terrazzo, epoxy, and concrete. The composition of the floor determines the kind of care it should receive. For instance, while porous surfaces require sealing, the sealing of nonporous floors is unnecessary.

SYNTHETIC RUBBER FLOORS

Floors covered with synthetic rubber tiles are nonporous and, therefore, waterproof; however, liquids containing oil, solvent, or grease may cause the material to crack and deteriorate. Rubber floors are easy to maintain, as they just require mopping to keep them clean. The cleaning solution used should be pH neutral, as alkalis and acids would mar these surfaces. These types of floors do not require sealing. Synthetic floors can be kept shiny by buffing them with a water emulsion floor polish. When wax or dirt buildup is embedded in the finish, the floor should be stripped with a mild de-waxer.

VINYL FLOORS

These are nonporous surfaces resistant to most chemical spills. Thick vinyl material is quite durable and can be purchased in a variety of patterns to resemble natural products. If the material is treated with special seals when made, it can be resistant to scratches and abrasions. No-wax vinyl surfaces do not need sealing, stripping, or finishing. Conventional vinyl floors can be treated with solvent-based waxes and buffed to a rich luster. Wax buildup can be removed with a mild de-waxing stripper. Dusting and a daily mop-and-rinse will remove most dirt and grime.

WOOD FLOORS

Wood floors are not common in most modern lodging properties, where carpeting, ceramic tile, and synthetic surfaces are the norm, but they may be found in older establishments and in some ski resorts and hunting lodges. Because of its porosity, wooden floors must be well sealed to prevent stains; once stained, the surface needs to be thoroughly sanded to remove the marks. Wood floors can also be damaged by mobile equipment with metal rollers and by moving heavy furniture without first protecting the surface. These surfaces can be treated with a combination sealer/finish made of waterborne polyurethane. When properly sealed and finished, wooden floors just require an occasional buffing to keep them shiny.

CARPETS

Preventing staining and wear is more important for carpets than it is for other types of floor coverings. For example, if the lobby of a lodging property is carpeted, the slush, mud, and gritty soil tracked in by guests quickly become embedded in the carpet fabric, causing it to stain and wear very fast. The best prevention for carpet deterioration is adequate protection. Placing walk-off mats in doorways and plastic runners over the most high-traffic sections of the carpet will lengthen its life and save labor hours in cleaning and maintenance.

Scheduled daily vacuuming of carpets is probably the best way to extend their lives. Most of the soil tracked into a building is dry—the kind that can be controlled by vacuuming. The absorption of dust, sand, and grit particles by vacuuming will prevent the erosion of fibers when they are compressed by the weight of traffic from people and carts. Vacuums with top-loading bags are preferable, as they ensure that the vacuum does not lose effectiveness as the bag fills.

Marks and stains can be removed by bonnet cleaning, by which carpet shampoo is sprayed on the surface to be treated and a rotary floor machine equipped with a bonnet is passed over until the stains are removed. When surfaces are heavily soiled, deep cleaning is necessary. Heavy soils can be treated using water extractors that automatically apply the cleaning solution and pick it up with an attached wet-vacuum system that recovers water and soil in a holding tank. Carpets should be cleaned with hot water, except for wool fabrics that require cold water. Dry foam and dry powder methods are less effective than water extractors, but it takes less time for the carpet to dry, so the area can be used sooner if necessary. Some products applied regularly to carpets are antimicrobial solutions to prevent the growth of bacteria and fungi, antistatic sprays to eliminate static electricity caused by low humidity or high winds, and fluorochemical treatments that resist soiling and prevent spills from becoming hard-to-remove stains.

UPHOLSTERED SURFACES

Upholstered armchairs and couches can be spot-cleaned with most of the same products used on carpets. Machines with special attachments are needed to apply the spot removers to narrow surfaces. Some spotters are fortified with enzymes to treat organic compounds; tougher soils, such as crayon, fresh paint, ink, and gum, require solvent formulas to dissolve the stains.

CERAMIC FLOORS

Because ceramic floors are very resistant to water spills and easy to clean, they are quite common in bathroom and kitchen. Usually, the terracotta that forms the tile is covered with a glossy coat that makes the surface 100 percent waterproof. A disadvantage with this type of floor is that they can be very slippery when wet. These surfaces are cleaned by sweeping and damp mopping. Sealing or finishing of ceramic floors is not necessary, except for the grout between the tiles.

MARBLE/TERRAZZO FLOORS

Marble is a crystalline limestone that is capable of taking a polish. Terrazzo is a floor material of broken stone (marble or granite chips) and cement that can also be easily lustered. Although very hard and durable, these surfaces are very sensitive to oils and acid and alkaline cleaners. A mild detergent is all that is needed to keep them clean. Because of their porosity, marble and terrazzo floors must be sealed, and when stripped, alkaline products should be avoided. The surfaces can be burnished to obtain a mirrorlike finish.

EPOXY FLOORS

Epoxy is a synthetic material that is durable, abrasion-resistant, and easy to maintain. Alkaline compounds diluted in water are used to clean epoxy floors. Epoxy surfaces can be kept shiny with a light finish application. Alkaline products are needed to strip the finish.

CONCRETE FLOORS

Concrete floors, made with a mixture of cement and sand, are usually used as outdoor surfaces, such as driveways, loading docks, and poolside areas. Cleaning is done by sweeping and hosing with water. Concrete is a porous compound that should be sealed to prevent liquid stains from seeping into it. Urethane-fortified products resist water and help protect against graffiti. An alkaline product diluted in water is required to strip the sealer.

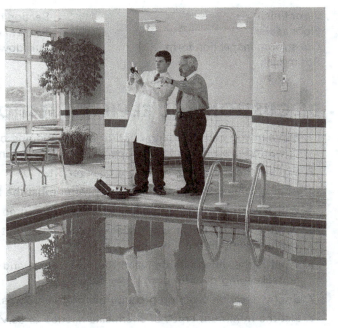

Ecolab Worker Analyzes Spa Pool Water
Courtesy of Ecolab USA Inc.

WALLS AND CEILINGS

Some wall and ceiling coverings that are different from those normally used on floor surfaces are paint, plastic laminate, fabric, vinyl, and wallpaper. Painted surfaces can be cleaned with mild detergent and water. Dusting and damp-wiping are all that it is required to keep plastic laminate clean, as it is nonporous and will not absorb stains. Fabric materials are very susceptible to mildew and stains. Walls covered with fabric should be spot-cleaned with chemicals rather than with water and detergent to avoid shrinkage. Vinyl covering can be purchased in many decorative motifs. It is durable and easy to clean with mild detergents. On the other hand, most wallpaper coverings cannot be cleaned with water, so they must be replaced if they are marked or stained.

Written procedures for all aspects of daily maintenance of surfaces should be established. In general, grease and dirt are acidic in nature and they are best cleaned with alkaline products. The more grease and dirt on a surface, the more alkalinity is needed in the cleaning compound to treat the area. When light soils are present, particularly on highly polished floors, a neutral product is required (pH range 7 to 8). The higher the pH, the more likely the floor polish will be damaged.

KEY TERMS

Floor finish

Floor sealer

Guestroom inspection form

Room rack

Section housekeeper work report

Team supervisor work report

Turndown service

DISCUSSION AND REVIEW QUESTIONS

1. Explain why housekeeping departments in lodging operations must compile standard operating procedures for the operative routines of the department.

2. Explain the purpose of the front desk report.

3. After receiving the front desk report, what must the housekeeping supervisor verify?

4. Which two reports are compiled from the information received on the front desk report?

5. What is the reason section housekeepers should not knock on all guestrooms of their sections early in the morning?

6. What is the difference between the A.M. report and the P.M. report generated in the housekeeping department?

7. Briefly describe cleaning procedures for guestrooms.

8. List the minimum types of chemicals needed to service a bathroom.

9. Why is the lost-and-found function usually administered by the housekeeping department in lodging properties?

10. What is the difference between a maintenance inspection checklist and a maintenance work order?

11. Describe the purpose of stripping, sealing, and finishing floors.

12. What are the advantages and disadvantages of ceramic floors?

MINICASES

SITUATION 1

As the assistant to the executive housekeeper of the 400-room Royal Hotel, you have been asked to open the department on Monday, June 15. On arriving to work at 5:30 in the morning, you receive the front desk report, which states that the number of occupied rooms the night of Sunday, June 14 was 385. Checking the adjusted daily schedule posted Sunday afternoon, you find that the number of section housekeepers scheduled to work this morning is 21. The workload for section housekeepers at the Royal is 16 rooms to be serviced in eight hours. What is your reaction to this situation? Would you call around to ask additional section housekeepers to report to work? If so, how many would you call to work? Or would you ask some section housekeepers to stay away because there are not enough occupied rooms for all the housekeepers scheduled to work today? If so, how many would you ask to stay away?

SITUATION 2

As executive housekeeper of a resort in Boca Raton, Florida, you have been asked to give your professional opinion on the type of floor covering you would recommend for three areas of the property that are going to be remodeled six months from now. The areas in need of new floors are the resort's coffee shop, the main lobby, and the employee locker room. The weather in Boca Raton is subtropical, with warm summers and mild winters. The property has two large swimming pools and the guests practice several water sports at the nearby oceanfront. For this reason, people staying at the resort often go to the front desk and concierge areas dripping water from their wet bathing suits. Sometimes they even go to the coffee shop counter in wet attire.

Present a written report to your supervisor indicating the types of floors that you recommend for the three areas, including the advantages and disadvantages of the new surfaces you advocate.

SITUATION 3

You have been hired as assistant to the executive housekeeper of a hotel in downtown San Francisco. One of the problems that you have found in the housekeeping department is that some of the team supervisors, fearful of running short of linen in their sections, consistently hoard linen items in their floor closets. This practice causes other teams to run out of linen in the middle of the daily activities, as the laundry room cannot generate enough clean items to go around.

Determined to solve this problem, you want to give specific instructions on how many linen items (maximum) can be stored in each floor closet. Each closet is designed to hold enough linen to service two sections. Each section consists of 16 guestrooms. Each room has two queen-size beds with two sheets and two pillows on each bed. The bathrooms are supplied with four bath towels, four hand towels, four washcloths, and one bath mat. You decide to allow a maximum of 1.5 linen par for each item in all floor closets. What is the maximum number of sheets, pillowcases, towels, and bath mats that the team supervisors can now stock in each floor closet?

Human Resources Management

Chapter 8: Personnel Administration

PART

4

CHAPTER

8

Operating Team, Drury Inn & Suites Flagstaff, Arizona
Courtesy of Drury Hotels

Personnel Administration

CHAPTER OBJECTIVES

- Understand the need to minimize employee turnover and absenteeism in the housekeeping department in order to maximize departmental income.
- Explain the process of selecting, hiring, and evaluating housekeeping employees.
- List some considerations to be followed when interviewing employees.
- Discuss procedures for testing and inducting workers.
- Describe the four major areas involved in housekeeping employee training.
- Discuss motivation theories applicable to housekeeping workers.
- Describe the concept of employee evaluation and compensation.
- Learn how to achieve worker satisfaction.
- Discuss the necessity of implementing guidelines for disciplining employees.
- Acquire awareness of cultural diversity, racial discrimination, and sexual harassment.

OVERVIEW

Employee turnover and absenteeism rates in the lodging industry are very high, substantially increasing the labor cost associated with constant recruiting and employee training. Successful executive housekeepers, however, can minimize turnover by following effective techniques for recruiting, hiring, and training employees. Practicing motivational methods and having in place adequate evaluation and compensation techniques can also create worker satisfaction and reduce turnover. Just as important as creating worker satisfaction is having in place fair, effective guidelines for disciplining those employees who do not perform within company regulations.

As the number of minority workers in lodging companies is very large, this chapter addresses the issue of cultural diversity and provides procedures to avoid racial discrimination and sexual harassment in the workplace.

THE NEED TO CURB HIGH EMPLOYEE TURNOVER AND ABSENTEEISM

The management of personnel in the lodging industry is complex. The business requires a large number of workers because most of the functions performed must be done by hand. Some years back, the use of robotics was forecast as a labor-saving panacea for lodging properties but, although some technological advances have been made, particularly in laundries and front desk operations, beds still need to be made, bathrooms still need to be cleaned, and guests still need to be served by employees. The industry is notorious for offering jobs that are quite demanding and for paying workers minimum wage, particularly in entry-level positions. Many people enter the field when they cannot find work elsewhere, perceiving their employment as a last resort rather than a career. This creates a chronic shortage of personnel as employees come and go in great numbers. It is not uncommon for lodging properties to experience employee turnover rates of over 100 percent per year. It is, therefore, critical that executive housekeepers maintain low levels of employee turnover and absenteeism.

There are two basic means to reduce turnover and absenteeism effectively: one is to follow the common technical rules of adequately recruiting, selecting, training, and evaluating personnel; the other consists of practicing effective methods of employee motivation, compensation, and the creation of an environment conducive to employee satisfaction.

PERSONNEL ACQUISITION

Ideally, a lodging property should employ only cheerful, good-natured people who smile easily and often, particularly when in contact with guests. Conversely, grouchy people, those who cannot keep their tempers, and those who feel sorry for themselves should not be hired at all. In all cases, the success of the operation depends on attracting applicants and placing them in the positions most appropriate to their skills and personalities.

Hiring applicants "off the street" may have a very negative outcome. If the wrong person is initially placed in the wrong position, turnover will result, as the person will inevitably leave the company, voluntarily or otherwise. Trial-and-error methods of employment should be avoided; instead, sound recruiting and hiring policies should be adopted.

RECRUITING HOUSEKEEPING EMPLOYEES

Housekeeping hires most of the department's employees on an as-needed basis; that is, they are asked to work depending on the daily occupancy of the property. Some employees, who are scheduled regardless of the property's occupancy, are hired **full-time**, such as supervisors, public areas or linen room attendants. Part-time employees agree to work usually less than 30 hours per week, generally receiving no major benefits other than wages. In most cases, part-time workers have an additional source of income, as they may be retirees, homemakers, or college students. Often, because of cost and fear of overstaffing, businesses turn to staffing companies for **temporary help**. One advantage of hiring temporaries is that it allows the employer to evaluate the temporary employees' qualifications and suitability for the job before offering them a full-time permanent position. Lodging properties should also have a number of people **on call**, who are asked to report to work when extra help is needed, such as when regular employees are ill or on vacation.

Union contracts, however, may have a significant impact on the composition of the company's work force. For example, a union contract may stipulate that all workers must be guaranteed a 40-hour work week; in this case, no part-time employees can be hired.

In all cases recruiting new employees is a special concern to both organization and newcomer. Management expects good performance and cooperation, while the new employee wants fair compensation, to be understood and recognized and, above all, to be helped during the induction process. In large hotels, the human resources department recruits employees. The order to recruit is initiated in the housekeeping department by filling an **employee requisition form** (Figure 8.1). This form indicates the position that needs to be filled and describes the specifications of the job and the required qualifications of the applicant. The **job description** is a detailed statement of the tasks required to get the job done. Figure 8.2 is a job description for section housekeepers. Each job description should include the minimum **employee qualifications** required and desired to ensure that applicants will be capable of doing the job for which they are applying. For example, the job description for laundry attendant may require that the applicant be capable of lifting 50 pounds (weight of laundry detergent pails used in the property) and may state that Spanish-speaking workers are preferred (since most of the other employees in the laundry speak Spanish).

After receiving the employee requisition, the human resources department advertises the position internally (**internal recruiting**) and externally (**external recruiting**). An organization that develops its personnel exclusively from within may be limiting itself by having to promote employees who may not be qualified for the position. On the other hand, capable employees already working for the company should be given a fair option to advance or change positions, and even departments, if they so desire.

Thus, the first step is to inform everyone in the department of the job opening. If no one is interested in applying for the position, employees may have friends or acquaintances who are looking for work. Usually, lodging companies reward workers for their referral of potential employees if these are hired and stay employed for a minimum of six months. Friends and relatives are usually well accepted by current employees, who are more likely to help the newcomers adjust to their new jobs. Another advantage of recruitment from within is that it avoids incurring recruitment costs. When the new opening is for a supervisory position, special efforts should be made to promote from within as a matter of fairness and to provide opportunities for advancement to the employees already with the company. Charts showing the various opportunities for career progression should be displayed for

FIGURE 8.1 Sample Employee Requisition Form

Date: _____ Department: _____

Position Requested: _____

New: _____ Replacement: _____ Number Required: _____

Classification: _____
(Full-time, Part-time, Temporary)

Working Hours: _____

Desired Starting Date: _____

Starting Rate of Pay: _____

Specification (general description of duties): _____

_____

_____

_____

_____

_____

Special Qualifications (desired or required): _____

_____

_____

_____

_____

_____

Department Manager: _____

employees to see. In the housekeeping department, the career path for a houseperson could lead from this entry-level position to section housekeeper, team supervisor, assistant to the executive housekeeper, laundry manager, and possibly executive housekeeper.

The most common external recruitment method is newspaper advertising. These ads are particularly successful in attracting the unskilled and young people looking for part-time and temporary employment. The advantage of this is that young, unskilled people can usually be adequately trained to perform the requirements of the job; the disadvantage is that once they have been trained, they may decide to change jobs and leave the department. Radio advertising reaches listeners who do not or cannot read newspapers.

When a supervisory or management position needs to be filled, private employment agencies are often a valuable source of recruits, but in most cases the property must pay a

FIGURE 8.2 Sample Section Housekeeper Job Description

Supervisor: Team supervisor.

Job responsibility: To service guestrooms as specified below. To fulfill any work assignments as requested by management.

Type of job: Full-time but dependent on room occupancy.

Position responsibility:

1. Arrive at the linen room on time and in uniform. Clock in.
2. Pick up guestroom section master key, section housekeeper report, and service cart.
3. Start cleaning section, avoiding waking up or disturbing stay-over guests. Follow the order:
   a. rooms already departed.
   b. rooms showing request for service.
   c. expected checkouts.
   d. stay-over rooms.
   e. requests for late service.
4. Knock on guestroom door twice and announce yourself. Leave door open and place service cart blocking the entrance for security purposes.
5. Prepare room for cleaning:
   a. open windows.
   b. turn on all lights, radio, and TV to make sure they work.
   c. ascertain condition of the room, reporting any damage to supervisor immediately. Leftover items are turned in to lost-and-found.
   d. set thermostat at 70°F.
   e. write a work order for any item in room that needs maintenance.
   f. if guests have not checked out, place away neatly all clothing, papers, documents, or any other belongings.
   g. empty out the trash and change wastebasket liners.
6. Proceed to make the bed:
   a. strip the bed, keeping items off the floor. Inspect mattress, pads, box spring, blanket, bedspread, and pillow for stains or torn spots and replace if needed.
   b. place the bottom sheet and tuck it at the head and sides. Miter bottom and top sheets and blanket at the foot of the bed and tuck them along the side. Place bedspread over the blanket, turn it about 15 inches back from the headboard, and place pillow over it. Roll back spread and pillows over the headboard. Repeat operation on other side of bed. Smooth out lumps and creases after the bed has been made.
7. Proceed to clean the room:
   a. brush lampshades with a dry cloth or feather duster.
   b. spray doors, furniture, and fixtures with cleaning solution or furniture polish and damp-wipe with dust cloth.
   c. wipe air vents, windowsills, light bulbs, telephones, and other surfaces with a damp cloth. Wipe out drawers. Clean or replace all recycled items. Spray mirrors and TV screen and wipe with dry cloth. Center all drapes, lamp shades, and pictures.
   d. vacuum carpet, including under the bed.
   e. apply deodorant to curtains and carpet.
   f. If the room has a balcony or patio, dust the furniture and sweep the floor.
8. Proceed to clean bathroom:
   a. check all lights and inspect faucets for leaks. Dump the wastebasket.
   b. place bowl cleaner in commode and brush it clean. Wipe outside of commode with a germicidal solution.

    c. standing inside of tub, clean bath walls, soap dish, plumbing fixtures, and shower door with all-purpose cleaner. Wipe dry. Clean tub or shower floor, pull out tub stopper and wipe clean.

    d. clean vanity and sink, including the sink stopper.

    e. spray mirror with cleaning solution and wipe dry.

    f. wipe bathroom floor with cloth and germicidal solution, including behind the door.

    g. remove lint from ventilation and fan grills.

    h. replace bathroom supplies and amenities.

9. Place section housekeeper card on desk or credenza, take a critical final look, and notify team supervisor that the room is ready for inspection.

10. File P.M. report before end of the shift, indicating status of all rooms in the section. Clean up equipment.

11. Restock service cart for following day's operation.

12. Turn in guestroom section master key. Clock out.

Management reserves the right to modify this job description and to assign other tasks to section housekeepers as circumstances require.

Required Job Qualifications:

Able to stand heavy sustained physical activities, including lifting moderate weights, frequent bending, and constant use of arms. Physical agility and dexterity to be able to service 16 guestrooms in eight working hours is a must.

Preferred qualifications:

Education: able to read and write English.

Experience: over six months' previous work experience as section housekeeper.

Personality: pleasant, able to interact with guests and fellow workers.

Appearance: well groomed.

Mental qualifications: able to follow instructions. Self-starter.

substantial fee for their services. Public employment agencies may be sources of good employees in some cases. The state employment services are non-fee referral agencies for workers, and so are organizations for the physically impaired. Most physically impaired individuals are very dependable and efficient in the performance of simple, repetitive jobs. In some cases, companies may benefit from tax credits by hiring workers from federally supported programs.

Schools and colleges are good sources of recruits with special skills. Local community colleges may offer vocational courses in housekeeping or laundry operations. High schools may have work-study cooperative programs. Most hotel/restaurant management programs require students to complete hundreds of hours in pre-graduation employment in the industry. Bulletin board advertising in these schools usually results in applications for employment. Some colleges and universities have summer internship programs that allow undergraduate students to practice in hotels and resorts prior to graduation. The students can be used as supervisors or management assistants or they can be put in charge of special projects, such as taking inventories, developing job descriptions, or getting involved in clerical work.

SELECTING HOUSEKEEPING EMPLOYEES

The initial contact with prospective employees begins with their filling out an **application form**. This form is a means of securing standard information about applicants. No person can be denied the opportunity to submit an application for employment; questions to be included in application forms depend on the company but, in all cases, every question asked should serve a purpose. No question should be asked that is not useful for research purposes or for determining the applicant's eligibility for the job. The U.S. Equal Employment Opportunity Commission has been set up to enforce the Civil Rights Act, which protects against discrimination on account of race, color, religion, sex, or national origin. Because of increased emphasis by state and federal governments on avoiding discrimination in employment, application forms must be carefully worded to avoid requesting any pre-employment information that could be considered discriminatory.

Questions such as those listed in the left column that follows are considered unlawful prior to hiring and should not be part of an application form. Questions in the right column are acceptable.

Unlawful application form questions	May ask or require
What race are you?	
Name of your spouse	Names of relatives employed by company
Marital status	
Where does your spouse work?	
Please attach a photograph of yourself	May be required after hiring for identification
Place of birth	
What is your native language?	If job related, what foreign languages do you speak?
Which country do you originate from?	
Of what country are you a citizen?	Are you a U.S. citizen?
Are you a native-born U.S. citizen?	Do you have a permanent immigration visa?
	Can you prove that you can legally work in the U.S.?
Are your parents naturalized U.S. citizens?	
Which is your religion of preference?	Can you observe regularly the required days and hours of work?
Do you have any disabilities?	Have you any physical, medical, or mental impairments that would restrict your ability to do the work?
Date of birth	Are you between 40 and 70?
	Are you over 18?
Have you ever been treated for AIDS?	
Type of military discharge	Military service; dates, branch of service, job-related education and experience
Do you observe religious holidays?	Can you observe regularly the required days and hours or work?
Have you ever been arrested?	Have you ever been convicted of a crime? (If crime is job-related, hiring may be refused.)
Do you own a car?	Do you have reliable means of getting to work?

The property's personnel department usually conducts the **prescreening interview**. The purpose of this initial interview is to screen out those applicants who do not meet the criteria for the job advertised as specified in the company's job description. For example, a person who is physically incapable of servicing 15 guestrooms in eight hours will automatically be disqualified. The person in charge of pre-employment screening must be well trained in interviewing techniques, as a high percentage of people applying for jobs tend to exaggerate their skills and abilities, to misrepresent their backgrounds, and to conceal or minimize their weakest qualities. Applicants who are not selected should be notified as soon as possible of the company's decision and their applications kept on file for future reference, mainly for a different job in the company for which they may be qualified.

The personnel department should immediately proceed to check the references of those candidates selected for interviewing. Checking references may reveal issues such as extreme absenteeism, irresponsibility, and not giving adequate notice, or may detect a person who always wants to work in a new property and will quit as soon as a new establishment opens. References may be checked in writing, although in most cases previous employers will be reluctant to put on paper their honest opinion about the worker; written reference checking is usually limited to a verification-of-employment statement. Telephone conversations can often reveal much more about the applicant, particularly if the person contacted is an industry colleague. Although in most cases it is impractical, the best way to obtain accurate information about applicants is to have a personal meeting with their former boss.

Applicants who are working at the time of the interview may request that their current employers not be contacted for a reference check. This request should be honored, to avoid putting workers in an antagonistic position vis-à-vis their current bosses.

The Interview

Those employees who have cleared the reference check are invited to a personal interview. The goal of an interview is to find the best match between the person and the position to be filled. The interview also allows the candidate and the department head to meet face to face to explore the possibility of a mutual agreement for employment. In the housekeeping department, interviews may be conducted by supervisors, laundry managers, manager assistants, or the executive housekeepers themselves.

Interviewers should evaluate the applicant's technical skills, general temperament, and emotional traits. By asking technical questions related to the job opening, the interviewer should attempt to find out if the applicant is (or will be after training) qualified to perform the job in question. By asking personal questions, the interviewer should try to ascertain the candidate's attitude toward the job and the first impression that the applicant will give in meeting customers and fellow workers. Some of the technical characteristics may be ascertained from factors such as previous work experience and training, knowledge of the job, stamina, and alertness. Some of the personal traits to be sought are stability, reliability, initiative, and personal appearance. In essence, the interview is a two-way communication effort in which the interviewer states the nature of the job opening and the applicant presents his or her own qualifications to fill the job. Interviews should be conducted in a private, quiet place where the candidate can be made to feel at ease.

Here are some points to be considered in employment interviewing.

1. A checklist can be helpful to avoid overlooking important information. Questions should be prepared from the job description of the position to be filled.
2. The interviewer should allow at least half of the interview time to listen to the applicant's statements about himself or herself. To this effect, questions eliciting "yes" and "no" answers should be avoided. Make frequent use of "why?" and "how?"

3. Most housekeeping tasks are tough and require much of the worker's commitment and dedication. Interviewers should not sugarcoat the job to convince the applicant to accept the position, only to find later that the worker finds it unbearable.

4. Interviewers may be swayed in their decision to hire by the neat appearance and smooth talking of candidates (the **halo effect**), only to discover that they are not capable of performing housekeeping work.

5. Avoid hiring someone who is overqualified. These candidates often become frustrated with tasks below their ability level, and eventually quit.

The result of the interview should be communicated to the candidate as soon as possible. If the decision is positive, applicants should know immediately so they can give appropriate notice to their current employers and get ready to start work in the new job. If the decision is negative, applicants should be notified so that they can restart their search for a job in other establishments. In this case, the candidate should also be thanked for the time taken in interviewing with the company.

Deluxe Suite, Sheraton Shanghai
Courtesy of Starwood Hotels & Resorts Worldwide, Inc.

Testing

Some lodging companies regularly give tests to prospective employees as instruments of selection, particularly to those seeking supervisory and managerial positions. However, because tests are only an indirect method of measurement, they are not as valid as the direct measurement of people's abilities. Tests should never be given in lieu of interviews or direct performance observations. Psychological testing, nevertheless, can be a helpful tool to avoid hiring unqualified candidates. **Intelligence tests** used in the industry measure vocabulary and arithmetic skills; some are designed for supervisory and managerial positions and a few for workers at an entry level. Some **aptitude tests** applicable to the industry measure the applicant's hand dexterity; these are suitable for workers involved in manual tasks. Others test clerical aptitude and are recommended for bookkeeping, cashier, and secretarial jobs. **Interest tests** provide some measure of an applicant's relative interest for certain fields of work. The lodging industry could use interest tests to examine the candidate's interest in people, as this is a people industry.

When using tests as a method of selecting employees, keep in mind that tests have been found to be inherently discriminatory to anyone who has not had the full advantage of free exposure to American culture. For instance, the scores achieved by a candidate belonging to a minority group should not be compared with those of people in general but only to the scores of other members of the same minority group.

HIRING

Induction

After being accepted for employment, workers are usually asked to report to the personnel department for their induction into the company. The purpose of the induction process is to fill the necessary paperwork about the new employee, to answer questions, and to make the newcomer feel welcome. All documentation regarding the new worker should be completed. This procedure includes filling out the W-4 (tax withholding statement), I-9 (proof of legality to work), and health and welfare insurance forms. At this time newcomers are provided with the **employee handbook**. Properties that hire large numbers of employees should use **employment checklist forms** (Figure 8.3) to ensure that no part of the induction process has been overlooked. The employment checklist includes all prerequisites that need to be completed before employees are sent to their respective departments to begin work.

The induction process continues with the **orientation** of the new employee. The purpose of orientation is to acquaint the employee and organization with each other. During orientation, the philosophy of the company is explained, the benefits, pay rate, and deductions are discussed, and the dos and don'ts that the job entails, or general house policies as stated in the employee handbook, are described in detail. The initial orientation session should be followed with a second meeting after the new employee has had a chance to become familiar with the job—anywhere between two and four weeks later. At this time, any questions that the worker may have are answered.

After the orientation process has been completed at the personnel department, the new employee is escorted to housekeeping where a departmental orientation takes place. Here, the hours of work and the necessity of calling in as soon as possible in case of illness or emergency are explained, as well as where to check in and out, uniform procedures, grooming standards, and when breaks and meal periods are scheduled. The employee is then given a tour of the property and is introduced to his or her supervisor who, in turn, introduces the worker to other members of the department. Induction and orientation procedures, if properly conducted, substantially increase the odds of the employee's remaining in the company.

Most new employees in the housekeeping department are hired on a **probationary basis**, usually 90 days, to allow workers enough time to learn to perform their jobs efficiently. After a successful probationary period, usually when employees reach no-fault or no-errors standards, they become regular workers and are given a raise as an incentive to continue to perform well and

FIGURE 8.3 Sample Employment Checklist

Name: _____ Social Security Number: _____
Address: _____
City: _____ State: _____ Zip: _____

Item	Complete ☑
Application	☐
Resume	☐
Proof of residency (I-9)	☐
Health and welfare documents	☐
W-4 form	☐
Deductions from pay (if any)	☐
Hotel employee handbook issued	☐
Company orientation	☐
Payroll number assigned	☐
Name tag issued	☐

Employee has been turned over to _____ in the
_____ department for training and department orientation.

stay with the company. If, after the probationary period, reasonable standards of efficiency have not been met, employees are not allowed to continue employment in that particular position.

Induction and the Peer Group

The peer group is an important part of the new employee's orientation. New employees depend on their coworkers for approval and acceptance. For the newcomer, the pressure to conform is very strong. It is a good idea to involve the most representative members of the peer group in the orientation process. This practice will help the old employees and the new person get to know each other as soon as possible. In fact, the induction process should not be considered completed until the full acceptance of the new employee by the peer group has been totally accomplished. To end the hiring process, the personnel department should open an individual record file for each employee in which personal information (such as address, telephone number or whom to call in case of emergency) and work data (such as starting wage and title of the position) are recorded. The file is thereafter updated each time a change in status occurs, such as changes in pay rate, disciplinary actions taken, written warnings, promotions, special recognition, and so on.

TRAINING

The hospitality industry is notorious for attracting large numbers of unskilled workers, especially young workers coming right from high schools and colleges. In addition, members of the hospitality work force tend to change from one job to another, causing high turnover, and have a relatively low educational background. On the other hand, most hospitality jobs are under the constant scrutiny of the public, hinging on a face-to-face relationship where the inefficiency of one employee may lose a guest forever. A lodging property cannot afford to have an untrained or uninterested worker on the housekeeping payroll.

Training in the housekeeping department should encompass four major areas: **technical skills**, **employee attitude**, **personal development**, and **knowledge of the property**. Technical skills training includes teaching workers how to perform the tasks described in their job description without fault or error. In the case of a section housekeeper, for example, it means teaching the person how to service guestrooms, including setup procedures, making beds, vacuuming, dusting, surface cleaning, bathroom cleaning, maintenance of equipment, and security and safety. The employee will have reached regular performance standards when a minimum number of faults is found by the inspector checking the room attendant's section. Technical training contributes to the success of both the organization and the individual.

Attitude training should create awareness of the relationships among the employee and the guests, other employees, and the company. Workers must be courteous, friendly, and approachable, and show keen attention to detail. Sensitivity toward fellow workers must be taught, including toward people of other cultures, races, and religions. This will help develop teamwork within a diversified group, which is always the case in housekeeping. Employees should have a positive attitude toward the company and its management by positively representing the property and mirroring the philosophy of the establishment. Training should also be provided to workers to improve their personal potential and their abilities to make changes in their own lives. This type of training can range from personal grooming sessions to seminars and workshops that will aid in developing their reading and writing skills or to help them increase their perceptions of themselves as functional individuals. Finally, knowledge training should teach employees the layout of the property so that they can give directions to guests and inform them about hours of operation and main features of the different outlets. For example, a houseperson, if asked, should be able to tell a guest how to get to the swimming pool or what type of menu the coffee shop offers.

Lodging properties should have ongoing training programs in place. People in general tend to forget concepts or deviate from standing procedures as time goes by. Clear indications of the need to retrain personnel include an increase of oral and written complaints by guests. For instance, if management keeps getting negative comments about the quality of guestroom linens, employees in the laundry room should be retrained in washing and/or finishing procedures. Another indication of a need for retraining may be a drop in productivity. For example, if in the past section housekeepers have been able to effectively clean 16 rooms in eight hours and lately some of them incur overtime to finish their job, their room-cleaning methods should be examined to ascertain whether the standing cleaning procedures are adequately followed. These performance analyses should investigate the question, "Could the task be performed quicker, with the same level of quality?" If the answer is yes, the worker should be retrained to increase his or her productivity performance. There is, however, a difference between **deficiency of knowledge**, in which the employee doesn't know how to do the job better and should be retrained, and **deficiency of execution**, in which the employee knows how to do the task but decides not to perform it correctly for his or her own benefit. In this case, the employee should be called to order and asked to do the job according to established procedures.

The most efficient method of training in the housekeeping department is **on-the-job training**, in which new employees are assigned to watch how the work should be performed, usually by observing a supervisor or senior employee. Large lodging operations have designated trainers whose job is to train newcomers or retrain employees who are not performing up to standard. When employees need to be trained to operate new machines or equipment, vendors or representatives of the manufacturing company often conduct **demonstrations** at no cost to the employer; in this case the purchaser of the products. Training of supervisors and middle managers can be enhanced by sending them to conferences and workshops where new industry products are introduced and demonstrated. When employees already in the company are being prepared for advancement, companies should train them in the different operational aspects of the department by following a career ladder or schedule. Thus, committed employees who master each step of the cycle along the way may be promoted to management positions within the property or in other company establishments.

Training programs offer distinct advantages to employers and employees alike. The employer will benefit from an increased learning rate, since workers will become efficient sooner rather than learning on their own by trial and error. Workers learn to achieve high levels of productivity and quality performance when their training begins with learning only the best way to accomplish jobs. As training improves performance, employee self-esteem rises, and with it, the willingness to come to work and to increase earning power. Turnover and absenteeism are, thus, reduced.

The simplest and most efficient way to ascertain the effectiveness of training and retraining programs is by obtaining feedback from guest comment cards. If substantial negative comments are received, training programs must be strengthened. Guest comments should be read at employee meetings. Negative comments should be discussed, without naming the employee who caused the problem, and the entire group should be challenged to find an appropriate solution. The employee who received the adverse comments should be addressed privately.

Candlewood Suites Atlanta, IHG
Courtesy of Six Continents Hotels, Inc.

WORKER MOTIVATION

Employees are vital to the success of the lodging industry. A business that requires face-to-face interaction with people requires a work force that is motivated to deliver excellent service. But the work force usually available to the lodging industry has inherent fundamental problems, such as high turnover, an uninterested attitude, and low productivity. Housekeeping tends to attract individuals with little education who come from lower socioeconomic sources or from minority groups that often do not know how to read and in some cases are unable to speak English. The problem is compounded by the fact that most lodging companies have limited financial resources to increase their employees' compensation beyond inflation rates. On the other hand, employees look to improve their own quality of life by achieving a satisfactory standard of living through job security and adequate compensation. However, adequate compensation, although necessary, is not enough to motivate the work force. People also look for a challenge, recognition, and the opportunity to be part of an organization that is successful in itself. Therefore, to motivate employees the manager must understand what type of environment most effectively utilizes the workers' energy and directs them toward the accomplishment of a common goal.

The first step is to establish a climate of mutual trust and respect, meaning that employees should never be looked down upon from a position of superiority; instead, managers should be characterized as fair, caring, and approachable individuals. Good motivators must be capable of understanding people well and be sensitive to their individual needs and differences. Motivation is internal, complex, and individually patterned: what motivates one person might displease someone else, and vice versa. Future executive housekeepers must be aware of the classical theories of motivation and understand how they can be applied to housekeeping settings.

MASLOW'S THEORY OF MOTIVATION

Although first expressed in the 1950s, Abraham Maslow's thoughts on motivation are still quite relevant to employee motivation in the housekeeping department. It can be deduced from Maslow's work that high levels of motivation in employees cannot be achieved unless the employees' basic needs have been met. A worker's **physiological needs** must be satisfied first; that is, if housekeeping employees are working in very poor conditions, such as in a steaming-hot, unventilated laundry room, all attempts to motivate them will fail. Likewise, if the workers' **security needs** for survival are not granted, motivation will be impossible. This would occur if a housekeeping employee is allowed to work only 28 hours per week and, therefore, is unable to make enough money to pay his or her rent. The fulfillment of **social needs** is also necessary prior to motivating people. A Hispanic employee, for instance, would be unhappy working in housekeeping in the midst of an Anglo-Saxon workforce that refuses to accept him or her as part of the group. Conversely, an Anglo-Saxon worker working among unaccepting Hispanic workers will also be hard to motivate. **Self-esteem**, the fourth of Maslow's basic needs applicable to hourly employees, must also be satisfied before workers can be motivated. For example, a houseperson in the housekeeping department hauling trash to the dumpster all day long, whose job is not appreciated by management and coworkers, will be reluctant to be motivated.

Housekeeping managers must always realize that individuals have a scale of needs and that motivating them to be courteous, polite, friendly, or productive does not become pressing to them until their basic needs have been adequately satisfied. Motivation at the departmental level will be easier to achieve if all job descriptions and specifications include both the needs of the organization and the personal needs of the workers.

HERZBERG'S IDEAS ON MOTIVATION

Once employees' basic needs have been covered, housekeeping managers must provide their employees with opportunities that are intrinsically satisfying or that embody responsibility. Frederick Herzberg proposes that workers can be motivated by recognition, feelings of achievement, job responsibility, and opportunities for advancement and growth. In other words, if employees feel wanted and are happy in their jobs, they will willingly contribute to the goals of the organization. In a housekeeping department setting, the executive housekeeper can motivate section housekeepers by always assigning them the same section of guestrooms. This individual responsibility will create in them a feeling of ownership and pride. A **career ladder program** to promote people from within can be implemented in the department to establish the possibility of advancement from lower entry-level jobs to supervisory and management positions.

There is a marked difference between motivation and manipulation of employees. Managers who attempt to influence workers to do what they want done seldom succeed. Niccolo Machiavelli, the cynical sixteenth-century writer, observed that because humans are selfish, greedy, ungrateful, and manipulative, they deserve not to be trusted and must be manipulated in turn, a theory hardly conducive to employee motivation. On the contrary, managers who know how to create a climate in which the individual can function to maximum capacity will be successful in motivating employees.

DAVID McCLELLAND

McClelland, an American theorist in psychology, experimented with volunteers who were asked to throw rings over pegs without stipulating particular distance. Most people seemed to throw arbitrary, random distances sometimes throwing close to pegs, sometimes farther away. However, a small group of volunteers, who McClelland identified as strongly achievement-motivated, took some care to measure and test distances to produce an ideal challenge—not too easy, and not too hard. McClelland deduced from this experiment that people need a balanced challenge to achieve motivation. This premise can be applied to housekeeping employees: a worker who is given a very difficult task will be demotivated by his/her inability to accomplish it; on the other hand, an employee who finds his/her job too easy will not be motivated by it. An example will be to ask section housekeepers to service 25 guestrooms in an eight-hour shift or to allow them to clean just six rooms in the same period of time.

Practical Motivational Techniques

Besides understanding the different theoretic approaches to motivation, executive housekeepers can put in place practical programs and plans to motivate housekeeping employees. Removing obstacles that often hinder performance may help workers to accomplish their tasks. Too much paperwork, for instance, may be an obstacle to productivity; another could be a badly designed work area that does not take into consideration the human element. Lack of communication may create a feeling of uncertainty about what needs to be done, as people tend to perform correctly only when they understand what is expected of them. The simple act of listening often allows managers to hear useful comments from employees regarding work conditions, suggestions to improve work flow, and the existence of morale problems. The fact that the housekeeping department is often the least appreciated in the property may be the hidden cause of low employee motivation. Housekeeping workers may not gain the same appreciation that the front desk, sales, and accounting people do. It is common for housekeeping to be considered at the bottom of the operational totem pole, given that they are paid minimum wage and have little decision-making authority. On the other hand, these workers must perform the backbreaking job of cleaning 16 or 17 guestrooms in an eight-hour shift. In order to motivate the housekeeping work force, employees must be given credit for the work they do and be respected for what they represent.

Some lodging companies have experimented with alternative methods of motivating employees. By paying section housekeepers by number of rooms cleaned rather than by hours worked, some properties have achieved increased productivity and staff retention. Others have established four-day work weeks with 10 hours worked per day. Both methods may help if they are first tried and accepted by management and employees. In general, paying per room cleaned may generate problems of quality, as the section housekeepers will try to service the largest number of rooms in the least possible time. The 10-hour work day may result in workers who are too tired to do a good job.

EMPLOYEE EVALUATION AND COMPENSATION

EVALUATION

The purpose of employee appraisals is twofold: to provide feedback to workers about how they are performing their jobs and to establish a basis for compensation based on the quality level of their performance. The advantages of providing feedback to workers are substantial, as employees who do well need to be recognized for their efforts while those whose work needs improvement must be notified of their specific deficiencies in order for them to be corrected. Using ratings to determine wage payment and promotions helps motivate employees to work hard so they can reap the benefits awarded to those who do a good job. To be effective, evaluation methods must be fair, objective, based on preestablished standards of performance, and accepted by those being evaluated.

To overcome anxiety or hostility, workers should be involved in setting up the standards of performance against which they are to be appraised, provided that their goals are in line with those of the company. Rating scales are effective tools for appraisal; they consist of a series of descriptors to which a numerical score is attached to determine the effectiveness of workers in areas such as absenteeism, tardiness, grooming, following instructions, courtesy to guests, and so on. Figure 8.4 is a rating form with a scale of five points, where 1 indicates "superior" performance and 5 indicates "needs improvement." Most companies ask workers to fill out a rating form after a designated period of time, ranging from six months to a year, while the worker's supervisor or manager also fills out a form on the employee being evaluated. At a scheduled meeting, the perceptions of both the worker being appraised and the supervisor are compared and discussed. From that discussion, goals for the next evaluation period are agreed upon. The goals are again evaluated against actual performance after the next appraisal period has elapsed and new goals are set. Where performance is difficult to quantify, as when rating assistant managers or supervisors, the **critical incident method** may be used instead of the rating

FIGURE 8.4 Sample Employee Evaluation Form

Employee Being Evaluated: _____

Evaluator: _____

Period of Evaluation: From: _____ To: _____

Date of Evaluation: _____

Description	Superior		Rating	Needs Improvement	
Absenteeism	1	2	3	4	5
Tardiness	1	2	3	4	5
Grooming	1	2	3	4	5
Following Instructions	1	2	3	4	5
Courtesy to Guests	1	2	3	4	5
Getting Along with Peers	1	2	3	4	5
Productivity Level	1	2	3	4	5
Accepting Responsibility	1	2	3	4	5

Total Points This Period _____

Goals/Objectives for Next Evaluation Period

1. _____

2. _____

3. _____

4. _____

5. _____

_____   _____
Employee's Signature   Evaluator's Signature

scale. In this case, the rater may periodically record observations of good or bad performance that are discussed at the time of the rating.

Any appraisal method used in the housekeeping department should be a way of recognizing excellent performance and of identifying areas in which further training is needed, and should be done so that the person being evaluated sees the process as a means of self-improvement. That is, there should be a mutual discussion between superior and subordinate with regard to what conditions must be altered to change or upgrade performance. These changes or efforts to upgrade become the objectives to be accomplished for the next evaluation period.

The first formal appraisal of employees should be conducted at the end of their probationary period. Afterward, evaluation should be done periodically, typically every six months to a year. It is common for lodging companies to have **pay scales** that start with a probationary rate and go up in accordance with time on the job. For example, an employee can be started at minimum wage for the first 90 days (probationary period) and then be raised 50 cents to a dollar per year worked to a preestablished maximum hourly rate. Employees who exhibit extraordinary performance are awarded additional increases, regardless of time, based on their positive performance appraisals.

Because performance evaluations are emotionally charged events, reviews should be held in a private, neutral environment, such as in a small conference room. Evaluators should go into the review fully prepared and with an attitude that supports discussion, cooperation, and negotiation. It is better to sit beside the employee rather than across the table from her/him. The meeting should be long enough to clearly delineate the workers' strengths and weaknesses and show them how and to what degree they must improve their performance.

COMPENSATION

Compensation (pay increases) should be tied to performance. If an employee's productivity is high and the quality excellent, his or her compensation should be greater than that of an employee whose performance is well below standards. When compensation is tied to performance and the evaluation system is fair and unbiased, employees strive to do well at work in order to obtain better wages and benefits. Most employees establish a relationship between the rewards they obtain from their job and the effort they put into it. The ideal effort:compensation ratio should be 1:1, meaning that the effort put into one's work should equal the reward obtained from it. If workers see that other employees in similar positions produce less but receive equal or higher wages than they do, they will soon be demotivated. Managers should regard equity in compensation as a critical part of the motivational process.

CREATING WORKER SATISFACTION

One of the underlying purposes of motivating employees is to reduce turnover. Hovering at about 100 percent for line employees and often costing over $3,000 per hourly employee, turnover represents a substantial loss of income to lodging companies. Thus, the challenge is to create worker satisfaction so that employees stay with the company for extended periods of time. Besides using motivational techniques and providing equitable compensation and fringe benefits, what else can the executive housekeeper do to alleviate the problem of high turnover?

Conducting **exit interviews** is the first step in attempting to solve high turnover; that is, finding out why employees leave in the first place. Exit interviews help management identify reasons for turnover, paving the way to corrective actions. During the interview, departing employees should be asked to discuss the company's working conditions, pay rates, training, benefits, job security, and so on. If the turnover is severe, current employees should be surveyed periodically regarding wages, benefits, and working conditions. Once the problem is identified, goals and objectives for a turnover-reduction plan should be set. Some of the most common reasons for high turnover are poor hiring techniques, inadequate orientation and training practices, no opportunity for advancement, poor supervision methods, bad department image, and lack of performance standards. Besides correcting these technical slips, executive housekeepers must get employees to feel like valuable members of the total team, boosting their self-esteem by making sure that the department does not have an image problem. The creation of a career path program within the department will make employees feel that there are opportunities for advancement. Encouraging employees to earn professional certification will help them develop the necessary expertise for advancement. The Educational Institute of the American Hotel and Lodging Association (AH&LA) offers certification in hospitality housekeeping (CHHE) that provides recognition as professional housekeeping executives in the lodging industry. Providing literacy classes for those who cannot read empowers workers, who then feel more in control of their future. **Incentive programs** are intended to provide employees with such rewards as recognition and appreciation for the good work they perform. Commendation letters, gift certificates, bonuses, plaques, complimentary stays in the property, and designated parking spots are some of the incentives that may provide substantial employee satisfaction at no great cost.

Wellness programs, designed to prevent illness and enhance the well-being of employees, are effective in reducing absenteeism. These programs include periodic medical examinations, sessions to improve dietary habits, weight control practices, exercise and fitness sessions, free or discounted meals, stress management workshops, and immunizations. **Employee assistance programs** can help retain employees who are substance abusers by helping workers overcome drug and alcohol addiction. Referring affected employees to counseling agencies and supporting them in their rehabilitation will help improve the company's retention of employees. **Transportation assistance** can also be an effective incentive in keeping employees in the workplace. Because a great number of housekeeping employees do not own their own means of transportation, in cities where public transportation systems are reliable and can be used by employees to get to work, the company can provide financial assistance to purchase passes. In localities with poor or no public transportation, employers can provide vans for pickup and delivery of workers to a central location or organize a ride-sharing or carpooling program. With subsidies from state and federal government programs, lodging properties can offer **child-** and **prenatal-care assistance** for workers, especially young single parents. The practice of **participative management** often creates worker satisfaction among employees in that they see themselves as part of the decision-making process. As they contribute to operative decisions, they become committed to the outcome of these decisions and get involved in the successful accomplishment of common tasks.

When everything else has failed, the company may resort to create **retention bonuses** by offering a percentage of a year's pay, spread over a period of several years, to those employees who stay with the company. In sum, any efforts aimed at maintaining high levels of morale, individual attention, and respect for hourly employees will increase service standards and guest satisfaction and reduce employee turnover.

EMPLOYEE DISCIPLINE

The implementation of a standard method of discipline is just as important as motivation for employers and employees alike. Corrective actions for unacceptable or irresponsible behavior must be taken as soon as they occur. Common misconduct cases that take place in the housekeeping department are quarreling, insubordination, intoxication, excessive unexcused tardiness or absences, theft, and unauthorized or unlawful doings. Depending on the severity of the wrongdoing, discipline can range from a simple verbal warning to termination. The most effective method of disciplining employees is the **counseling session.** Counseling sessions should be conducted on a one-to-one basis to ensure confidentiality. In these sessions, the problem or problems should be addressed straightforwardly with the understanding that the only purpose of the meeting is to find a fast, permanent, and equitable solution to the matter in question. Listening to the employee (the other side of the story) is crucial as the worker, not the supervisor, often is in the right. It is important that at the end of the session a mutual agreement is reached and that there is a strong commitment on the part of the employee to correct the situation. Needless to say, if the employee persists in his or her wrong behavior, the company always reserves the right to apply punitive measures, as the building of positive discipline requires effective disciplinary actions. **B.F. Skinner's** theory of radical behaviorism is based on the premise that a behavior followed by an aversive stimulus results in a decreased probability of the behavior occurring in the future. Once the violation occurs, disciplinary action follows this sequence: oral warning(s), written warning(s), suspension, and dismissal.

CULTURAL DIVERSITY AND THE HOUSEKEEPING DEPARTMENT

The number of minority hourly employees working in the hospitality industry is very high; in some states, Spanish-speaking people employed in housekeeping are the majority. In some cases, this diversity in the workplace can represent challenging management problems regarding communication, training, and operational performance. In the Southwest, for instance, the entire housekeeping department may be staffed with non–English-speaking Hispanic workers. Cultural differences may also be serious obstacles to traditional management practices. Some minorities are deeply individualistic and resist standardization, in contrast to the Anglo-American inclination to follow clearly defined, established rules of behavior. While the North American culture has been built around a strong work ethic, with emphasis on the search for efficiency and aiming at constantly pushing back the current mechanical and technological frontiers, minorities are often preoccupied with concepts like individualism, family, and leisure. However, language barriers and marked cultural differences do not imply incompetence. There is no valid evidence of differences in most abilities related to the genetics of race or sex.

The vehicle that best promotes understanding is, without doubt, language. Managers and supervisors will be able to bridge the gap between cultures if they are capable of communicating directly with the people they oversee day after day. An elementary knowledge of the language that can be applied to daily housekeeping operations is therefore invaluable, particularly in establishments in urban areas with large concentrations of minorities. Students in hospitality management programs should elect to study a modern language, particularly Spanish, prior to joining the industry after graduation.

On the other hand, dealing with multicultural issues can be a rewarding experience. Using effective communication skills and patience, managers and supervisors can successfully reach, and train, a diverse work force. Listening attentively and speaking slowly and clearly in elementary English are a must. The best method of training minorities with no command of the English language is to follow a hands-on, learn-by-doing approach.

One approach to training a multicultural work force is using pictures, rather than written instructions. For instance, videos or photographs can clearly show how to operate equipment and perform routine tasks, like washing laundry or waxing a wooden floor. This approach eliminates the need for translation, as visual aids are universally understood. It is common today to find vendors who provide demonstration videos about their products free of charge.

When dealing with a diverse work force, setups and stocking consistency helps avoid mistakes. For instance, to create a common language among all housekeeping employees, all floor and closets should always be organized and stocked in the same way. Service carts should also be organized and stocked in the same way to create consistency and eliminate confusion. Using color-coded chemical products and waste receptacles is an excellent way to reduce safety problems. For instance, the color red is indicative of infectious waste, green means recyclable contents, and so on.

Cultural awareness is another important aspect of managing a diverse work force. Some groups arrive in the United States with a strong respect for authority and will never discuss or dispute a request if it comes from the boss. Others will never volunteer an opinion if they are not specifically asked to do so. Some are socially shy and may wait until they are away from the group to ask an important question. Some lodging companies have English for Vocational Purposes (EVP) classes conducted at their facilities to teach foreign employees how to communicate with supervisors and peers on the job.

Holiday Inn Express & Suites Minneapolis, IHG
Courtesy of Six Continents Hotels, Inc.

Racial Discrimination and Sexual HarassmentRacial problems in the workplace can lead to lack of productivity and costly lawsuits. Productivity can decline if some employees in the housekeeping department harbor resentments; others may decide to leave in search of businesses where racial tension is strongly discouraged. Lodging companies should have procedures in place to reduce friction between employees of different races and know how to respond when a racial incident occurs.

The property must have a written policy that prohibits discrimination based on race, national origin, sex, and physical impairment. It should also forbid discrimination in hiring, promoting, and terminating employees. Racial remarks or jokes should not be tolerated. The written policy must be communicated to all supervisors and employees, who should also be educated about the company's expectations regarding interracial behavior. When a racial incident does occur, action must be taken immediately to make sure that it does not escalate to a legal confrontation.

Sexual harassment is a subtle, hard-to-define form of discrimination. It is not unusual to find that as much as 40 percent of women in the work force have suffered some sort of harassment in the workplace in the form of uninvited pressure for sexual favors, of which cornering, touching, leaning over, or sending provocative notes are the most common. The U.S. Equal Employment Opportunity Commission declared in 1980 that sexual harassment violates title VII of the 1964 Civil Rights Act. In a June 1998 decision by the U.S. Supreme Court, the guilt of all demonstrated acts of sexual harassment in the workplace extends not only to the perpetrator but also to the employer for which he or she works. For this reason, it is important for companies to have anti-harassment plans in place to sensitize employees about sexual harassment by way of training materials, workshops, and speakers. In addition, the company's employee handbook must have clear descriptions of what may constitute sexual harassment, specifically acts such as staring, flirting, suggestive gestures, sexual remarks, touching, sexual propositions, and physical duress.

KEY TERMS

Application form

Aptitude test

Career ladder program

Child assistance effort

Compensation ratio

Counseling session

Critical incident

Deficiency of execution

Deficiency of knowledge

Employee assistance program

Employee attitude

Employee handbook

Employee qualifications

Employee security needs

Employment checklist

Exit interview

External recruiting

Full-time employee

Halo effect

Incentive program

Intelligence test

Interest test

Internal recruiting

Job description

Knowledge of the property

On-call employee

On-the-job training
Orientation
Participative management
Pay scale
Personal development
Physiological needs
Pre-natal care assistance
Pre-screening interview
Probationary basis

Rating scales
Retention bonus
Self-esteem needs
Social needs
Technical skills
Temporary help transportation assistance
Vendor demonstration
Wellness program

DISCUSSION AND REVIEW QUESTIONS

1. What is the difference between a part-time and a temporary worker?

2. What is the purpose of an employee requisition form?

3. Why could a company that develops exclusively from within be limiting itself regarding the composition of its work force?

4. Explain why an interviewer should not ask the question, "Do you own a car?"

5. What is the purpose of the prescreening interview?

6. (a) Why should housekeeping managers and supervisors ask prospective employees questions regarding their technical skills?

   (b) List three questions that a supervisor should ask people looking for section house-keeper work to find out if they are technically qualified to perform the job.

7. What is the main reason for housekeeping departments to hire employees on a probationary basis?

8. What four areas must be addressed when training workers in the housekeeping department?

9. What is the difference between deficiency of knowledge and deficiency of execution?

10. What are the advantages of implementing a career ladder program in the housekeeping department?

11. Name and describe four programs or actions that lodging companies may implement to create worker satisfaction.

12. Besides overcoming the language barrier, housekeeping managers must be able to bridge the gap between cultures if they are to reach workers of different cultural backgrounds. Explain why.

MINICASES

SITUATION 1

Review the following occurrences and be prepared to discuss them in an open forum. Was there sexual harassment or discrimination in these cases?

1. One of your supervisors, Dave, often comments on Minnie's appearance, telling her how good she looks in her clothes.

2. Elliott assigns time-consuming, complex projects to the men on his staff and short-term, simple assignments to the women. He believes he is doing the women a favor.

3. Co-workers Carla and Michelle earned comparable appraisals and equal raises until Michelle was promoted. Carla believes she was more deserving of the promotion because of extra effort and workload she has taken on. One day, Michelle confided to her that she was dating her boss who had pressured her into the relationship, saying that "it would pay off."

SITUATION 2

The housekeeping department of the Royal Hotel has been going downhill since the property opened five years ago. Morale is down, productivity is low, and the department's annual employee turnover rate is over 100 percent. Most housekeeping workers are from Asia and Central America; the majority of them do not speak English and are technically unskilled when first hired. Communications between hourly employees and the English-speaking-only supervisors is very poor. Some of the workers are single mothers who live far from the hotel and do not own a car; a few of them may be substance abusers. The company is very concerned about the current state of affairs and decides to create satisfaction among the workers to improve the situation. Funds have been allocated to correct the problem. You have been sent to the Royal for one year, on an on-loan basis, to help management improve the current status.

Present a written proposal to management suggesting actions they should take to address the high turnover problem and lack of employee morale.

SITUATION 3

Jennifer usually has some excuse for not showing up for work. The excuses during the past three months included four dental appointments, four car breakdowns, and three occasions for which she was unable to find a babysitter. You, as Jennifer's supervisor, find it difficult to schedule your department as a whole because of Jennifer's spur-of-the-moment absences. Mrs. Robinson, another supervisor in your department, has told you in confidence that Jennifer is an unmarried employee who collects government financial aid for her two dependent children. Because the financial aid is conditional upon Jennifer's earnings, Mrs. Robinson thinks that she is trying to keep her work hours low enough to keep qualifying for government aid. What would be your approach to resolving this situation?

CASE STUDY 1

Christine Woods has been hired as executive housekeeper of a 500-room hotel located near Atlanta's Hartsfield International Airport. Christine holds a degree in hotel and restaurant management from a leading university in the discipline and has four years of experience in front office operations with a nationwide hotel chain. Christine's employer selected her from 43 other candidates because her academic record showed that she had done very well in a housekeeping management course in college. The recruiter thought that this qualified her to reorganize the housekeeping department of the hotel.

Christine spent her first two weeks on the job looking into the department's records and having one-on-one meetings with supervisors and hourly employees, One of the major problems, she soon found out, was the high turnover and absentee rates in the department. According to human resources, the estimated average cost for replacing a room attendant at the hotel was $2,100. This cost included advertising for the position, hiring and training the worker, and providing additional supervision during the induction period.

The exit interviews conducted had identified some of the reasons for leaving. Room attendants claim great frustration on the job as the main cause. An employee who quit recently tried to explain the problem: "Each one of us had to fend for herself. Every morning, I had to scramble for linen to stock my cart. Some other housekeepers hid washcloths in their lockers to have them available when needed." Housemen complained that often they had to fight over a vacuum cleaner to have the hallways cleaned. A section housekeeper said, "I take pride in cleaning my rooms but never get a bonus while others are sloppy workers and get the same wage that I get." A room attendant with more than five years' work in the hotel offered a comment: "The workload of 13 rooms per one-hour shift is ridiculous. I could easily finish 16 rooms a day if they paid me more money. I've already got 10 rooms done by lunchtime and slow down for the remaining three until it is time to clock out."

Overall morale is low among the housekeeping workers. "They treat us like dirt," said one of the housekeepers. "The front desk and maintenance people think that they can boss us around." The front desk and engineering departments in turn accused housekeeping of not being able to communicate professionally.

Christine is now faced with high absentee and turnover rates, lack of esprit de corps among workers, poor interdepartmental communication, and numerous guest complaints.

Assignment

Specify the steps Christine Woods should take to change to better the internal and inter-departmental performance of housekeeping.

CASE STUDY 2

After graduating from a hotel and restaurant management program, you have been hired by a nationwide lodging company and sent to work the first year in a resort property in the Southwest. Having completed the period of training successfully, the company has promoted you to executive housekeeper of a downtown hotel in a large city in New England. The property is a four-star, 500-room hotel offering meeting facilities, a restaurant, bars, and a health center. The hotel also has the following problems:

Absenteeism. Prior to your arrival, the housekeeping department has consistently reported between 40 and 60 hours of overtime daily for section housekeepers. The previous housekeeping director contended that this is primarily due to transportation problems. He claimed that many of the workers do not have their own transportation and must rely on the city's transit system that is very unreliable. According to one of the housekeeping workers, "If only there was a bus route nearby, my life would be a lot easier. Most of us live 25 minutes from work."

Turnover. The turnover rate of section housekeepers is 150 percent annually. Estimates of replacing a room attendant range from $2,900 to $3,900. The exit interviews conducted by the personnel department have pinpointed some common reasons for the high turnover rate. Some room attendants claim that they can make more money at other hotels in town, which also guarantee a minimum of 35 hours of work per week to most employees.

Guest complaints. The general manager gets a continuous flow of guest complaints about room cleanliness. She contends that the section housekeepers don't know how to clean guestrooms effectively. The inspection system of assigning a numerical value to a 1 to 5 scale doesn't seem to be working.

Productivity. Currently the room attendant workload per day is 13. Workers in most four-star hotels in the area are cleaning 17 rooms per shift. According to the outgoing executive housekeeper, "We would have raised the number of rooms but we didn't want to compromise our standard of cleanliness any further. They are currently making $8.50 an hour and across the street people are making $9.00 per hour; this could also be a factor."

Assignment

From the information given, establish a motivational plan of action, including specific ways of applying Maslow's, Herzberg's and Skinner's theories.

Administrative Controls

Chapter 9: Controlling Operations

PART

5

J.W. Marriott Quito, Ecuador
Courtesy of Marriott International, Inc.

JW Marriott Quito

Controlling Operations

CHAPTER OBJECTIVES

- Understand the purpose of operating budgets in the housekeeping department.
- Learn the process of compiling operating budgets.
- Explain the process of calculating the justification for section housekeeper man-hours.
- Explain the structure of the profit and loss statement.
- Discuss how to obtain productivity indicators in the housekeeping department.
- Learn how to work out the weekly forecast for section-housekeeper work.
- Describe how to control payroll.
- Learn about automation in the housekeeping department.

OVERVIEW

This chapter discusses the control of resources inherent in the job of executive housekeeper. The control function begins with the compilation of an annual operating budget for the rooms division of the property, of which the housekeeping department is a part. The executive housekeeper must project labor and operating expenses for the upcoming year that, once approved by upper management, become the operational expense parameters.

Because most department expenses are a function of occupancy, their totals must be justified. The justification of man-hours for section housekeepers is based on the number of rooms to be serviced and the workload criteria for room attendants.

As the year progresses, the housekeeping department receives monthly profit and loss statements showing the revenue of the rooms division and expense totals by category. The director of housekeeping uses the information to monitor costs and readjust expense amounts if they are larger than expected. Statistical information can also be used to control costs and productivity in the department by comparing the results obtained with budget indicators. The chapter ends with a discussion of automation applications for the housekeeping department.

HOUSEKEEPING OPERATING BUDGET

An operating budget is essentially a financial plan that allocates funds for expenditures by department for a determined period of time, generally one year. It is also a means of control that provides a measure for performance. Budgeting in large lodging operations requires a full cooperative effort of all department heads and the property's controller, who is usually in charge of preparing the final document before it is presented to the general manager for approval. Budgets are generally compiled for one-year time spans and are divided into 12 months, although some companies divide the year into thirteen 28-day periods to avoid distortion in the comparison of working periods (not all months have the same number of working days). Preparation of the operating budget in large lodging properties requires several months of planning and is usually finalized just before the budgeting cycle commences. The budget year can begin on January 1 (calendar year), or at the start of the company's fiscal year. Once top management has established its guidelines and amounts for each department, the respective departmental budgets are distributed down through each level. One of these levels is the housekeeping department.

The housekeeping department budget is part of the rooms division budget, which also includes the front office. The executive housekeeper's participation in determining the amounts allocated to the housekeeping department is essential if she/he is to be held accountable for the departmental control of expenses.

The basic structure of budgets for revenue-generating divisions is: **Revenue** (Sales) – Costs (Expenses) = **Departmental Income** (Departmental Profit). The revenue of the rooms division consists of the dollars to be generated by the sale of rooms at a certain unit price (number of rooms sold × **average daily rate or ADR**). For example, if the projection for selling rooms is $160,000 in a year and the ADR projected is $175 for each room sold, the anticipated annual revenue will be $28,000,000 (160,000 × 175). The costs of the rooms division consist of the expenses incurred by the housekeeping and front office departments. Typically, they include **salaries and wages** and **other expenses**. The percent of expenses is obtained by dividing the projected cost of expenses in dollars by the projected revenue. For example, if we project

Lobby, Sheraton Shanghai
Courtesy of Starwood Hotels & Resorts Worldwide, Inc.

spending $950,000 for guest supplies and the projected revenue is $28,000,000, the ratio will be 0.034, or 3.4 percent (950,000 ÷ 28,000,000). Conversely, if we know the percentage and want to find out the cost of expenses in dollars, we would multiply the percent by the revenue divided by 100; in this case, 3.4 × 28,000,000 = 95,200,000 and 95,200,000 ÷ 100 = 952,000.

The first step in the budget process is the compilation of the **consolidated room sales summary** in which the rooms division director, director of sales, and front office manager are directly involved. Although the executive housekeeper is usually not involved in this step, he/she should understand the process. The summary is a projection of revenues for the 12 months of the upcoming year based on the forecasted percentage of occupancy and average daily rate. The projections are calculated from the room bookings at hand, historical data from previous years, upcoming local events, state of the local economy and, in some cases, the weather prediction for the area. Figure 9.1 is a consolidated room sales summary for a 400-room hotel that includes the predicted percent occupancy, number of rooms, average daily rate, and total revenue. In this example, the average occupancy for the year is 83 percent, the number of rooms to be sold 121,184, the average daily rate (ADR) $85, and the projected revenue $10,371,804. Last year's figures for January through October are real; those for November and December are tentative, as these months had not yet elapsed at the time the budget was prepared.

Once the division's revenue is forecasted, the executive housekeeper and front office manager ascertain the expenses predicted for the year. Typical expense categories of the rooms division are: front office salaries, housekeeping salaries, payroll taxes and employee benefits, travel commissions, **outside services**, cleaning supplies, **linen replacements**, guest supplies,

FIGURE 9.1 Sample Consolidated Room Sales

Month	Upcoming Year Budget				Last Year's Budget			
	Occupancy %	Rooms	ADR	Revenue $	Occupancy %	Rooms	ADR	Revenue $
January	65	8,060	75	604,500	65	8,060	71	572,260
February	80	8,960	79	707,840	80	8,960	75	672,000
March	78	9,672	81	783,432	78	9,672	77	744,744
April	80	9,600	84	806,400	80	9,600	80	768,000
May	88	10,912	89	971,168	88	10,912	85	927,520
June	89	10,680	90	961,200	89	10,680	86	918,480
July	95	11,780	92	1,083,760	95	11,780	88	1,036,640
August	93	11,532	91	1,049,412	93	11,532	87	1,003,284
September	90	10,800	89	961,200	90	10,800	85	918,000
October	87	10,788	89	960,132	87	10,788	85	916,980
November	81	9,720	82	797,040	81*	9,720	78	758,160
December	70	8,680	79	685,720	70*	8,680	75	651,000
	83%	121,184	85	10,371,804	83%	121,184	81	9,887,068

*Estimated

telephone, postage, **printing and stationery** supplies, uniforms, **laundry supplies**, customer goodwill, and auto expense. Of these categories, front office salaries, travel commissions, postage, customer goodwill, and auto expense (airport van) are front office expenses. The categories of payroll taxes and employee benefits, telephone, printing and stationery supplies, and uniforms are shared by the two departments. The remaining categories—housekeeping salaries, outside services, cleaning supplies, linen replacements, guest supplies, and laundry supplies—pertain to housekeeping only. The amounts to be allocated to each expense category are ascertained taking into consideration the percentages from previous years and factors such as predicted increases in salaries and wages, adding extra employees to the department, upgrading cleaning and/or guest supplies, replacing an unusual amount of uniforms or linens, and so on. The challenge for department heads when requesting expense allocations is to keep the cost percentages as low as possible while maintaining an optimum level of service and quality.

Once the budget has been finalized and approved by management, it becomes the plan of operation for the upcoming year. The director of housekeeping must henceforth operate the department within the budget's limitations so that the percentages of amounts spent in each expense category do not exceed the percentages budgeted. It is important to understand that the cost percentages are a function of the revenue. For example, if the projected cost of guest supplies has been set at 2 percent of a $10,000,000 revenue, the dollar allocation for guest supplies for the year will be $200,000 (10,000,000 × .02). However, if the revenue is less or more than projected, the dollar allocation has to be adjusted accordingly. For instance, if the revenue drops to $9,500,000, the allocation for guest supplies becomes $190,000 (9,500,000 × .02). If the revenue reaches $10,500,000, the allocation changes to $210,000 (10,500,000 × .02).

Whenever any substantial deviation from the budget occurs, the executive housekeeper will be asked to explain the variance. If the variance is found to be correctable, a plan of action is usually agreed upon between the director of housekeeping and upper management. Figure 9.2 is a sample budget for the rooms division of the Royal Hotel. The revenue for the upcoming year has been projected 5 percent higher than the current year's to reflect an increase in room rates. The occupancy percentages, however, have been kept the same as in the current year, assuming that a slowdown in the local economy does not allow a larger occupancy. Salaries and wages have been increased by 0.5 percent from last year's in housekeeping and by 0.3 percent in the front office, anticipating a rise in pay. Payroll taxes and employee benefits will be up 0.2 percent overall as predicted by the hotel's controller. The cost percentages for all categories of "other expenses" have been kept as in the previous year except for "guest supplies" and "laundry supplies." Guest supplies have been increased by two tenths of one percentage point to reflect an upgrade of guest amenities, while the percent cost for laundry supplies has been reduced to 0.2 percent from 0.5 percent following the installation of a computerized chemical feeding system for the laundry washers. The departmental profit (income) projected is obtained by subtracting all expenses from the revenue. In this example, the income has been projected to be 74.3 percent of the revenue, down from 75.2 percent the previous year. A departmental profit of 74.3 cents for every dollar of room sales is a good target for rooms divisions in the lodging industry.

To justify the expenses in the category of salaries and wages, both executive housekeeper and front office manager must submit a statement showing the amounts needed to pay employees in both departments. The allocation to cover salaries is easy to work out as it consists of adding up the yearly pay of salaried employees. To figure out the wages for fixed employees (those who work regardless of the hotel's occupancy), the executive housekeeper must

FIGURE 9.2 Sample Rooms Division Budget (Summary)

	Upcoming Year		Last Year	
	Dollars ($)	Percentage (%)	Dollars ($)	Percentage (%)
REVENUE	10,371,804	100.0	9,887,068	100.0
Salaries & Wages				
Front Office	549,706	5.3	494,353	5.0
Housekeeping	985,321	9.5	889,836	9.0
Total	1,535,027	14.8	1,384,189	14.0
Taxes & Benefits	435,616	4.2	395,483	4.0
TOTAL PAYROLL	1,970,643	19.0	1,779,672	18.0
Other Expenses				
Travel Commissions	207,436	2.0	197,741	2.0
Outside Services	200	—	200	—
Cleaning Supplies	41,487	.4	39,548	.4
Linen Replacements	103,718	1.0	98,871	1.0
Guest Supplies	228,180	2.2	179,741	2.0
Telephone	20,744	.2	19,774	.2
Postage	10,372	.1	9,887	.1
Printing & Stationery	20,744	.2	19,774	.2
Uniforms	2,000	—	2,000	—
Laundry Supplies	20,744	.2	49,353	.5
Customer Goodwill	20,744	.2	19,774	.2
Auto Expense	20,744	.2	19,774	.2
TOTAL OTHER EXPENSES	697,113	6.7	674,437	6.8
TOTAL EXPENSES	2,667,752	25.7	2,454,109	24.8
DEPARTMENTAL PROFIT	7,704,048	74.3	7,432,959	75.2

refer to the property's staffing guide to calculate the number of hours that employees will work per shift and multiply the hours by the average wage that workers are paid. For example, if the hotel schedules four public areas attendants daily at an average hourly rate of $10.25 and they all work eight-hour shifts, the annual cost for public areas attendants will be $119,720 ($4 \times 8 = 32$; $32 \times 365 = 11,680$; $11,680 \times 10.25 = 119,720$). This calculation would be different if, for instance, the number of public areas attendants was fewer on weekends or if the daily hours worked were also fewer. Besides public areas attendants, the category of fixed employees in the housekeeping department usually includes linen room workers and the evening team.

SECTION HOUSEKEEPERS' MAN-HOUR JUSTIFICATION

To ascertain the wages of section housekeepers, and laundry workers, calculations must be made depending on the room occupancy of the hotel, as these employees report to work based on the number of rooms that need to be serviced daily. Figure 9.3 is a sample man-hour justification for section housekeepers. The purpose of this statement is to warrant the amount that must be obtained for the concept of room attendant wages in the upcoming budget. The form includes the forecasted occupancy broken down into months, the number of eight-hour shifts needed to service the occupied rooms at the rate of 16 per worker, the total number of work-hours (**man-hours**), and dollar amounts for each month. The difference between the amount needed to pay the section housekeepers next year ($369,413) and the amount in the budget for the concept of housekeeping salaries and wages ($985,321) will cover the expense for salaries and wages of the department's management team, housekeeping supervisors and housepersons, and fixed personnel, as well as cost for overtime, holiday and vacation pay, and bonuses. These expenses will also have to be justified separately. If the property has an on-premise laundry, the cost of labor, based on the projected room occupancy, is usually worked out in the same manner by the laundry manager.

The calculation of the "taxes and benefits" category is generally done by the property's controller and is based on the cost of employee meals, payroll taxes, insurance, and other benefits. In practice, the controller will apply a percentage to the "total salaries and wages" category based on previous years' costs plus any increment to expenses foreseen for the upcoming year.

THE PROFIT AND LOSS STATEMENT

Once the year is under way, every hotel division and department receives a monthly status report generated by accounting called the profit and loss statement (P & L). This statement shows the hotel's revenue and expenses for the month and includes a **variance analysis** column that indicates the changes in revenue and expenses from budget by category. The purpose of the analysis of variance is to alert department heads of percentage changes from budget. If the cost percentages are higher than projected, the causes for the difference must be identified and explained to management and a plan to correct them in the future implemented. Figure 9.4 is a sample profit and loss statement for the rooms division for the month of March, showing a column with the actual results, a column with the budgeted amounts, and the percentage variance between the two, which can be positive or negative. A positive variance in revenue and profit indicates that the sales have been larger than forecasted and that the departmental profit percentage has been better than predicted. A positive variance in costs indicates that the expense percentages have been larger than planned; negative variances indicate the opposite.

FIGURE 9.3 Sample Section Housekeeper Wage Justification*

Month	Occupancy %	Rooms	Shifts	Hours	Average Wage Rate	Expense $
January	65	8,060	504	4,032	5.95	23,990**
February	80	8,960	560	4,480	5.95	26,656
March	78	9,672	604	4,832	6.00	28,992
April	80	9,600	600	4,800	6.00	28,800
May	88	10,912	682	5,456	6.10	33,282
June	89	10,680	668	5,344	6.10	32,598
July	95	11,780	736	5,888	6.15	36,211
August	93	11,532	721	5,768	6.15	35,493
September	90	10,800	675	5,400	6.15	33,210
October	87	10,788	674	5,392	6.15	33,131
November	81	9,720	608	4,864	6.20	30,157
December	70	8,680	542	4,336	6.20	26,883
	83%	121,184		60,592		369,413

*The workload for each room attendant is 16 rooms to be serviced in one 8-hour shift.
**400 × .65 = 260; 260 × 31 = 8,060; 8,060 ÷ 16 = 504; 504 × 8 = 4,032; 4,032 × 5.95 = 23,990.

FIGURE 9.4 Sample Rooms Division Variance Report

	Variance Analysis for the Period March 1 to March 31				
	Actual $	Percentage (%)	Budgeted $	Percentage (%)	Variance
REVENUE	794,200	100.0	783,432	100.0	+.1
Salaries & Wages					
Front Office	41,690	5.2	41,552	5.3	−.1
Housekeeping	74,850	9.4	74,426	9.5	−.1
Total	116,540	14.6	115,948	14.8	−.1
Taxes & Benefits	30,753	3.9	32,904	4.2	−.3
TOTAL PAYROLL	147,293	18.5	148,852	19.0	−.5
Other Expenses					
Travel Commissions	16,050	2.0	15,669	2.0	—
Outside Services	1,500	.2	200	—	+.2
Cleaning Supplies	5,150	.6	3,134	.4	+.2
Linen Replacements	6,020	.8	7,834	1.0	−.2
Guest Supplies	17,830	2.2	17,236	2.2	—
Telephone	1,500	.2	1,567	.2	—
Postage	640	.1	783	.1	—
Printing & Stationery	1,654	.2	1,567	.2	—
Uniforms	200	—	150	—	—
Laundry Supplies	1,710	.2	1,567	.2	—
Customer Goodwill	400	—	1,567	.2	−.2
Auto Expense	890	.1	1,567	.2	−.1
TOTAL OTHER EXPENSES	53,544	6.7	52,841	6.7	—
TOTAL EXPENSES	200,837	25.3	201,693	25.7	−.4
DEPARTMENTAL PROFIT	593,363	74.7	581,739	74.1	+.4

In Figure 9.4, the results in all categories, as indicated by the respective percentages, are as planned or better, except for "cleaning supplies" and "outside services," where the percentages obtained are positive and therefore over budget. The executive housekeeper will need to investigate the causes for the increases in cost percentages. For the cleaning supplies, there are several possibilities, such as inflated purchasing prices, inferior quality materials, pilfering, improper mixing of chemicals, or overuse of products. The extra cost of outside services could be due to an oversight in budget planning or to an extraordinary expense caused by an unforeseen event. For instance, a fortuitous flood in the hotel lobby could have required the services of a carpet cleaning company. The departmental profit line at the bottom of Figure 9.4 also indicates that the overall performance of the housekeeping department for the month of March was better than predicted by four tenths of one percent (74.7 − 74.3 = +.4).

Some important statistical figures can be obtained from the budget. The average revenue generated by one section housekeeper hour worked can be obtained by dividing the estimated revenue by the estimated section housekeeper hours. In this case, 10,371,804 (see Figure 9.2) ÷ 60,592 (see Figure 9.3) = $171.17. The average number of minutes needed to clean one room can be obtained by dividing the section housekeeper hours by the forecasted rooms and multiplying by 60. In this case, 60,592 ÷ 121,184 (see Figure 9.3) = .50; .50 × 60 = 30 minutes.

The **cost per occupied room** is a good determinant of expenses per room sold. The cost can be obtained by dividing each expense category for a certain period of time by the number of rooms sold during that period of time. For example, if during the month of March the cost of guest supplies was $17,830 and the rooms sold were 9,672, the cost of guest supplies per room sold would be $1.84 per room. This figure, compared to that projected in the budget, will provide information about whether or not too much money is being spent on guest supplies. In this particular case, the annual budget was set at $228,180 (see Figure 9.2) for guest supplies for 121,184 (see Figure 9.3) rooms sold, or $1.88 per room sold. The cost for guest supplies per room sold for March ($1.84) was slightly lower than budgeted ($1.88).

PRODUCTIVITY CONTROL

Productivity is a measure of output compared to input. Examples of output are the number of rooms serviced in a certain period of time or the amount of linen washed in an eight-hour shift. Inputs are the investments made by a business to provide products or services, the materials used to have the job done, and the work of the company's employees. In the lodging industry, the overall result of productivity is measured by the profit, that is, revenue minus expenses. The average departmental profit of the rooms division in the lodging industry is around 75 percent; that is, for every dollar made from selling rooms to guests, 25 cents should be cost and the remaining 75 cents departmental profit.

Indispensable factors to reach good levels of productivity, apart from the influence of department heads, are appropriate investments in the design, machines, and equipment of the facilities. The effects of internal factors, particularly those of supplies and labor, on productivity can be controlled by executive housekeepers. Supplies management is a good example of cost savings through efficient techniques. For instance, every dollar saved by purchasing the right product at the right price is an additional dollar added to the bottom line. Labor management also contributes to increased profits; a worker who has been adequately trained and is motivated

Crowne Plaza Belem, Brazil, IHG
Courtesy of Six Continents Hotels, Inc.

to perform effectively can increase the work output by using a minimum amount of time to accomplish the task. Section housekeepers servicing effectively 16 guestrooms in one eight-hour shift instead of servicing 15 will provide better productivity to the company and, therefore, an increase in the company's profit.

Productivity, however, must go hand in hand with quality. It is to no advantage to achieve high productivity if the product is defective. To reach quality control, the housekeeping department must adhere to specifications and inspections. Inspections take up labor hours and are therefore expensive but, if planned carefully to keep costs low, they can be very effective in ensuring proper quality levels. As discussed before, a useful ratio to control productivity in the lodging industry is: *revenue ÷ hours of work required = dollars per labor hour*. Another indicator of productivity is: *hours of work used ÷ units produced = mean hours per room serviced*.

WEEKLY LABOR FORECAST

After the labor expense percentages have been determined in the annual budget, labor cost controls must be in line with the preestablished levels of occupancy and employee workloads. The weekly labor forecast (Figure 9.5) projects the section housekeeper hours needed to service the forecasted occupied rooms for a particular week, in this case, one week in March. By dividing the estimated revenue for the week by the section housekeeper hours, the revenue generated per hour worked is obtained. Likewise, by dividing the section housekeeper hours by the forecasted rooms occupied and multiplying the result by 60, the average number of minutes to clean one guestroom is also obtained. The results are compared to the amounts stated in the yearly budget

FIGURE 9.5 Weekly Section Housekeeper Forecast

				Date: Monday _____ through Sunday _____			
	Monday	Tuesday	Wednesday	Thursday	Friday	Saturday	Sunday
Occupancy %	84	86	86	82	70	70	72
Rooms	336	344	344	328	280	280	288
Shifts	21	22	22	20	17	17	18
Hours	168	176	176	160	136	136	144
ADR	84	98	94	90	72	74	78
Revenue	$28,224	$33,712	$32,336	$29,520	$20,160	$20,720	$22,464
Total Section Housekeeper Hours			1,096				
Total Revenue			187,136				
Total Occupied Rooms			2,200		Budget		
Revenue/Hours			$179.74		$171.17		
Hours/Occupied Rooms			.50		.50		

for the same concepts. If the amounts are close to the budgeted amounts, the number of section housekeepers scheduled for the week is acceptable. If they aren't, a reduction in the number of scheduled hours will be necessary. It must be kept in mind, however, that the control of productivity using the ratio "estimated revenue/section housekeeper" hours could be easily distorted if the ADR differs markedly from the ADR projected in the budget. In the example shown in Figure 9.5, the ratio revenue/section housekeeper hours equals $170.74 and the ratio section housekeeper hours/occupied rooms is .50 (30 minutes). Compared to the $171.17 and 30 minutes worked out in the budget, the amounts are very close and, therefore, acceptable. We may conclude that the productivity of the section housekeepers for the scheduled week coincides with the productivity statistics stated in the annual budget.

PAYROLL CONTROL

Executive housekeepers must develop a formal system of accurate reporting of payroll to the accounting department. The report is a record of hours worked daily by all employees in housekeeping. The system must include a means of control of overtime work. An effective way to control overtime work is to request that all supervisors obtain authorization for all extra time before it occurs. The hours worked by hourly employees are in most cases recorded on **time cards** or on digital clocks. Workers are asked to punch a time clock in and out at the beginning and end of their shift. During orientation, these procedures must be explained to employees in detail, such as not clocking in until they are in uniform and ready to work and clocking out at the time they stop working. Some companies allow one half hour for lunch on company time; others require workers to clock in and out before and after lunch. Breaks of 15 minutes are always on company time. Management should not ask employees to perform any duties off the clock, as this is against labor laws. Punching a time card in or out for another employee should be cause for disciplinary action. Time machines record hours in military time, starting at 00:01 and ending at 24:00. The actual time worked by an employee is determined by subtracting the smaller time from the larger.

At the end of every work week, the summarized hours worked on the time cards are recorded on a **time sheet** *or* computer program from which actual pay is calculated by the payroll office. Besides the hours worked, time reports should also indicate hours to be paid for vacation time, sick pay, or overtime pay. If workers are asked to perform duties of a different job category, they should be paid at the higher wage rate for that category, as would apply if, for example, a section housekeeper performs the duties of a supervisor for a certain period of time while the supervisor is on vacation.

COMPUTERIZED HOUSEKEEPING MANAGEMENT

More and more lodging companies are using automation to manage operations in housekeeping departments. Executive housekeepers can use technology to perform tasks such as controlling inventory supplies, scheduling operational routines, and tracking departmental man-hours and costs. There are software packages on the market that can perform personnel management tasks such as compiling personnel records, employee absences, training programs, and reports of on-the-job accidents. Other software applications can be supplements to quality assurance programs to evaluate employee performance. Preventive maintenance packages can schedule tasks well in

Drury Inn & Suites, Flagstaff, Arizona
Courtesy of Drury Hotels

advance, such as stripping floors and cleaning carpets and upholstery. The computer can be programmed to print daily work schedules.

Perhaps the most useful application of automation to housekeeping departments is the tracking of cleaning and guest supplies, equipment, and linen inventories and usage. If housekeeping can control the use of materials, the purchasing function can be improved by buying the right amount of products to eliminate the possibility of over- or understocking supplies.

Other applications of computers are word processing and the ability to produce graphs and charts to help directors of housekeeping organize past-performance data and forecast projections to be presented to upper management. Word processing enhances the quality of the correspondence generated in the housekeeping department, including reports, memoranda, e-correspondence and letters. Computer programs, however, can be very labor-intensive because of the time needed to input data. On the other hand, the payoffs can be considerable, as answers can be obtained by simply striking a key rather than having to perform elaborate calculations.

The first step in selecting a computerized housekeeping management software system is to determine the needs of the department. The second is to select a system that will fulfill the essential requirements to have the job done. Finally, the vendor chosen should be able to provide technical support and employee training. All in all, computerized systems must provide a way to facilitate and improve the management of housekeeping operations in a cost-efficient manner.

KEY TERMS

Average daily rate (ADR)
Consolidated room sales summary
Cost per occupied room
Departmental income
Laundry supplies
Linen replacements

Outside services
Printing and stationery supplies
Rooms sold
Time cards
Time sheet
Variance analysis

DISCUSSION AND REVIEW QUESTIONS

1. What is the difference between a budget prepared for a calendar year and one prepared for a fiscal year?

2. Which two departments are usually included in the rooms division's operating budget?

3. What is the projected annual departmental income for a resort that plans to sell 130,500 rooms at an ADR of $77.50? The anticipated total expenses for the year are $3,050,600.

4. Classify the following expense categories into (a) front-desk-only expenses; (b) housekeeping-only expenses; (c) shared expenses: front office salaries, housekeeping salaries, payroll taxes and benefits, travel commissions, outside services, cleaning supplies, linen replacements, guest supplies, telephone, postage, printing and stationery supplies, uniforms, laundry supplies, customer goodwill, auto expense.

5. If the projected revenue for the upcoming year is $9,000,500 and the authorized percentage for laundry supplies is 0.6 percent of the revenue, how many dollars should be allocated for this expense category?

6. If the actual rooms revenue for the month of March was $500,400 and the actual expense amount for cleaning supplies was $7,500 for the same period, what was the expense percent of this category?

7. For the same month of March, what would have been the variance percent for the expense category of guest supplies if $19,000 had been budgeted and the actual cost was $21,000?

8. What was the average number of minutes spent per room cleaned for a certain week if the number of rooms serviced was 2,100 and the section housekeeper hours for the week were 989?

9. List possible causes for a negative variance obtained for any given period in the category of guest supplies in the housekeeping department.

10. Explain how you would use the cost per occupied room statistic to help you control expenses when working in the housekeeping department.

11. What is the purpose of time sheets?

12. List possible applications of computers in housekeeping operations.

MINICASES

SITUATION 1

The results of last year's operations at the Royal Hotel are:

Net Revenue $10,100,500
Front Office Salaries 535,000
Housekeeping Salaries 899,000
Taxes and Benefits 394,000
Travel Commissions 202,000
Outside Services 1,500
Cleaning Supplies 35,300
Linen Replacements 64,000
Guest Supplies 240,000
Telephone 18,000
Postage 9,500
Printing and Stationery 21,400
Uniforms 3,500
Laundry Supplies 58,900
Customer Goodwill 21,000
Auto Expense 17,700

Calculate the dollar amount and percentage of the Royal Hotel's rooms division departmental profit.

SITUATION 2

As executive housekeeper of the Royal Hotel, you have been asked to provide preliminary budget information for the upcoming year on the category of "Housekeeping Salaries and Wages." The Royal is a 400-room hotel, the projected occupancy is 78 percent for the year, and the workload for each section housekeeper is an average of 16 rooms per one eight-hour shift. The total housekeeping salaries and wages for personnel other than section house-keepers is $540,000.

Calculate the total salaries and wages for your department for the upcoming year.

SITUATION 3

Compile the weekly section housekeeper labor forecast for the week of July 3 (Monday) through July 9 (Sunday).

The Royal Hotel has 400 guestrooms.

The workload per room attendant is to service 16 rooms in one 8-hour shift.

The projected ADR for Monday through Thursday is $118 per room per day. The ADR for Friday and Saturday is $85 and for Sunday $99.

Find: Total section housekeeper hours

Total revenue

Total occupied rooms

Revenue/hours productivity indicator

CASE STUDY 1

As the executive housekeeper of London's Royal Court Hotel, you receive the following information from the rooms division director, Mr. Speedy:

- Projected room revenue for the year $12,000,000
- Average hourly rate projected for section housekeepers $9.00
- Expected average occupancy for the year 85%
- Cleaning supplies expenses for the year 0.2% of revenue
- Guest supplies expenses for the year 1.1% of revenue
- Laundry cost for the year .3% of revenue
- Linen replacement for the year .7% of revenue

The hotel has 375 rooms and the workload for section housekeepers for a regular eight-hour shift is 15 rooms each.

Assignment

Mr. Speedy asks you to submit, on the double, the following figures:

1. Total man-hours for section housekeepers for the year.
2. Total section housekeeper wages for the year.
3. Ratio of wages for the year to the annual projected revenue.
4. Projected average minutes per room cleaned.
5. Projected cost in dollars for: cleaning supplies, guest supplies, laundry, and linen replacement.

CASE STUDY 2

You have just been hired as executive housekeeper of a 310-room Hyatt hotel in Florida. After welcoming you, the general manager, knowing that you have a Hotel and Restaurant Management degree, asks you to prepare a draft section housekeeper cost for the upcoming year. You receive from the controller the following information:

- Projected occupancy for January through May 80% each month
- Projected occupancy for June through October 94% each month
- Projected occupancy for November through December 75% each month

- Average daily rate (ADR) $174
- Average hourly rate for section housekeepers $11.25
- Workload per eight-hour shift for each room attendant 16
- For statistical purposes, consider that all section housekeepers work eight hours per shift on average.

Assignment

1. Work out the room nights forecasted for next year.
2. Work out the total revenue forecasted for next year.
3. Work out the man-hour and cost for section housekeeper wages for next year.
4. Work out the ratio of total section housekeeper wages to the hotel's total revenue.

CASE STUDY 3

The role of physical inventories in controlling costs

John Simpson is the assistant executive housekeeper of a 390-room economy inn in downtown St. Louis. John has been asked by his boss to monitor the use of laundry chemicals consumed by the establishment because the cost percentages have been climbing steadily in the last three months. It is late evening on Monday, May 31. John has found the following amounts of laundry chemicals in both the main storeroom and the laundry room:

Main Storeroom

15 cases of detergent at $90 each case
15 cases of neutralizer at $65 each case
16 cases of softener at $31 each case
7 pails of bleach at $7.50 each pail
1 bucket of starch at $13.50

Laundry Room

5.75 cases of detergent
2.25 cases of neutralizer
8.50 cases of softener
0.50 pails of bleach
0.25 buckets of starch

The beginning inventory for laundry supplies on May 1 was $6,051.75. Purchases of laundry chemicals on May 9 totaled $890.15. The hotel sold 9,067 rooms for the month at an average daily rate of $65.10. The average daily rate was as budgeted. The budgeted laundry chemicals cost percentage was 0.2.

Assignment

1. Find the actual laundry chemical cost percentage for the month of May and analyze and critique the result.

Risk and Environmental Issues in Lodging Properties

PART

6

Le Meridien Barcelona, Spain by Starwood
Courtesy of Starwood Hotels & Resorts Worldwide, Inc.

Safety, Security, and Infectious Diseases in Property Operations

CHAPTER OBJECTIVES

- Discuss the management of safety in property operations.
- Understand the importance of safety committees and employee training programs.
- Explain the risks of fire in lodging properties and describe fire-prevention systems.
- Learn about security issues in lodging operations, including theft, bomb and terrorism threats.
- Describe guestroom and property-wide security systems.
- Discuss how infectious diseases spread in lodging properties and how to prevent the cross-contamination of microorganisms.

OVERVIEW

Risk management in lodging operations involves the reduction of operational hazards and the minimization of crime. This chapter deals with the reasons behind the need to involve property operations personnel (housekeeping and engineering departments) in the risk management of lodging properties. Effective ways to control accidents, eliminate safety hazards, deter theft, and prevent and contain fires are to train employees and to take specific proactive steps to prevent risk in the workplace.

Because physically impaired guests may often be at greater risk in emergency situations, some recommendations for this traveler segment are listed. The chapter ends with a discussion on how to fight microorganisms and the need to educate employees on preventing the spread of contagious diseases.

SAFETY IN THE HOUSEKEEPING DEPARTMENT

There are three important reasons why fire and accident prevention for employees and guests are management functions. The first is legal: the Occupational Safety and Health Act (OSHA) requires employers by law to keep their places of business free from hazards that may cause harm or injury to employees. The act assures every working person in the nation safe and healthful working conditions; therefore, housekeeping managers must comply with OSHA regulations to keep workers safe. OSHA inspectors can enter an employer's premises without notice to conduct inspections, review records, and question workers about safety. When serious injury or death is involved, criminal charges can be filed against the property.

Another reason is financial: statistics provided by the National Safety Council indicate that the number of injuries that occur in the service sector is staggering, costing companies billions of dollars annually. In addition, thousands of lost workdays cause a huge loss of human productivity and are, therefore, the source of a considerable financial burden on organizations. Accidents are the reason that worker's compensation premiums go up whenever mishaps occur in the workplace. Worker's compensation is insurance required by the states to cover injuries sustained at work. The worker's compensation insurance premium payments are determined by the employer's safety and health records. Besides, courts of law tend to award substantial amounts of money when injured guests and employees file civil lawsuits against businesses for accidents or mishaps.

The third reason is ethical. As employees and guests expect to find a safe place to work and stay, lodging operators must see to it that their properties are free from harm, injury, danger, or risk and that the organizational climate is conducive to the personal well-being of their workers.

When accepting the position of executive housekeeper or chief engineer, it is a good idea to request a site inspection by the company's insurance carrier to determine if the departments are complying with standard safety regulations. The first step toward implementing a safety program is developing **job-safety analyses** for those tasks that might involve any risk of injury and accident. After describing the potential hazards that the task may involve, safety tips about how to perform the job should be provided to workers. Job analyses are particularly necessary for jobs that involve working with industrial machinery, such as laundry washers, dryers, mangles, and mechanical saws.

SAFETY TRAINING PROGRAMS

Property operations managers should institute **safety-training programs** designed to instruct housekeeping and engineering employees in safe work practices. Specific instructions to guard against hazards and dangers unique to their job assignments should also be provided. The National Institute for Occupational Safety and Health (NIOSH), as well as other agencies in most states, provide help, assisting employers in the development of programs on safety standards and practices and providing printed information on regulations and recommendations to maintain health and safety in the workplace. Some of the safety standards that can be adopted by the housekeeping department may include: eliminating accident and fire hazards, providing first-aid supplies and equipment, handling hazardous chemicals correctly, keeping stairs and railings stable, adopting safety factors to operate laundry equipment, having proper grounding for electrical outlets, and so forth. Examples of specific proactive steps to prevent injury may include immediately fixing loose handles, missing tiles, and torn carpets; avoiding having wet, slippery walkways at all times; and keeping tub and shower surfaces and room furniture in perfect condition.

Deluxe Room, Le Meridien Barcelona, Spain
Courtesy of Starwood Hotels & Resorts Worldwide, Inc.

Implementation of safety programs should start at orientation, when employees should be taught about the safety philosophy of the department (and company), as well as what is expected of them in order to perform their jobs safely.

Housekeeping and engineering departments of large lodging establishments often form **safety committees** consisting of three or four employees for the purpose of preventing accidents from happening and investigating accidents after they take place in the workplace. Members of the safety committee regularly inspect all areas, such as the linen room, hallways, service elevators, the laundry room, and employee areas, looking for possible safety and fire hazards. When a potential safety risk is found, the committee requests that the cause be promptly corrected. Examples of potential safety risks are: missing floor tiles, cracked glass panes, inappropriate worker clothing, obstructed fire exits, improperly vented dryers, defective vacuum cleaner cables, wet floors, wrinkled mats or rugs, nonfunctioning fire and smoke detectors, and so on. Another responsibility of the safety committee is investigating the causes of accidents, establishing and keeping records of occupational injuries, and developing strategies to help prevent future mishaps. Employees should also be trained in how to operate equipment and how to lift loads safely by keeping weights close to the body, bending the knees, and keeping the back straight. Table 10.1 lists some safety tips for workers. By reducing the number of accidents in the departments, insurance premiums, lawsuit costs and workers' compensation payments can be effectively contained.

Often, the availability of immediate first aid can save the life of a worker or guest. The housekeeping and engineering departments should keep a well-supplied first-aid kit on hand. In large lodging operations, having a CPR- and first-aid-certified supervisor should be a priority. In all cases, employees should be instructed how to (or how not to) handle injured people and to call a physician immediately.

Guest bathroom safety is particularly important because of possible safety hazards in this area; for example, the potential of scalding due to high water temperature, of slipping on wet surfaces, and of electric shock. Scalding can be prevented by setting the temperature at about

TABLE 10.1 Sample List of Safety Tips for Housekeeping Workers

1. Use gloves as often as possible in the workplace.
2. Use goggles when decanting hazardous chemicals.
3. Wipe all spills immediately, particularly on tile floors.
4. Walk; do not run.
5. Report all hallway obstructions.
6. Discard chipped or broken glassware safely.
7. Use pan and brush to sweep up broken glass.
8. Never touch electrical switches with wet hands.
9. Do not use equipment that has frayed electrical cords.
10. Store heavy material on lower shelves and lighter material above.
11. Keep stored material away from sprinkler heads and light bulbs.
12. Do not use chairs or boxes to reach for stored material.
13. Keep loads close to body when lifting.
14. Bend knees and keep a straight back when lifting heavy objects.
15. Never try to give liquids to an unconscious person.
16. Control bleeding by pressing on the wound with a clean towel.
17. Do not use bare hands to push or pull trash in wastebaskets.
18. Handle soiled linen with care to avoid contact with sharps.
19. Always use gloves to handle blood spills or stains.
20. Report any actual or potential safety hazard to your supervisor.

110 degrees at taps. This temperature can be delivered in showers by installing valves or shower heads with heat sensors that automatically mix hot and cold water to achieve comfort levels. The slipping of guests can be prevented by installing grab bars and keeping the slip resistance rating of shower and tub bottoms, and bathroom floors high. Bathroom electrical outlets should be installed with ground fault circuit interrupt (GFCI) receptacles designed to cut off the circuit to eliminate electrical shock, as bathrooms are often wet.

FIRE PREVENTION IN LODGING OPERATIONS

Risk management in lodging properties must include fire prevention and deterrence. Fires in lodging properties are quite common, even though most hotels, motels, and resorts are equipped with state-of-the-art equipment to suppress fires when they occur. Fires can be prevented by fireproofing guestroom furnishing; curtains, carpets, pillows, blankets, and upholstery purchased should be labeled as fire-retardant or flameproof, as cigarette smoking in bed by guests is the typical cause of fires in guestrooms. Foam rubber products are particularly dangerous as they ignite easily and burn rapidly. Excessive accumulation of lint in dryers, painter's supplies, and oily rags can also start fires by **spontaneous combustion**. Oily kitchen cloths should be kept in metal containers and washed or disposed of as soon as possible; painter's products such as linseed oil should be stored in tight containers. Frayed guestroom lamp cables and damaged cords, switches, or plugs may start smoldering fires, as may overcrowded outlets that overload fuses or circuits.

Fire-safety programs should include fire protection instruction, including fire drills. Fire departments in most localities will participate in employee training by showing films on fire prevention, lecturing on the effects of smoke (generally smoke kills, not the fire itself), and demonstrating the use of fire equipment. Fire safety programs should train employees in combating small, controllable fires, operating fire extinguishers, closing doors to contain large fires, keeping fire exits free of any materials, reporting immediately the smell of burning equipment or the presence of smoke, evacuating the building in an orderly manner if the fire alarm sounds, notifying guests of fire if asked to do so, and so on. All property operations workers must be told, at orientation, where the nearest fire alarm, fire extinguisher, and fire exit are located. Above all, employees must be trained not to panic in case of a fire but remain calm in all cases. **Panic emotion** can cause people to feel disoriented, preventing them from acting rationally. Guestrooms should be provided with diagrams of evacuation routes and instructions explaining what to do in case of fire.

SECURITY IN LODGING OPERATIONS

One of the greatest concerns of the lodging industry today is the issue of security. Lodging properties in the past boasted one house detective to keep crime in check; today, it is not uncommon for large properties to hire a team of officers to maintain security in the establishment.

Lodging properties can have their own in-house security department or contract the security function to private companies. By having in-house security staff, the property can exercise greater control over the security officers and train them to the specific characteristics of the establishment. Contracting the service to a security organization, on the other hand, can result in considerable savings because of lower payroll costs and freedom from administrative and supervisory responsibilities. Small companies can resort to using off-duty police officers, who have already been thoroughly trained and usually know the area's delinquents. Besides security manpower, lodging properties must provide security training for employees and often are compelled to invest substantial resources in closed-circuit TV surveillance, in-room safes, and impenetrable room-entry systems.

As with safety, there are legal, ethical, and financial reasons to keep guests, employees, and the company's possessions secure. Innkeepers have the legal and moral obligation of providing reasonable care for guests and staff. The costs of property stolen from guests and company, and from lawsuits resulting from criminal activity, can be very high. Security awareness for guests and training of employees must be ongoing concerns of management in order to prevent theft. Examples of guest security awareness are reminding travelers to keep valuables in the property's safe, asking them to use locks and chains, and recommending they look through the peephole before opening the door. The main outcome of any security training program should be ensuring that a property's entire staff understands its security role. Some specific training goals can be to close every guestroom door found open, to notify the security department of suspicious characters loitering in hallways, and to report anything unusual inside guestrooms, for example, weapons of any type, illegal drugs, bloodstains on walls or carpet, etc. Employees must be trained to be alert for objects left unattended in public areas and to report suspicious individuals present in employee-only areas, particularly if they are acting suspiciously. If approached with security questions about the property, employees must be told to report such inquiries to a supervisor or manager immediately. The departments should also train their staff in emergency-management procedures; that is, in case of bomb threat or a bomb explosion. Practicing thorough checks on potential employees is also a must.

Security-conscious properties should provide printed instructions on table cards for guests explaining how to deter crime and, in some cases, including a direct telephone number at which to contact the security department in case of emergency. Some lodging companies routinely assign single female travelers to rooms that are close to elevators so they don't have to walk down long hallways; others place female guests on their club floor, access to which requires a special key. Some lodging companies instruct switchboard operators not to connect phone calls to rooms without the caller knowing the guest name.

EMPLOYEE THEFT

Estimates of employee theft in the workplace are very high. While accurate statistics are difficult to obtain, it is believed that half of all employees steal from their employers. This is particularly credible in the hospitality industry where wages are low and working conditions leave much to be desired. Housekeeping and engineering employees have ample opportunities to steal and pilfer—they can steal from guests, as they have master keys to access the guests' rooms; and they can pilfer company property, particularly guest and cleaning supplies, linens, and tools. Often, employees steal because of sheer need, as their minimum wages are not sufficient for them to make ends meet. Other times disgruntled workers, feeling frustrated by the way they have been treated,

Four Points Sheraton Shanghai
Courtesy of Starwood Hotels & Resorts Worldwide, Inc.

decide to get even by taking away the company's possessions. In other cases, employees steal simply because security is lax and everybody else is doing it.

MINIMIZING THEFT

Employees who steal use several methods to get supplies out of the property. The most common is using bags, purses, or parcels. An effective way of controlling this type of theft is by implementing a **parcel-pass system** by which employees leaving the property must show security officers a signed authorization to remove any items from the premises. A designated entrance/exit for employees that is controlled by security can be very effective, deterring individuals from exiting the premises through unmonitored doors. However, employees concealing items under their clothing are very difficult to detect and management does have to rely on observation by supervisors or on anonymous tips from loyal workers to pinpoint the culprits. Housekeeping and engineering managers should also establish effective controls on linens, supplies and tools, insisting on monthly physical inventories, strict issuance procedures, and on allowing admittance to storerooms and floor closets to authorized employees only. The engineering department should establish a system for controlling the issuing and retrieving of tools and expensive materials and for conducting unscheduled inventories.

Another method of stealing is by filling trash bags with linens and supplies and depositing them near the trash dumpster, to be picked up after work or by an outside accomplice. Any trash container left outside the garbage compactor or dumpster should be considered suspicious. Employees should also be asked to park away from the building so that no goods may be easily placed near vehicles.

Properties that use keys rather than cards must establish an effective way of limiting access to guestrooms, floor closets, and storerooms by establishing a **key-control system**. The loss of a floor master key or grandmaster key or key card can be disastrous to the department. Keys must be accounted for at all times by logging them in and out at the beginning and end of shifts. Housekeeping staff should be instructed to report any faulty lock on an emergency basis; in no case should a room be handed over to the front desk as ready if its access control device is inoperative. The engineering department should have a system of high priority in place for security-related requests, for example, when a guestroom lock is reported as malfunctioning.

Theft by employees can also be effectively curtailed by establishing theft-prevention measures in the department. The first step is to make sure that application forms are carefully scrutinized and that references of all employees hired are thoroughly checked. Gaps in employment history, for example, may indicate an attempt to hide a job from which the applicant was fired because of theft. References can be effectively checked by establishing an information network by telephone with other executive housekeepers in the area for mutual cooperation. Once employees are hired, it must be clearly stated at orientation and in the employee handbook that theft will be an automatic cause for dismissal. Usually, the safety committee is also in charge of security matters, such as investigating patterns of theft, conducting security inspections around the property, and maintaining records of crime incidents.

THEFT BY GUESTS AND INTRUDERS

The proverbial filching of towels by guests is as common today as it has ever been. In some cases, cash-only guests take with them bathroom appliances, coffee makers, blankets, pillows, clock/

radios, telephones, TV sets, and, in rare cases, the entire furniture of rooms by parking a van behind the room sliding door/window. Guest theft can be reduced by the establishment's not admitting travelers who don't own a credit card. In any case, section housekeepers should be trained to report immediately any missing item from rooms or when observing a guest's suitcase loaded with linen or other items. The detection of empty suitcases or trunks and the presence of suspicious characters loitering in hallways should also be reported. Section housekeepers should also be instructed to never open a guestroom door to anyone claiming to have forgotten the key in the room; instead, room attendants should kindly request the person to obtain an extra key at the front desk. It is particularly important to train housekeeping and engineering employees to spot and report suspicious activities taking place on guest floors, hallways, public areas, and in the back of the house.

SECURITY IN GUESTROOMS

TV sets and light appliances in guestrooms should be bolted down or secured to the wall, furniture, or electrical socket. Entry doors should close automatically and be fitted with latching bolts that lock the door when it is closed. Besides the latching bolt, guestroom doors should have deadbolts, chains, and peepholes. Sliding glass doors on balconies should be provided with "charley bars" that, when extended down, prevent prying the door open from the outside. Special attention should be given to the connecting doors between rooms. Besides the primary lock on the connecting doors, an additional security chain or deadbolt that can be activated by the guest from within each room should be installed.

Room keys, in use for decades, are not effective to deter crime from occurring; as a matter of fact, lodging properties using traditional guestroom keys are considered to be at a competitive disadvantage. That is the case because it is practically impossible to prevent crooks from keeping room keys if they rent a room, then keep the key upon checkout, and come back in the evening to enter the same room when the current guest has gone out. This problem can be completely corrected only by changing the locks each time keys are missing, which requires substantial labor costs and additional manpower. Fortunately, most lodging properties in the U.S. have abandoned the use of traditional keys, although this practice is still common abroad. Card entry systems, on the other hand, are designed so that every guest checking into the property receives a card with a combination different from that used the previous night. In fact, the computer terminal issuing cards at the front desk is capable of providing millions of combinations for entrance to the room. Card entry systems can also register around the clock the time and what specific card was used to enter the room. That is to say, printed records can indicate the time guests and staff used the card at any time during the day or night. Besides, if a master card is lost, the entire floor or floors can be reset very quickly.

Some entry card systems are designed to encode two different tracks, enabling the property to control access not only to the guestrooms, but to other designated areas such as pools, health clubs, elevators, and in-room safes. State-of-the-art cellular control systems can be programmed to issue cards that can limit employee access to rooms by name, time, and date. For example, a section housekeeper card can be programmed to access a group of rooms at certain times during the day and on specific days of the week only.

The guest's personal valuables can be effectively protected by providing a small safe in every guestroom. Most in-room thefts take place when guests leave jewelry, travel checks, cameras, or cards unattended while they are swimming in the pool or having a meal in the dining room. In-room safes can be operated with keys, cards, or touch-pads, on which guests can punch their own safe-opening codes. While the smallest in-room safes should be able to hold a camera or camcorder, business properties need to install briefcase-size or larger units to accommodate portable computers.

The housekeeping department is usually in charge of providing babysitting services to guests traveling with children. The job of babysitting should be offered as a voluntary service to trusted, reliable, long-tenured housekeeping employees. When outside babysitting is used, the executive housekeeper must make sure that the agency has an impeccable record and that it is bonded.

THE THREAT OF TERRORISM

Besides typical domestic threats to security in the lodging industry, one must add nowadays the curse of international terrorism. The terrorist attack in Mumbai, India, is an example of how a luxury hotel can be devastated by terrorism. In a recent study, seven out of ten hotel general and security managers said that their employees were not adequately trained to respond to a terrorist emergency. While threats and attacks can occur in any hotel or resort, the properties that cater to western diplomats or military personnel can be attractive to terrorists. Companies like Marriott and Starwood Hotels and Resorts have reacted to calibrate their security efforts with government's warnings and alerts; other hospitality companies will surely be stepping up their terrorist-related security measures as well.

Intercontinental New York Times Square
Courtesy of Six Continents Hotels, Inc.

The tactics used by terrorists can be bomb threats, suicide bombings and armed teams infiltrating the establishment to take hostages or cause as much harm as possible. This new reality is forcing lodging companies to supplement traditional security with security technologies, such as perimeter surveillance provided by cameras and, in sophisticated cases, ground-based radar and all-weather day-night laser-illuminated devices to vector in on and track approaching suspects. In selected areas within the property, networks can be configured to alert automatically for objects left behind or for intrusion in restricted areas. A command and control center with monitored visual displays would be necessary for an effective control if intelligence-enabled sensors, cameras, and ground radar are installed.

In case of bomb threats, procedures to respond should be included in the property's emergency plans. Persons likely to receive the threat should be trained to memorize the exact words of callers, to ask them when the explosive is set to go off and the reasons why the device was placed, and to remember the accent of the caller. Although potential terrorists are difficult to recognize, lodging employees should be trained to notice anything unusual, including potential terrorist scouts who try to case locations months prior to an attack, and to watch for abandoned packages. If approached with security questions about the property, employees must report such inquiries to management or security personnel.

FIGHTING THE RISK OF INFECTIOUS DISEASE

In the hospitality industry, great attention is generally accorded to fighting bacteria that can cause food-borne illnesses, but not enough consideration is given to the fact that microorganisms are also present in guestrooms and public areas of lodging properties, where they may contaminate guests and employees. Property managers need to have a basic knowledge of how microorganisms spread and of infection control so that they can be part of employee education programs and provide effective sanitation services. For example, although employees often have serious concerns about contracting a disease while at work, particularly the HIV/AIDS infection, they often don't know that the HIV virus can rarely be contracted by casual contact, by sharing bathrooms or utensils, or even by shaking hands with infected individuals. However, hospital and healthcare workers who have intense exposure by direct contact with patients' body fluids and needles should be instructed about these potential dangers.

There are three kinds of microorganisms that may cause illnesses: **viruses, bacteria,** and **fungi**. Viruses are infective agents, smaller than common microorganisms, which require living cells for multiplication. Viruses can cause poliomyelitis, hepatitis, AIDS, and the common cold if they find their way into the human body, where they may multiply. Most bacteria are the simplest group of plant organisms that are involved in fermentation and putrefaction of matter and, unfortunately, the production of disease. Bacteria cause illnesses such as cholera, dysentery, tuberculosis, enteritis, and typhoid. Given the right conditions, bacteria can grow by cellular-division in incredibly large numbers and at a very fast pace. For instance, under ideal conditions, one bacterium can reproduce over two million bacteria in seven hours. Fungi belong to a group of organisms that include molds and mildew. These minute mushroom-like growths thrive in damp, dark places, including shower walls, laundry rooms, and around toilets.

Viruses can be fought by vacuuming carpets daily, wiping surfaces with cloths containing a germicidal, and having employees wash their hands frequently or wipe them with a hand sanitizer. The best way to fight bacteria is by keeping foods (such as welcome cheese platters in guestrooms) out of the **danger zone** (40–140°F), washing hands with antibacterial hand soap, and sanitizing wiping cloths and floor mops. Bacteria usually spread by **cross-contamination,** which involves using a medium to transport microorganisms from place to place. The typical spread of bacteria takes place if a floor mop is used in a public restroom and then again without being sanitized, say, on the employee cafeteria floor. Mold and mildew can be eliminated by keeping areas as dry as possible and using cleaning products that contain bleach or bleach derivates. Sunrays are natural killers of microorganisms.

Luckily, most germs do not cause humans to become sick; as a matter of fact, only some, the **pathogenic germs**, can be deadly. Nevertheless, and just in case, lodging properties must provide employee training and effective cleaning services to prevent the spread of infection. There are three effective methods of reducing the spread of germs in the workplace. The first, **sanitation**, consists of cleaning surfaces, articles, and material to reduce germ count to a safe level according to public health standards and codes. The second, **disinfection**, deals with using cleaning products to selectively kill specific types of germs. **Sterilization** requires steam to eliminate germs in a pressurized container. A variation of sterilization, although not 100 percent effective, consists of washing items such as guestroom glasses at high water temperatures, usually between 160 and 180°F.

A large number of contaminating agents can be found in public and guestroom trash receptacles. Some examples are needles, razor blades, and body fluids. Every person who handles a trash container should be instructed not to compress the content with the hands and to keep the trash bag away from the body to reduce the risk of being stuck by sharps. The use of gloves when handling trash is necessary.

Housekeeping managers in hospitals must be knowledgeable about how to handle medical infectious waste, which may include cultures and stocks, blood, and sharps. Regulations on how to dispose of infectious waste vary from city to city and state to state. Directions common to all hospital facilities are provided by OSHA's Bloodborne Pathogens Regulation, implemented in 1992. Section housekeepers and hospital personnel should be trained to remove soiled linens from beds carefully to avoid sharps and to prevent spreading germs. Soiled linen should be placed directly into a soiled-linen bag rather than first putting it on the carpet or on furniture. To clean up dried blood spills on walls or floors, a worker wearing gloves should spray the area with a strong disinfectant and wipe it with a cloth.

Public areas attendants who clean bathrooms and restrooms should be instructed not just to clean but to disinfect as well. The products needed to disinfect these areas are a bowl cleaner/disinfectant, a glass cleaner, a germicidal all-purpose cleaner, and a cleaner/disinfectant for mopping floor surfaces. Germ cross-contamination can be effectively avoided by not using toilet brushes and cleaning rags used for cleaning toilets and urinals on other bathroom or restroom surfaces. In guestrooms, the tub, shower, shower curtains, sink, and counter top should be disinfected daily.

Germs may also be transmitted by employees. In order to avoid the spread of micro-organisms, workers should be instructed to wash their hands with bactericidal soap and hot water or use hand sanitizer after using the bathroom. Gloves and cleaning rags should also be cleaned and disinfected before being reused in a different cleaning job.

BEDBUG INFESTATIONS

Bedbugs, eradicated years ago from lodging properties using strong pesticides, particularly DDT, seem to have made a comeback. At the time of writing this book, these insects have spread to several public buildings in the New York City area, including hotels and the United Nations edifice. The infestation is so widespread that a conference has been hosted by the Real Estate Board of New York to discuss the matter. Because the insects come out at night to feed, they are difficult to detect by room attendants making beds. During the day, they hide in cracks, baseboards, and mattress seams.

In case of infestation, operators of lodging properties should request the services of licensed professional companies and follow their recommendations to control the problem. Pest-control companies like Ecolab have introduced bedbug treatment programs aimed primarily at the hospitality market. Besides the use of chemicals to fight the pest, dogs are trained to sniff out where the bugs may be burrowed and employees are instructed on how to inspect for the insects on a daily basis. The use of impermeable mattress covers can prevent the spread of bedbugs into beds not yet infested.

LEGIONNAIRES' DISEASE

Legionellosis is a potential infectious disease caused by aerobic bacteria that thrive in a temperature range of 25-45°F. The disease took its name from an outbreak of pneumonia among people attending a convention of the American Legion in Philadelphia. The bacteria were traced to the cooling tower of the hotel from, which they entered the building through the air-handling system. To prevent outbreaks of this type, the engineering department in lodging operations must treat the water used in places like cooling towers, humidifiers, fountains, and spas, where wet conditions can provide a breeding ground for these microorganisms.

KEY TERMS

Bacteria
Cross-contamination
Danger zone
Disinfection
Fungi
Job-safety analysis
Key-control system
Panic emotion

Parcel-pass system
Pathogenic germs
Safety committee
Safety training program
Sanitation
Spontaneous combustion
Sterilization
Virus

DISCUSSION AND REVIEW QUESTIONS

1. Give three reasons why fire and accident prevention are functions of management.
2. How would you describe OSHA?
3. In which jobs are job-safety analyses particularly necessary?
4. What are the main advantages of implementing safety training programs in the workplace?
5. What are the purposes of forming safety committees in the workplace?
6. List four fire hazards common in housekeeping departments.
7. Why should housekeeping employees be trained in security awareness?
8. What are common ways for housekeeping and engineering department employees to steal or pilfer company property?
9. Why are guestroom lock-and-key systems considered to be obsolete?
10. What is the difference between disinfection and sterilization?

MINICASES

SITUATION 1

You have been hired by a large lodging hotel in downtown Phoenix, Arizona, as executive housekeeper. The general manager has pointed out to you that the property has been suffering from repeated theft in guestrooms and from severe pilfering of guest and cleaning supplies. The director of security has made clear in one of the staff meetings that there is not much that she can do about the situation because of the lack of basic departmental structure regarding security.

Prior to investigating what is going on, prepare a list of possible loopholes that the department may have regarding security.

SITUATION 2

John and Pearl Padilla, husband and wife, checked into a motel on a Sunday afternoon. Two days later, as they came back from dining out, they were attacked by a man who had gained entrance to their room. Both guests were beaten up, after which the assailant took the couple's jewelry and cash. It was found later that Mr. Padilla had left his room key in the bar they visited before returning to the motel. The key was attached to a heavy brass base together with a plastic label with the motel's name and room number. The bartender at the counter had said: "I briefly saw the key laying on their table but I thought they were dancing and would come back to pick it up." John had asked the clerk on duty at the front desk for a second key, saying: "I cannot find my key. I must have left it in my room before leaving this evening." The Padillas filed a lawsuit against the motel the following day.

a. Was the hotel found guilty by the jury at the trail?

b. Explain why, in your opinion, the hotel was found guilty (or not guilty).

SITUATION 3

Betty Palin befriended a good-looking young man in the bar of the resort where she was staying. After dancing a little and having some drinks, the man asked Ms. Palin to accompany him to his room, room number 205, where they could have a nightcap before the night was over. Betty accepted and both left the bar at about 1 A.M.

At 2:30 A.M, the night clerk received a frantic call made by Betty Palin from room 205 saying that the man registered in that room had robbed her of her fur coat, jewelry, credit cards, traveler's checks, and cash she had in her purse. The value, she said, was over $5,000. The front office clerk called the police. It was later found that the man had rented the room by paying in cash at check in and furnishing the hotel with a false address. He was never found thereafter.

a. Who is to be blamed legally in this situation?

b. Why?

CASE STUDY

The plaintiff and her friend entered a restaurant in a hotel and sat at a table across from a group of three individuals already having dinner. The three diners began engaging in coarse conversation, aimed to be overhead by and to shock the plaintiff and her companion. At one point, the restaurant manager asked the group to quiet down, but the abusive shouting continued.

Sometime afterwards, as the three members of the group were getting up to leave, one of the individuals directly insulted the plaintiff. After an exchange of words, the defendant struck the plaintiff on the face with a clenched fist, bruising her mouth and nose. The plaintiff called the attacker a racial expletive, encouraging the attacker to strike the victim again. The restaurant supervisor stood by watching but did not intervene or call security since he did not feel the situation warranted it.

As the fight continued, the plaintiff's friend ran to the counter to dial for the police but was told that the phone was not for public use. Later, she did manage to call 911. The attacker and friends were scared away and left the area. The plaintiff filed suit against the hotel, alleging that management had failed to provide security measures to protect her.

Assignment

1. Discuss the case and determine whether the hotel was at fault.

Solar panels, Marriott Jordan Valley
Courtesy of Marriott International, Inc.

Energy and Water Conservation in Lodging Properties

CHAPTER OBJECTIVES

- Create awareness in lodging management students of the need for energy conservation.
- Describe techniques used in lodging properties to conserve water.
- Discuss methods commonly used in lodging properties to conserve electricity.
- Learn about the procedures practiced in lodging establishments to conserve energy used in heating and cooling systems.

OVERVIEW

Future lodging managers must understand that conservation of water and energy has become a necessity in the regular operation of lodging establishments. The ever-increasing use of resources in a society focused on growth, together with an expanding population, are gradually depleting the planet's basic resources. In addition, operators will continue to face higher costs for water and energy, making it difficult to generate an acceptable operations bottom line and, consequently, a fair return on investment.

This chapter, besides creating awareness of the need of water and energy conservation, discusses the methods and techniques commonly used in lodging properties to minimize the use of these critical resources.

THE NEED FOR WATER AND ENERGY CONSERVATION

The demand on world resources has skyrocketed with the increase in world population and the efforts of emerging economies to catch up with the Western world's industrialized levels. At the same time, due most likely to the change in global climate, water scarcity has reached catastrophic proportions in many parts of the planet. It is estimated that nearly one billion people don't have access to enough safe drinking water. Some statistics on water-related problems are staggering; for example, it is believed that at any given time half of the world's hospital beds are occupied by patients suffering from **water-borne diseases** and that one out of four deaths under the age of five worldwide is due to water-related illnesses.

In the United States' Southwest, water scarcity is severe, with Lake Meade, for example, reaching its lowest levels since 1937. At the same time, the Las Vegas metropolitan area and the Valley of the Sun of Phoenix, Arizona, have had massive increases in population, resulting in enormous increases in water consumption. Climate change has also caused persistent droughts, with rainfall down 89 percent of its average levels in the upper Colorado River basin. This pattern is becoming common also in other parts of the country, forcing communities to resort to drilling wells to depths of 3,000 feet or more. This, in turn, causes water tables to drop, which creates irreversible conditions in riparian zones and, even worse, dries some of the creeks and small rivers used in the past to supply water to farmers and city dwellers. The fact is that the high cost and low availability of water have become a concern to many, including managers in lodging operations.

The production and distribution of electricity is also facing important challenges. Although the United States holds vast deposits of coal to power its electricity-producing plants, the mining, transportation, and burning of this resource require large capital investments and cause severe pollution problems. Other sources of energy to generate electricity present operating difficulties as well. Nuclear energy, once thought to be the solution, raises public concerns about safety; the possibility of a meltdown of Three Mile Island's proportions once thought to be remote has become a reality in Japan's Fukushima disaster. Another concern is the disposal of radioactive waste, a byproduct of electricity-generating plants.

Electricity production from solar sources is still in its developing stages, representing but a small percentage of the total output. A significant disadvantage of solar power is its installation costs, making it prohibitive in **developing countries**. On the other hand, the generation of electricity using solar sources is quite clean since it causes no atmospheric pollution. Lodging companies should investigate if some of the incentive programs offered by the U.S. government warrant the installation of photovoltaic or concentrated solar power systems. Wind mills can generate electricity by powering **turbines**. There are increasing numbers of wind farms that are connected to electric power transmission networks. This type of energy is plentiful and renewable, producing no greenhouse gas emissions during operation. There is resistance, though, to its visual impact on the landscape and to the occasional killing of some raptor birds. By far, the most efficient method of generating green electricity is the **hydroelectric plant**. Water power, however, supplies only a small percentage of the country's energy needs.

Electricity is distributed via a colossal grid consisting of tens of thousands of miles of cables, many generating plants powered by different energy sources, and thousands of power stations and substations distributed around the country. However, the general consensus is that our national **electric grid** is outdated and needs a major overhaul without which the danger exists that power outages could cripple vast areas of the country.

Oil and gas deposits, once thought to be endless, are being consumed rapidly by Western as well as emergent countries, particularly China and India. Although new deposits are being discovered, their exploitation will require in most cases deep off-shore drilling with the potential of destroying the environment. The cost of a barrel of oil has been increasing over the last 20 years and has reached more than $100 at the time this book is written. It is feared that any future convulsion in the oil markets will trigger further escalation in price.

With this state of affairs, it seems vital to lower the consumption of water and energy-generation resources as much as possible. Because the hospitality industry hosts thousands of travelers daily, energy management in lodging properties is of critical importance, meaning that resources used in lodging establishments must be used wisely. Hospitality companies with energy conservation programs are viewed favorably by an ever-increasing number of guests who are conscious of the need for sustainability. Some companies have adopted strict construction codes to address energy efficiency in buildings, for example, insisting on the minimization of BTUs and wattage usage per square foot per year. A commitment to conservation and energy management by lodging properties will reduce consumption substantially, contributing to the reduction of the usage of our water and energy resources while lowering operating costs significantly.

WATER SYSTEMS AND CONSERVATION

A reliable supply of potable water to lodging operations is provided by local utility companies. Internally, some basic precautions must be taken to ensure an effective supply. If the establishment is a high rise, the water supplied usually doesn't have enough pressure to reach the upper floors. In this case, a pump or a series of pumps must be installed to propel the water to all stories. If the pumping system is deficient, water surges in showers and faucets can

Photo-cell-activated faucet by Sloan
Courtesy of Sloan Valve Company

occur that can annoy guests. When the water supplied has excessive levels of calcium and magnesium salts, it is said to be hard. These minerals can cause lime buildups in pipes and plumbing fixtures and poor results in silverware and linen washing. This problem can be eliminated by installing a **water softener** consisting of a tank or series of tanks filled with a filtering resin, usually **zeolite**, that purifies the water before it is used.

In most cases, waste water is removed from buildings by gravity. Drain pipes conduct the waste downwards to the sanitary sewer systems through which it flows to the city's treatment plant for recycling. Some older properties with below-sewer-level basements may have to dispose of waste water after it collects in a well. In this instance, a **sump pump** needs to be installed in the pit to bring the waste to sewer level. These pumps, if submerged, tend to clog from time to time, making them very difficult and dangerous to clean because of the fetid fumes that may be present in the well.

WATER CONSERVATION

It is understandable that water consumption in lodging properties is very high. Imagine a 400-room hotel using old-fashioned toilets being flushed three or more times a day when the room is occupied at the rate of four gallons per flush. If the room were to be occupied 365 days a year, the number of gallons used would be 4,380 ($3 \times 4 = 12$; $12 \times 365 = 4,380$). To this amount, the water used in the bathtub or shower and sinks must be added, together with an average of 25 gallons per guest per day for items washed in the laundry room. Some studies give the consumption of water per occupied room per day as 55 gallons on average; others raise it to over 300 gallons in some properties. At the same time, the cost of water keeps climbing. As an example, hotels and motels in Flagstaff, Arizona, are charged at the time this book goes to print $4.09 per 1,000 gallons of water. This price has gone up substantially over the years and will continue to increase as time passes.

A water conservation program in lodging properties should begin with the initiation of employees and guests in awareness on how to conserve water as an overall effort to save the environment. Signs can be posted in public and employee areas reminding everybody that water is a precious, finite resource. The engineering department can be instrumental in minimizing water consumption in lodging properties where leaks are a major cause of waste. A preventive maintenance program should be aimed at stopping **ghost flushing** and leaks in toilets, faucets, and showers by routinely checking all units. The water used in toilet flushing can be reduced by adjusting the mechanism in the tanks or by installing devices to reduce the water used. In Europe, toilets in guestrooms have

Button valve by Sloan
Courtesy of Sloan Valve Company

Waterless urinal by Sloan
Courtesy of Sloan Valve Company

two push buttons, one for regular and another for smaller discharges. Waterless urinals in public restrooms can save thousands of gallons of water annually. An alternative to waterless equipment is to fit public urinals with an automatic flush operated by passive **infrared sensors**. This system can also be applied to faucets in sinks. Plumbing fixtures can be fitted with **flow-reducing aerators** to minimize water use. Retrofitting old toilets with low-flow units and shower heads with new models using 50 percent less water is usually cost efficient and yields paybacks in a short period of time. The device for shower heads consists of a round, inexpensive piece of metal with a hole smaller than the diameter of the supply pipe that reduces the number of gallons per minute used. Installing **tunnel washers** in large laundry operations can reduce water usage by two-thirds, as does the use of a water reclamation system. To prevent evaporation and loss of heat, swimming pools should be covered when not in use. The water discharged from swimming pools can also be recycled and used for irrigation purposes.

ELECTRICITY SYSTEMS AND CONSERVATION

There are three terms related to electricity that future hospitality managers must understand—**voltage, wattage,** and **amperage**. Voltage is the electromotive force of electricity expressed in volts; for example, the intensity of the current when it leaves a power plant may be of thousands of **volts**, while that provided for lighting purposes is only 110 volts in the U.S. Wattage refers to the number of **watts** required to operate an electrical device; for example, a 60-watt light bulb will consume 60 watts per hour while a 100-watt bulb will consume 100. The billing unit for energy delivered to consumers is expressed in **kilowatts** (one thousand watts). Amperage is the strength of an electric current measured in **amperes**; for example, the motor of a vacuum cleaner may take 7 amperes from the current being supplied to it, while a different vacuum cleaner with a stronger motor may take 12 amperes from the electric flow.

Most lodging companies in the U.S. receive their electricity service from utility companies that supply power to their properties at an average force of 480 volts. The electricity is then distributed throughout the building using step-down transformers that reduce the voltage to 120 volts for lighting and 220 volts and higher for motors. In buildings, the current travels through cables that are grouped into circuits. The circuits begin at electrical panels where **breakers** or **fuses** are installed that will jump (breaker) or melt (fuse) if the demand on a particular circuit is too great for the cable to carry. In this case, if the electricity were not cut off by the breaker or fuse, the cable might ignite and cause a fire hazard. Most, if not all, electrical outlets in commercial buildings are grounded using GFCI receptacles, thus being capable of cutting off power if the plugged-in object or appliance demands too much electricity from the circuit.

ELECTRICITY CONSERVATION

As with water, electricity conservation begins with creating awareness in employees and guests to minimize the use of power. It begins with asking everyone to turn off lights and equipment whenever possible. When the property is not operating at 100 percent occupancy, room usage should be restricted by floor or wing so as not to supply full electrical service to unoccupied areas. The housekeeping staff should be trained to be energy conscious; for example, they should turn off lights and television sets when guests are not in the room and reduce the use of lights while cleaning the area.

Reducing the wattage of light bulbs will save energy, although care must be taken not to inconvenience guests by dimming lights too much. By changing incandescent (old type) light bulbs to fluorescent ones, a minimum of 50 percent of electricity can be saved; in addition, their life span can be extended considerably. Electricity conservation in large spaces, such as ballrooms, parking lots, and covered garages, can be improved by using **electric discharge lamps,** which are both durable and energy efficient. This type of light bulb is filled with a gas that glows when heated by the current. To provide lighting only when it is needed, **space sensors,** timers, and photocells can be used to save energy. In Europe, guests are obliged to insert their room door-opening card in a slot located at the entrance to turn on the electricity. When they leave, the power is disconnected after they take the card with them.

Electricity costs can be lowered by using equipment during **off-peak hours** (usually in the middle of the night), for example, by operating the laundry washers and dryers or the kitchen's ovens during this period. Because motor efficiency is a function of the capacity in turning electricity into mechanical energy, its initial cost, and the wattage used per hour, chief engineers should analyze the savings that a motor can yield before making a purchasing decision. For example, a motor can be more expensive to buy but could generate enough savings in electricity usage to offset its higher cost over time; on the other hand, a motor can be inexpensive but generate less mechanical energy or use too much electricity in the process. The cost of electricity can also be lowered by implementing preventive maintenance programs that include periodical motor cleaning, lubrication, and adjustment of the driving belts.

HVAC SYSTEMS AND CONSERVATION

HEATING SYSTEMS

Heat used in lodging properties is generally produced by systems using water, steam, or electricity. To heat water or to create steam in a central plant, oil, gas, or electricity is used. A hot water heating system consists, basically, of a boiler, where the water is heated to temperatures between 110 for mild days to 220°F when it is cold outside, a closed circuit of pipes to circulate it, and a series of **radiators** or **fan coils** where the heat is irradiated or transferred by blowing air into the spaces to be warmed. The water returns back to the boiler by mean of a **circulating pump** for the process to start all over again. Steam is generated using the same system as for hot water, although in large cities it can be supplied by utility companies. Steam systems require traps to prevent the steam from circulating back to the boiler before it cools off. At this point, the steam condensates into water, which is collected in a receiver tank from which it is sent back to the boiler by a pump.

When using electricity as fuel, electric resistances or elements are inserted in a boiler that cause the water to heat up. The advantage of this system is that a flue is not needed in the boiler since there is no combustion involved in the process. A major disadvantage is the high cost of the electricity used. Natural gas burns cleanly but, obviously, it requires a conduit to expel the combustion fumes from the building. Utility companies charge for natural gas per **therm** consumed. A therm is equivalent to 100,000 **BTU**s (British thermal units). As a practical comparison, the term therm is to natural gas what wattage is to electricity and gallon is to water? that is, a unit of consumption. Fuel oil is usually used in large lodging establishments operating in cold climates. This system needs more maintenance and causes more pollution than burning natural gas and requires an on-site storage tank where the fuel oil is delivered by truck.

In decentralized systems, electricity used in single baseboard heaters is a safe and clean method of generating heat but its cost can be very high. For this reason, it is generally used in small lodging establishments located in mild climates. Some properties use individual units rather than a central plant to generate heating, especially in guestrooms. The units are usually **heat pumps** that are powered by electricity and can deliver both hot and cold air by simply reversing their mechanical cycle. The unit is either placed outside or inside the guestroom. The advantage of using decentralized units such as these is that they don't require a large area for a central plant nor the installation throughout the building of an intricate system of pipes, ducts, radiators, or fan coils. Some disadvantages are the noise of the motor running close to guests when they are in the room and the high level of maintenance that these units require.

HEATING CONSERVATION

The purpose of supplying heating to buildings is to keep their temperature within a certain range, usually between 70 and 74°F. When some of this heat is lost, the heat-generating unit must keep working to maintain the temperature at comfort levels. Thus, the more heat lost, the more energy consumed.

Heat can be lost by **ventilation, infiltration**, or **transmission.** The fresh air forced into buildings to ventilate spaces and the exhaust fans used to get rid of stagnant air tend to displace the warm air inside buildings towards the exterior. To minimize this effect, chief engineers should calibrate fresh-air intake and exhaust fans to minimize heat loss. To avoid excessive infiltration of cold air into buildings through openings, self-closing or rotating doors and windows with efficient glass layers should be installed to prevent heat loss. Single-pane windows may lose as much as fifteen times more heat than a well insulated wall. In most cases, retrofitting window glass to a higher quality is warranted as the expense will be recovered in a short period of time.

Heat is also lost by transmission through roofs and walls. Obviously, a poorly insulated building will lose more heat than a well insulated one. **Heat transmission transfer** can be quantified and its computation can be useful to calculate the difference in heat loss in BTUs using different types of insulation. The formula is:

$$T = A \times U \times (T_2 - T_1)$$

where T = BTUs lost per hour
A = Area of heat transfer
U = Heat transmission coefficient
T_2 = Temperature inside (warmer)
T_1 = Temperature outside (colder)

The U value of an insulator indicates how much heat will pass through it during a specific time interval. A lower U factor implies better insulation material. In practice, the formula determines the BTUs per hour lost per square feet per °F. For example, if we want to determine the BTUs lost per hour through a 50-square foot window with a U factor of 0.20 and temperatures of 70°F inside and 30°F outside, the answer should be 400 ($T = 50 \times 0.20 \times (70 - 30)$).

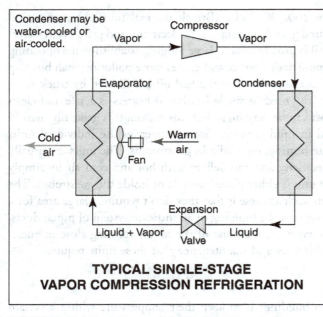

FIGURE 11.1   Vapor Compression Refrigeration Cycle

Besides the calibration of ventilation and exhaust equipment and the prevention of heat loss through infiltration and transmission, other means of conserving heat in lodging properties include the maintenance of heating units (boilers, blowers, etc.) and the insulation of pipes used to distribute the hot water or steam.

REFRIGERATION AND AIR-CONDITIONING SYSTEMS

The typical refrigeration cycle is based on a closed circuit that includes an **evaporator**, a **compressor**, and a **condenser** linked by a pipe. The circuit is filled with a refrigerant fluid of low boiling point, such as ammonia, sulfur dioxide or a non-halogenated hydrocarbon, such as methane. In a vapor-compression refrigeration cycle (see Figure 11.1), the chilled refrigerant circulates through the evaporator coil, absorbing heat from the space to be cooled. As the heat is absorbed, the space is cooled while the liquid refrigerant evaporates. The warm refrigerant vapor flows to the compressor, where its pressure and temperature are raised. In the condenser, the heat absorbed is released and the refrigerant turns again into a chilled liquid state. From the condenser the liquid gas travels to the evaporator, where the cycle begins all over again. In decentralized systems, cooling units placed in individual guestrooms consist of the same components—that is, an evaporator, a compressor and a condenser. When heat pumps are used, these units can provide chilled air as described above and heat from an electric resistance by reversing the mechanical cycle.

Large lodging establishments use the absorption refrigeration cycle system to cool guestrooms and large areas. In this more complex centralized system, water is the refrigerant. The cold water produced is conducted through a series of pipes to individual cold-water coils through which air is moved to cool the space. As the water releases cold, it warms up, returning to the chiller to start the process once again. Large units use **water-cooling towers** to cool the warm water flowing from the absorber and condenser units before returning it back to the condenser. The purpose of adding cooling towers to these systems is to increase the chilling capacity of the absorption refrigeration cycle.

AIR-CONDITIONING CONSERVATION

As with heating conservation, an effective equipment-maintenance program, ventilation calibration, infiltration control, and good insulation will minimize the loss of chilled air in lodging properties. In addition, conditioned air can be conserved by reducing **solar effects**, that is, by preventing the sun from directly hitting windows and walls. This can be accomplished by installing awnings and canopies or by planting trees or bushes to deflect the sun's rays. This is particularly important in very hot climates such as in the American South. The isolation of **internal sources** that generate heat can also help conserve chilled air. Kitchen and laundries are strong producers of heat and should be isolated by installing separating doors between these areas and the front of the house.

KEY TERMS

Amperage
Amperes
BTU
Building ventilation
Circulating pump
Compressor
Condenser
Developing countries
Electricity breaker
Electric discharge lamp
Electric grid
Evaporator
Fan coil
Flow-reducing aerator
Fuse
Ghost flushing
Heat pump
Heat radiator
Heat transmission transfer
Hydroelectric plant

Infiltration
Infrared sensor
Internal heat-generating sources
Kilowatt
Off-peak hours
Solar effect
Space sensor
Sump pump
Therm
Tunnel washer
Turbine
Volts
Voltage
Water-borne disease
Water cooling tower
Water softener
Watts
Wattage
Zeolite

DISCUSSION AND REVIEW QUESTIONS

1. How is the drilling of water using deep wells affecting the environment?
2. What are the disadvantages of using coal for energy generation?
3. Why is the use of nuclear energy dangerous in energy generation?
4. What is the main advantage of using the sun for energy generation?
5. Why are there environmental problems associated with the use of nuclear energy?
6. What can a lodging property do to minimize the consumption of potable water?
7. What are the advantage and one potential disadvantage of reducing the wattage in light bulbs?
8. Why are fuses placed at the start of an electrical circuit?
9. Give three ways of conserving electricity in lodging operations.
10. What are one advantage and one disadvantage of using electricity to generate heat?
11. Can the same heat pump deliver hot air and cold air?
12. Describe the cycle of a vapor-compression refrigeration system.
13. Give three ways to conserve conditioned air in a lodging establishment.

14. Insulation material A has a *U* coefficient of 1.01. Insulation material B has an insulation coefficient of 0.80. Which of the two is most efficient?

15. In a vapor-compression refrigeration cycle the refrigerant reaches the evaporator in a liquid state. Is this statement true or false?

MINICASES

SITUATION 1

Five years into your career in the hospitality industry, your company has promoted you to manager of a casino in Reno, Nevada. Your chief engineer, Mr. Ricardo Howey, needs to purchase a motor to power one of the exhaust fans for the property. The engineer wants to replace the current motor's brand with a new-brand one that he believes is more efficient. You are not sure that changing brands is wise and decide to research the matter on your own. The information you gather is:

Current motor:

Cost	$375
Life expectancy guaranteed by manufacturer	10 years
Energy consumption:	Kwatt/hour

New motor:

Cost	$300
Life expectancy	9 years
Energy consumption	5.50 Kwatt/hour

Given that the motors will run round the clock and that the cost of electricity is $0.2005 per Kwatt/hour, decide which brand should be purchased. Perform the cost analysis based on an annual timeframe.

SITUATION 2

For the same property as above, Mr. Howey proposes now to change the light bulbs in five hallways to save electricity. Here is his plan:

Current lighting:
- 100 light bulbs
- 100 watt/hour energy consumption per unit

Proposed lighting:
- 100 light bulbs
- 75 watt/hour energy consumption per unit

If the cost of electricity still is $0.2005 per Kwatt/hour, how much will the new light bulbs save annually if you approve the change? (Calculate the saving without factoring in any labor cost involved in changing the light bulbs.)

SITUATION 3

Betsy Yordy, the new assistant manager of a hotel in Tucson, Arizona, has been asked to determine the consumption and replacement cost of the four hundred fifty 75-watt incandescent light bulbs currently in use in the hotel guestroom hallways with compact fluorescent light bulbs. The internal corridors require that the light bulbs are switched on 24 hours a day. The current average cost of each kilowatt-hour paid by the property is $0.09331.

If the cost of one fluorescent light bulb is $1.90 and its wattage is 60, how many days will be necessary to amortize the purchase of the new light bulbs from the savings obtained by lowering the bulbs' wattage? Betsy is not considering the cost of replacing the light bulbs or the effect of the life of both bulb types.

CASE STUDY 1

Natalia Casado, general manager of a resort in Palo Alto, California, was asked by her corporate office supervisor to lower energy costs during the coming winter. Natalia decided to put in effect all the energy-conservation techniques learned in her hospitality property management class. She began by finding out how many BTUs per hour could be saved by upgrading the glass windows in the resort's dining room. She decided to apply the formula recommended by her professor to determine insulation results:

$$T = A \times U \times (T_2 - T_1)$$

where T = BTUs lost per hour
A = Area of heat transfer
U = Heat transmission coefficient
T_2 = Temperature inside (warmer)
T_1 = Temperature outside (colder)

Natalia considered changing the four single-pane, 10×15 ft dining room windows with a heat transmission coefficient of 1.13 with insulating double-pane glass having a 0.65 coefficient. As a base to go from, she decided to limit her calculations to the month of March. She learned from the local weather bureau that the maximum temperature in Palo Alto for the month of March was 65 and the minimum was 43. For her calculation, she assigned an average daily temperature of 52°F.

Assignment

1. How many BTUs per hour would be saved for the month by changing the windows to the new specifications while maintaining the inside temperature at 69 degrees?

CASE STUDY 2

Mark Toeniskoetter has been appointed assistant to the general manager of a busy downtown hotel in southern California. In addition to his normal duties, he has been assigned the special project of lowering the cost of water by suggesting ways to conserve consumption. The property's general manager's comments were that the bill has been steadily increasing for the past three years even though charges by the utility company had not been raised and hotel occupancy had been steady.

Mark started by conducting a thorough, systematic, month-long walking survey—an inspection of the building conducted on site. His findings were as follows:

- Average number of faucets found dripping daily in the 30-day period: 35; estimated water loss per faucet: three gallons per day.
- Average number of toilet ghost flush found: 16; estimated water loss per toilet: 16 gallons per day.
- Water per flush for each guestroom toilet: six gallons.

In addition, all shower heads had been retrofitted five years ago with flow controllers to minimize consumption. Mark knew that the 450-room hotel was running at 78 percent occupancy annually and that the average person per occupied room was 1.45. He arbitrarily assigned an average of four flushes per person per day for toilet use.

Mark's plan consisted of starting a program to change valve seat washers of dripping faucets, hoping to reduce the daily average number of leaks from 35 to 6. In addition, he planned to reduce the number of ghost-flushing toilets to a maximum of six per day. He also proposed to adjust the vacuum flush mechanisms of all toilets to reduce the gallons of water per flush from six to 3.5 in all guest rooms.

Assignment

1. Present a water consumption reduction proposal to the general manager indicating the number of gallons of water that would be saved annually if Mark's plan were adopted by management.

Golf course, The St. Regis Monarch Beach
Courtesy of Starwood Hotels & Resorts Worldwide, Inc.

Environmental Management and Sustainability

CHAPTER OBJECTIVES

- Learn about environmental problems.
- Describe how to implement a recycling program in lodging operations.
- Understand the need to dispose of hazardous materials safely.
- Explain what to do to improve indoor air quality.
- Discuss how to attract environmentally conscious travelers.
- Debate the issue of sustainability in the lodging industry and learn about green certification procedures.

OVERVIEW

Managers of housekeeping and engineering departments are in the privileged position of being able to make an impact on planet **sustainability** by reducing energy use, recycling materials, and disposing properly of harmful substances. In this chapter, we discuss the need for environmental awareness as well as specific ways in which lodging properties can be made eco-friendly, thereby helping the earth, attracting concerned guests, and, ultimately, improving the bottom line. The chapter also includes information on green lodging certification.

ENVIRONMENTAL CONCERNS

For the last twenty-five years, scientific studies have caused growing apprehension about the earth's environment. One of these concerns has been the realization that the planet's **ozone layer** is deteriorating. This layer is a protective blanket that shields life on earth from lethal ultraviolet radiation from the sun. Scientists affirm that the loss of ozone is caused mostly by the use of chemical compounds such as **chlorofluorocarbons** used as propellants, refrigerants, and solvents. At the same time, **carbon dioxide** and methane gases emitted by industrial plants powered by coal and vehicles propelled by fossil fuels are causing a greenhouse effect, elevating the temperature on the earth's surface dramatically changing the climate.

Another environmental problem is waste disposal, particularly chemical and oil byproducts, generated by an ever-increasing world population. In America alone, waste per person per day is estimated to be 3.5 pounds. The total amount of solid waste produced by American society annually is thought to be around 450 million pounds. In addition, more than 200 million tons of hazardous waste require special treatment so as not to pollute underground water when discharged into public wastewater systems. Traces of noxious substances, particularly from discarded prescription drugs, corrosive materials such as drain cleaners, and liquids like motor oil and antifreeze, can infiltrate the drinking water supply. Toxic particles from public trash incinerators not equipped with effective pollution control devices can also pollute the atmosphere. Occasionally, indoor air pollution in lodging properties may be caused by the presence of dangerous substances such as chemical cleaning compounds. These environmental hazards are altering the earth where we live and the air that we breathe, threatening our own health and safety and those of thousands of other living species. Most scientists today believe that humans must adopt strategies to begin recovering the sustainability of planet earth.

This state of affairs has created widespread public concern for environmental quality. Many people feel that the country needs tougher environmental regulation and that more money should be spent on environmental protection. Specific to our industry, more people are willing than ever before to patronize establishments that care about the environment. As a result, many lodging companies are gaining an edge by implementing "green" procedures. This new approach requires increased awareness and knowledge of environmental issues on the part of managers, as well as the development of managerial skills and strategies to convert operational procedures to environmentally friendly ones. The housekeeping and engineering departments can implement programs to recycle materials, dispose of hazardous waste, and minimize in-door air pollution.

RECYCLING

Some experts suggest that recycling could reduce the amount of solid waste going to landfills by 70 percent. Japan has one of the most comprehensive waste management and recycling programs. Japanese citizens recycle about 40 percent of the country's total solid waste, including 50 percent of all paper and 50 percent of glass bottles. In the United States, to address the solid waste problem, the **Environmental Protection Agency (EPA)** has identified some possible solutions, such as reducing waste before it is originated and recycling byproducts as raw materials for making other products. Specifically, property operations managers can minimize the cost associated with hauling garbage to a landfill by strategically placing labeled bins around the property for the disposal of reusable products. This should include guest areas, as many travelers appreciate the idea of recycling waste even when they are away from home. Common solid byproducts that can be recycled are:

aluminum cans

tin cans

glass bottles and jars

newspapers

plastic

grass clippings, leaves, and twigs

Those that are considered nonrecyclable include mirror glass, crystal, light bulbs, and polyethylene plastics. One of the most difficult problems with recycling is the disposal of plastic packaging. Because they are not biodegradable, plastics will stay in landfills for centuries. Some companies have made a switch from plastic to other paper-based products, for example getting rid of take-home or to-carry styrofoam containers.

Paper bales, Marriott recycling
Courtesy of Marriott International, Inc.

There are some potential savings from recycling. Corrugated cardboard, for instance, can be sold for over $100 a ton. Local recycling companies will also pay for newspapers and aluminum cans. Savings can also be realized for every ton deferred from landfills as some close and as tipping fees rise for transporting the waste to out-of-state dumps.

In addition, executive housekeepers can cut the costs of cleaning supplies used to maintain the facilities by using **source-reduced products**. Source reduction can be defined as pre-cycling, as it prevents waste from occurring before it starts. Source reduction involves considering the final destiny of products when making decisions on what to buy: for instance, products that are designed to last longer, and that require efficient dispensing methods and less packaging. For example, the use of drinking glasses made of glass instead of plastic in guestrooms can reduce waste substantially. The bottom line is to purchase products that minimize waste.

HAZARDOUS WASTE DISPOSAL

Americans throw away over four million tons of hazardous waste per year, part of this discarded by lodging establishments. Prolonged exposure of humans to toxic substances can increase the

risk for diseases such as cancer and severe respiratory illnesses and, in some cases, death. Products labeled as toxic, poisonous, corrosive, or dangerous should be stored carefully and disposed of safely. Toxic products should not be poured into sanitary or storm drains because they can contaminate the water. If placed out with the regular trash, they contaminate the atmosphere if they are disposed of in incinerators. Particularly noxious when burned are synthetic foams and some solvents and cleaning agents whose atoms destroy the ozone layer when they reach the stratosphere. For this reason, haz-

Ecolab Oasis green cleaning products
Courtesy of Ecolab USA Inc.

ardous products should be disposed of following manufacturer instructions. Some noxious products commonly found in housekeeping and engineering departments are paint and paint strippers, drain cleaners, wood finishes, and antifreeze and motor oil discarded by guests in general trash containers.

Property operations managers should follow some basic steps to implement a source-reduction program, such as analyzing the purchasing of supplies that are recyclable and that minimize waste while maintaining high performance, controlling product usage where possible, and buying concentrated supplies, which usually go farther and cost less than prepared products. Executive housekeepers should also remember that basic cleaning jobs can be performed with green cleaners such as vinegar, vegetable oil-based soaps, borax, and baking soda. Although they may not be convenient as using ready-made cleaning products, they are safer, less expensive, and do not have a negative impact on the environment. Companies such as Ecolab offer cleaning products labeled as biodegradable or green. Pump dispensers with hand triggers are much safer than some aerosols, whose gas propellants, released into the air every time the product is used, affect the ozone layer. The engineering department should have a program in place to dispose of hazardous waste such as paint, solvents and oils, acid wastes, pesticides used on bushes and trees, and any substances with high levels of mercury, lead, or arsenic.

INDOOR AIR QUALITY CONTROL

Indoor air pollution can have negative health effects on guests and employees. Lodging properties built as tightly sealed buildings, if polluted, can cause workers and guests to suffer headaches, dizziness, allergies, and other problems associated with poor air quality. Indoor air pollution may be caused by the presence of dangerous substances, such as chemical cleaning compounds. The problem is accentuated if polluted indoor air is recirculated. Chemical analyses of air from "sick buildings" frequently show compounds known to be human irritants. In most cases, toxic levels are low and difficult to detect, but when several pollutants are present at the same time, even at below-toxicity levels, they can cause symptoms of irritation and discomfort in humans.

Some of the chemicals used in the housekeeping department may be air pollutants, for example, products containing formaldehyde, which is used as wood, linen, and carpet treatment, some cleaning products, and most pesticides and drain openers. Microbial contamination can also result in a potentially serious health condition known as hypersensitivity pneumonitis. The contamination may be caused by bacteria or mold present in damp carpets, furnishings, and ventilation systems, or simply by allergenic microorganisms such as mites suspended in dust. The most effective way to improve air quality is to control the sources of pollution by not using toxic chemicals in the building and by increasing ventilation and cleaning. Housekeeping departments should have a policy in place to open windows whenever possible to circulate in fresh air from outdoors, although this may not always be practical, particularly if the air-conditioning or heating system is in operation at the time. Regular vacuuming of carpets and furnishings can also be effective, as dust mites thrive in areas where moisture and skin scales are deposited, such as carpets and sofas. Faulty vacuum bags, however, can spread more allergens than they remove. To prevent air contamination when vacuuming, **high-retention vacuum cleaners**, which hold particles larger than 0.1 microns should be used.

GREEN LODGING FACILITIES

Hotel companies are recognizing the fact that environmentally helpful improvements in their establishments may lead to economic benefits and competitive opportunities. By implementing programs aimed at minimizing waste and reducing energy consumption, they lower operating costs and help the environment. By advertising to guests the actions taken, they can gain customer loyalty and enhance their public image. The housekeeping department can help regain the sustainability of the planet by implementing recycling programs for employees and guests by reusing as many items as possible. Some ways to do this are making cleaning rags out of worn towels, giving partially used soaps to local charities, and using ceramic mugs rather than foam cups; purchasing recyclable and biodegradable products; and composting yard debris, such as twigs, dry leaves, and grass clippings.

Some lodging companies have introduced the concept of environmentally friendly rooms, often called **green rooms**, that appeal to the over 40 million "green travelers" or environment-conscious guests the industry claims exist. These eco-friendly properties stock rooms with amenities packaged in recycled containers that are themselves recyclable, with recycled paper supplies, and with soaps that are biodegradable, that is, made from vegetable fats and oils without chemical additives. Some hotel chains, focusing on targeting travelers with respiratory ailments, have gone as far as installing special filters in the air-intake ducts in guestrooms and filtering the water in the sink and shower. The extra fee charged to guests for these niceties is gladly paid by travelers sensitive to indoor-air quality.

Green prototype, Marriott Courtyard Hotel
Courtesy of Marriott International, Inc.

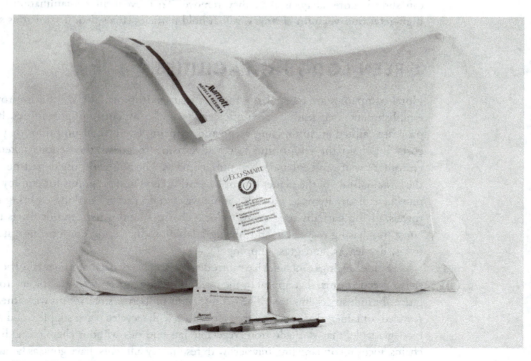

Green Eco-Smart amenities, Marriott
Courtesy of Marriott International, Inc.

Another way to minimize the generation of waste and save energy is to place desktop signs in guestrooms asking travelers to request changing sheets and pillow cases if they are staying over, and giving them the option of reusing the bathroom towels. This drastically reduces the poundage of linen to be laundered, with the consequent reduction in water, energy, and chemical product usage and cost. The American Hotel/Motel Association provides on request laminated notices endorsed by the U.S. Environmental Protection Agency for use in lodging establishments to inform guests of this save-the-environment program. Besides helping the environment, lodging properties can save around $5 per occupied room per day when they give their guests these choices. In addition, a survey conducted by the international consulting firm Deloitte Touche shows that about 34 percent of travelers seek out hotels that are environmentally friendly and 28 percent of those surveyed said they would pay an extra fee to stay in a green lodging facility.

Marriott International has been in the forefront at innovation, implementing recycling and energy-saving programs in 90 percent of its properties. One hotel in particular, the Edinburgh Marriott hotel, has replaced its incandescent light bulbs in all guestrooms with low-energy ones and provides green meeting rooms where paper, pens, and flipcharts are made from recycled material. Other Marriott-branded hotels in the United Kingdom have successfully reduced carbon emissions and greenhouse gases by 7.3 percent to earn carbon trust standard certification, a government program launched in response to the U.K.'s Climate Change Act.

Marriott's strategy to reduce its carbon footprint 25 percent by 2017 includes using solar power in up to 40 properties and working with its top suppliers to buy greener products across its $10-billion supply chain. The company, since the inception of its energy-conservation program, has installed 400,000 low-flow shower heads and toilets worldwide. To date, 24 Marriott Golf managed hotels in North America have become Certified Audubon Cooperative Sanctuaries, and the company is planning to expand the program to 17 of its international golf properties. The Audubon certification verifies that golf facilities protect the environment by enhancing natural areas and wildlife habitats.

GREEN LODGING CERTIFICATION

Lodging companies that adopt a significant program aimed at protecting the environment can obtain certification from organizations which will endorse their properties' efforts towards the preservation of the planet's ecosystem. **Green Seal** is a nonprofit, third-party certifier and standards development entity in the United States providing independent, objective, science-based guidance to the marketplace and to consumers. It is an ecolabelling organization that meets the Environmental Protection Agency's (EPA) criteria for third-party certifiers. A Green Seal certification mark on a lodging property means that the establishment has gone through a stringent process to show that it has reduced its impact on the environment and human health. The organization provides technical assistance and recognition to organizations that wish to green their facility management practices. Green-Seal-certified hotels and resorts can be found in most states and the District of Columbia.

Green Lodging Programs have been developed by states to provide travelers a green option for their lodging needs. For example, the California Green Lodging Program is currently being operated by the Department of General Services as a part of the state travel program. The program's goals include diverting waste from landfills, conserving energy and water, and improving indoor environmental quality. California state employees are encouraged to explore green lodging options when on state business on the premise that travelling green has many benefits, including reducing carbon footprints and saving limited resources. Some of the reasons given why green lodging properties should be patronized are:

- Average-size hotels purchase more products in one week than 100 families do in a year. The program's goal is to encourage properties to procure at least 50 percent environmentally preferable products.
- Waste generation can be as high as 30 pounds per room per day. The goal is to recycle as much as 80 percent of these materials.
- The hospitality industry spends 3.7 billion a year on energy. Electricity use accounts for 60–70 percent of the utility costs of a typical hotel. The goal is to introduce companies to energy-efficient products and practices that will reduce energy consumption and lower energy costs.
- Two percent of California's food waste comes from the hotel and lodging industry (112,000 tons per year). The goal is to divert a large percentage of this waste to charities in need or to compost.
- A typical hotel uses 218 gallons of water per day per occupied room. The goal is to use water-efficient fixtures to reduce water and sewer use by 25 percent.

Energy Star is a joint program of the US Environmental Protection Agency and the U.S. Department of Energy helping lower energy costs and protect the environment through energy-efficient products and practices. Energy Star offers energy-management strategies that help measure energy performance, set goals and financially reward improvements. EPA also recognizes top-performing buildings with certification providing them with the Energy Star logo to be displayed.

The **U.S. Green Building Council (USGBC)** is a nonprofit community of leaders working to make green buildings available throughout the United States. Its **Leadership in Energy and Environmental Design (LEED)** certification provides independent third-party verification that a building project meets the highest green building and performance standards. The program emphasizes that sustainable building strategies should be considered early in the development cycle, beginning with an initial LEED assessment to bring the project team together to evaluate and articulate its goals and define the certification level sought. The environmental and financial benefits to earn LEED certification are:

- Lower operating costs and increased asset value
- Reduced waste sent to landfills
- Conservation of energy and water
- Healthier and safer environment for occupants
- Reduced harmful greenhouse emissions
- Qualification for tax rebates, zoning allowances, and other incentives offered by cities
- Demonstration of an owner's commitment to environmental stewardship and social responsibility.

Green Globe provides services and certification after verification by independent auditors, who assess the sustainability performance of travel and tourism businesses and their supply chain partners. The Green Globe standards are a collection of 337 compliance indicators applied to 41 sustainability criteria. The Green Globe standard is reviewed and updated twice per calendar year.

Companies across the U.S. like Doubletree Hotels and Resorts are aligning their business practices to meet the standards of their respective state Green Lodging programs, Green Seal, Energy Star, and Green Global certification.

SUSTAINABILITY

Sustainability has become the test for long-term maintenance of well-being in terms of environmental survival. The answer to the test will depend on the decisions society makes, since the total environmental impact ultimately depends on how resources are being used. There have been positive reactions from all sides, with many entities, governmental, public, and private, tackling this impending global crisis. Most of the initiatives are focused on **stewardships of place**, some dedicated to minimizing or eliminating greenhouse gas emissions by reaching carbon neutrality, and others by greening their businesses with the dual purpose of helping the earth's ecosystems and growing their environmentally conscious customer base.

The population of the world has reached the seven billion mark and in the coming decades will continue to grow, particularly in underdeveloped countries. Today, wealthy nations use many times more resources per capita than poorer countries, but as global income rises, increased consumption worldwide will stress the planet more than population growth. Data indicate that humans are not living within the carrying capacity of the planet; on the contrary, human activity on earth is having a significant, escalating impact on the biodiversity of world ecosystems, reducing its biocapacity. In other words, the underlying driver of direct human impact on the environment is human consumption. It seems that the challenge of sustainability is to curb and manage consumption in the Western world while raising the standard of living of the developing world without increasing its resource use and environmental impact. Hospitality administrators can contribute greatly to this.

KEY TERMS

Carbon dioxide

Chlorofluorocarbons

Energy Star

Environmental Protection Agency (EPA)

Green Globe

Green Lodging Program (state)

Green room

Green Seal

High-retention vacuum cleaner

Leadership in Energy and Environmental Design (LEED)

Ozone layer

Source-reduced product

Sustainability

Stewardship of place

U.S. Green Building Council (USGBC)

DISCUSSION AND REVIEW QUESTIONS

1. Describe two ways to address the nation's solid waste problem as identified by the Environmental Protection Agency (EPA).
2. Explain the advantages of using source-reduced products regarding product waste.
3. Why shouldn't toxic products such as paint thinners be discarded with the general garbage generated in the housekeeping department?
4. What do you understand green lodging facilities to be?
5. Which chemicals, commonly used in housekeeping departments, may be potential air pollutants?
6. What are the major problems challenging the sustainability of the planet?
7. Which are three initiatives to preserve the environment that lodging properties can take?
8. Give one environmental and one financial reason why hotels and resort should obtain green certification.
9. What do you understand by stewardship of place?
10. How could a lodging property contribute to reaching carbon neutrality?

MINICASES

SITUATION 1

You have been hired by a large lodging property in downtown Phoenix, Arizona, as assistant to the general manager. The company has decided to market the hotel as an eco-friendly property and you have been asked to prepare a draft detailing the initiatives you recommend for this purpose. Do so, including actions to be taken by both the housekeeping and engineering departments.

SITUATION 2

Lilly Sachse is the general manager of a successful resort in North Carolina. As operator, she has managed to control costs and maintain a healthy bottom line for the last five years. Her continued excellent performance has resulted in substantial annual bonuses. Last month, Lilly had a meeting with a group of concerned local citizens about the fertilizer that the resort was using on the 18-hole golf course located near the city's water reservoir. According to the group, the fertilizer used contained a strong component that could contaminate the reservoir if the chemicals reached the underground water table. They suggested that the resort use a biodegradable product containing no noxious chemicals.

After consultation with the company's lawyer, Lilly found out that there are no federal or state regulations compelling golf courses to use biodegradable fertilizers. Contamination test results for the potable water supply were negative. Nevertheless, Lilly wanted to comply with the request made by the concerned citizens and she asked the resort's purchasing agent to inquire about buying an environmentally friendly product. She was notified that the fertilizer would cost twice as much as the non-biodegradable chemical.

Fearing that her annual bonus would be substantially smaller because she increased the cost of next year's budget and reduced the overall income of the resort, Lilly decides to keep using the current fertilizer.

Was Ms. Sachse's decision illegal? Was it unethical? How would you have acted? Why?

SITUATION 3

Write a précis combining the following topics:

1. What is sustainability and what has motivated society to pay attention to it?
2. What do you think has led companies to integrate sustainability into their business strategies?
3. What can companies do in order to build sustainable business strategies?

Active listening A communication technique that requires the listener to understand and interpret well what a speaker says.

Adjusted daily schedule A modification of the standing work schedule based on the property's daily occupancy.

Alkalis Chemicals used in commercial laundries to neutralize acids in the washing solution.

All-purpose cleaner A liquid cleaner of neutral pH-balanced formula.

Amenities Nonreusable guest supplies.

A.M. guestroom check An inspection of guestrooms conducted as early as possible in the morning by the housekeeping department to ascertain whether the information provided in the night clerk's report was accurate.

Amperage The strength of an electric current measured in amperes.

Ampere A unit of current strength.

Antichlors Chemicals added to rinses to ensure that chlorine bleach is totally removed from the washed fabrics.

Application form Written or digital form filled out by prospective employees.

Aptitude test A measurement of the applicant's hand dexterity, such as how to operate machinery, or clerical aptitude, such as the ability to operate a computer.

Art Deco A design style in which earth colors are usually used.

Authoritarian leadership style A type of management in which the manager dictates the tasks to be performed.

Average daily rate (ADR) The average rate obtained from the selling of rooms during a certain period of time.

Average hourly wage The wage per hour paid to workers on average.

Backing (carpet) Material to which the carpet pile is secured.

Back vacuum Vacuum cleaners with adjustable straps used for cleaning vertical or high surfaces.

Bacteria Simple group of non-green vegetable organisms that are involved in the fermentation and putrefaction of matter and the causing of disease such as salmonella and cholera.

Bathroom linen Bath towels, hand towels, washcloths, and bathmats.

Bed-and-breakfast Establishments, usually small, that cater to travelers seeking a homey, personal environment.

Bed linen Washable items used to make the bed, mainly sheets and pillowcases.

Bed structure The total number of beds of a lodging property.

Bleach A chemical that is very effective in killing bacteria, whitening linens, and removing stains.

Breaks Heavy-duty alkaline compounds designed to break soil in the soak cycle.

BTU (British thermal unit) A unit used to describe the heat value of fuels.

Building ventilation The fresh air forced into buildings to ventilate spaces.

Burnisher A machine used to burnish nonresilient floors such as terrazzo or tile.

Caddy Plastic basket used by room attendants to carry guest amenities and cleaning supplies.

Capital expenditure budget Budget used to record the fixed assets needed for the upcoming fiscal year.

Carbon dioxide (CO_2) A gas generated as a byproduct of combustion emitted by industrial plants powered by coal and from vehicles propelled by fossil fuels.

Career ladder Program to promote people from within the company.

Case furniture Wood pieces such as chests of drawers, credenzas, and armoires.

Casinos Establishments, generally first class, that provide elaborate facilities for gambling.

Chemical dispenser A mixing station for liquid cleaning chemicals.

Child assistance A program to help workers with child care such as nurseries in the workplace.

Chlorofluorocarbon A chemical compound used in propellants, refrigerants, and solvents.

Circulating pump A pump used in heating systems to return water to the boiler.

Classical scientific management Management theory proposed by Frederick Taylor for improving efficiency and productivity in the workplace.

Cleaning supplies Items used for cleaning purposes that are part of the operating budget, such as window cleaners and floor waxes.

Coercive power A manager's administration of punishment to modify a worker's behavior.

Compensation ratio A method of paying employees based on their work output.

Competitive shopping form A record kept of price, service, and quality of cleaning supplies from at least two different vendors.

Complementary colors A combination of two hues to optimize the appearance of walls, floors, and fixtures in guestrooms.

Compressor A machine used in refrigeration systems to condense gas with water or air at prevailing temperatures.

Condenser An apparatus used in refrigeration systems where heat is released, causing the refrigerant to turn into a chilled liquid state.

Consolidated room sales summary A projection of revenues for the 12 months of the upcoming year based on the forecasted percentage of occupancy and average daily rate.

Cost of labor The expense of labor determined by multiplying the number of hours worked by the average hourly wage.

Cost per occupied room A determinant of expenses per room sold obtained by dividing each budget expense category by the number of rooms sold.

Cost per use The cost of using a linen item after considering its durability, laundry costs, and purchase price.

Counseling session A face-to-face meeting between a supervisor and an employee at which problems on the job are discussed.

Crib A child's bed with enclosed sides.

Critical incident A method focusing on the observation of good or bad performance of employees to be discussed at the time of periodical evaluations.

Cross-contamination The spread of bacteria from one medium to another via a contaminated cleaning rag or floor mop or hands.

Cruise ships Vessels that provide luxury lodging services and amenities.

Damask A twill-woven fabric blend with a glossy, silky appearance.

Danger zone Temperature range, typically between 40 and 140°F in which bacteria can multiply rapidly.

Deep cleaning Periodic in-depth cleaning of an area (usually guestroom).

Deficiency of execution Situation in which the employee knows how to do the task but decides not to perform it correctly.

Deficiency of knowledge Situation in which the employee doesn't know how to do the job correctly.

Democratic leadership style A type of management in which the manager seeks to reach consensus after group discussion.

Departmental income The result of subtracting the total of a department's expenses from the departmental revenue.

Department equipment Heavier, mobile equipment used in the housekeeping department for cleaning or transportation purposes such as vacuum cleaners. These items are categorized as fixed assets.

Department head An employee in charge of a department in lodging properties. The position of executive housekeeper is that of department head.

Detergent A chemical substance used as cleaner.

Developing countries A term generally used to describe nations with low levels of material well-being.

Disinfection The process of cleansing from infection by destroying pathogenic microorganisms.

Dual-purpose sleeping equipment A piece of furniture that provides both seating space and sleeping capacity.

Dust ruffle Cloth skirting placed between the mattress and the box spring that extends around the sides of beds.

Economy property A budget property providing the basic needs of the traveling public.

Electricity breaker An automatically operated electrical switch designed to cut off electricity to protect a circuit from damage caused by overload or short circuit.

Electric discharge lamp A type of electric light bulb filled with a gas that glows when heated by a current.

Electric grid A network for electricity distribution.

Elton Mayo An Australian psychologist and industrial researcher who proposed the human relations movement theory.

Employee assistance A program aimed at retaining workers who are substance abusers.

Employee attitude Training of employees to create awareness of the relationship between the worker and the guest.

Employee handbook A list of rules and regulations about the property given to workers at the time of hiring.

Employee qualifications Minimum conditions required to ensure that applicants will be capable of doing the job for which they are applying.

Employee requisition A request forwarded to the human resources department for hiring employees.

Employee security needs Maslow's premise that motivation is impossible if workers' basic needs are not met.

Employment checklist Document to ensure that no part of the new worker's induction process has been overlooked.

Emulation Effort to equal or excel the behavior of a superior.

Energy Star A joint program of the EPA and the U.S. Department of Energy to help lower energy costs and protect the environment.

Environmental Protection Agency (EPA) An agency of the federal government charged with protecting human health and the environment.

Equipment layout The optimum placement of equipment in laundries to avoid cross traffic.

Evaporator In refrigeration systems, a coil where the chilled refrigerant absorbs heat from the space to be cooled.

Evening team Workers scheduled to work in the housekeeping department after the end of the morning shift (usually between 3 and 11 P.M.).

Executive committee The directors of divisions who, in large lodging properties, are involved in operational policy-making decisions.

Executive housekeeper Person in charge of managing the housekeeping department. In large lodging properties, the executive housekeeper reports to the rooms division director or resident manager. In smaller establishments, he/she reports directly to the general manager.

Exit interview A technique used to find out why employees leave the company.

External recruiting The advertising of open positions outside the property, such as by newspaper ads.

Extract cycle Washing sequence in which the moisture is spun out from the load.

Extractors (carpet) A machine used to clean carpets.

Face weight In carpets, the number of ounces of yarn per square yard.

Fan coil A coil is a pipe through which hot or cold water or steam flow. The fan is used to propel air across the coil to generate hot or cold air.

FF&E (Furniture, Fixtures & Equipment) Items with a five- to seven-year life span that are used in guestrooms, public and employee areas, such as tables and TV sets.

Fixed assets Items with a long-term life span that can be depreciated, such as mattresses and chairs.

Fixed team Hourly workers, such as cleaning areas attendants, scheduled regardless of the occupancy of the property.

Flexible work hours A scheduling system that allows employees to begin and end their shifts at times convenient to them.

Flocking The process of embedding the pile fibers into a layer of adhesive material applied to the backing of carpets.

Floor finish A chemical applied to floors to make them slip resistant and give them a glossy, shiny look.

Floor sealer A chemical compound used to protect floors from wear and tear and liquid spills.

Flow-reducing aerator A device placed at the tip of water faucets to help reduce water usage.

Flush cycle Washing sequence to soak the linen and dissolve the soils.

Folder stand A stand allowing one worker (rather than two) to fold items.

Folding table A surface used to fold terrycloth items.

Four-day work week Scheduling of workers 10 hours per day, 4 days a week rather than 8 hours per day, 5 days a week.

Franchised property An establishment that contracts the right to conduct business displaying the logo of a particular chain while adhering to the company's requirements regarding service and amenities provided to guests.

Frederick Taylor A U.S. economist and educator who proposed the theory of scientific management.

Front office Generally, the department managing operations of the front desk, reservations, and bell services.

Full-time worker An employee regularly scheduled to work more than 30 hours per week.

Fungi Group of microorganisms characterized by absence of chlorophyll, such as mold and mildew.

Fuse A metal wire or strip that melts when excessive current flows through a cable.

Ghost flushing A periodic partial flushing of a toilet bowl caused by a defective stopper.

Green Globe An organization providing sustainability services and certification.

Green lodging programs Plans developed by states to give travelers a green option for their lodging needs.

Green room A guestroom stocked with eco-friendly amenities such as biodegradable soaps and recycled paper supplies.

Green Seal A nonprofit organization and third-party certifier providing independent guidance to properties that wish to green their facility management practices.

Ground warp The main body of bath linen such as towels.

Guestroom cleaning team A number of room attendants (usually four to six), a houseperson, and a supervisor in charge of cleaning and servicing a predetermined number of guestrooms.

Guestroom inspection form A check list used to inspect rooms by team supervisors or inspectors.

Guestroom team cleaning A technique of pairing two section housekeepers for cleaning guestrooms (rather than just one room attendant per section).

Guest supplies Amenities provided to guests that are part of the operating budget, such as shampoo and coat hangers.

Halo effect Appearance and smooth talk of job seekers that sway interviewers in their decisions to hire.

Hamper A large basket used to transport linens to and from washers and dryers.

HazComm OSHA's regulation to ensure that the hazards of all chemicals produced in the U.S. or imported are evaluated, and that information concerning their dangers is made known to employers and employees.

Heat pump   A heating or air-conditioning unit powered by electricity used in decentralized HVAC systems.

Heat radiator   A heating device consisting of a coil of pipes through which steam or hot water passes.

Heat transfer   The flow of heat from a warm to a cool environment.

Heat transmission   The loss of heat through walls or window panes.

Henri Fayol   A French engineer who developed a theory of business administration in which a manager must practice the functions of planning, organizing, directing, coordinating, and controlling.

High-retention vacuum cleaner   A machine that can hold dust particles larger than 0.1 microns.

Hopper   A light truck to transport trash or soiled linen.

Hospitality industry   Companies providing services to guests such as lodging, restaurants, event planning, theme parks, cruise lines, and other segments related to or associated with tourism.

Hotel   A facility offering lodging, food, and amenities to travelers.

Housekeeping department   A lodging establishment's department providing operational services and upkeep of guestrooms, laundry, and other public and back-of-the-house areas.

Housekeeping teams   The different teams included in the housekeeping department's staffing matrix.

Houseperson   A worker in housekeeping teams in charge of helping section housekeepers with general tasks.

Human relations management   A theory based on the premise that management must be concerned with the social and psychological aspects of the relationship between the company and its employees.

Hydroelectric plant   A complex for the generation of electric energy derived from water falling on rotating turbines.

Incentive program   Technique intended to provide employees with such rewards as bonuses, recognition, and appreciation for the good work they perform.

Independently owned property   Lodging establishments that are usually managed by their owners.

Infiltration   The flow of warm or cold air into buildings through openings such as open windows or doors.

Infrared sensor   Automatic flush devices used in public urinals, toilets, and hand-washing sinks.

Inn   A small-size establishment that provides lodging and, usually, food and drink to travelers. They are typically located in the countryside or along highways.

Innersprings   Metal coils in mattresses that support the weight of the sleeper.

Institutional lodging   Housing facilities that are integral parts of institutional organizations, such as retirement homes, universities, or hospitals.

Intelligence test   A questioning of prospective workers to measure intellectual skills.

Interest test   A questioning of prospective employees to measure the applicant's relative interest in a certain kind of work.

Internal heat-generating sources   Areas producing heat such as kitchens and laundries.

Internal recruiting   The advertising of open positions inside the property.

Job description   A detailed statement of the tasks required to have the job done.

Job safety analysis   The identification of possible hazards in the workplace

Job sharing   A scheduling technique that allows two or more employees to accomplish a job regardless of who does it at any particular time.

Jute   A fabric used to build the baking of carpets.

Key-control system   Program in place to control for the prevention of loss of keys.

Kilowatt   A measure of electricity consumption consisting of 1,000 watts.

Knowledge of the property   Training of hired workers on the layout of the property and on the services offered at the property.

Large-area vacuum   Oversize vacuum cleaner used in hallways and lobbies with extensive areas of carpeting.

Laissez-faire management style   A type of management in which subordinates have complete freedom to make group or individual decisions.

Laundry manager   An employee in charge of laundry operations who reports directly to the executive housekeeper.

Laundry supplies   The products used in laundry operations such as breaks and antichlors.

Laundry team   Workers scheduled to work in the laundry room.

Leadership in Energy and Environmental Design (LEED)   An organization providing independent third-party certification that a building project meets the highest green building standards.

Linen chute   A conduit in high-rise properties used to send soiled linen directly to the laundry room.

Linen poundage   Weight of all items that need to be processed at 100 percent occupancy.

Linen replacement   An amount budgeted for replacing discarded or stolen linens in laundry operations.

Linen room   A location where clean linens are stored and issued.

Linens   Washable items that are processed, in most cases, each time that they are used.

Long-range objectives   Goals planned to be achieved over a long timeframe, such as refurbishing a hotel within the next three years.

Luxury property An establishment offering world-class service that is committed to the ultimate in hospitality.

Maintenance checklist A form or computer program used to conduct maintenance inspections.

Management company An organization that manages lodging properties in exchange for either receiving a basic fee or retaining an agreed-upon percentage of the revenue or income.

Management team In housekeeping, salaried employees who manage the housekeeping department, including the laundry room.

Mangle Machine used in commercial laundries to press linen.

Man-hours A phrase used when planning hourly workers' hours needed to perform a specific task, such as cleaning guestrooms or determining the number of hours used to accomplish a specific task.

Master inventory list A control summary indicating the existing inventory of all linen items.

Maximum quantity The greatest number of units that should be in stock at any given time.

Mid-market property A lodging property category between those of economy and luxury committed to providing excellent services to guests. Four-star and four-diamond establishments are classified as mid-market properties.

Minimum quantity The lowest number of units that should be in stock at any given time.

Mobile bed A bed on wheels, usually called a rollaway.

Mobile rack A stainless steel rack on wheels used to transport clean linen.

Momie cloth An inexpensive material used in napery.

MSDS (material safety data sheet) Information about a chemical provided by the manufacturer when the product is purchased.

Motel Lodging properties located for easy access by motorized vehicles that offer lower prices than those charged by hotels.

Multi-unit chain Chain units operating under the direct control of the company's headquarters.

Murphy bed In-wall bed commonly used in parlor rooms.

Muslin Bed linen fabrics made with carded fabrics.

Napery Table linen: tablecloths and napkins.

Needle punching The process of making carpets by compacting the fibers and the backing.

Neutralizer rinse Chemical used to neutralize the alkaline residue prior to applying a new finish to floors.

Night clerk's room report A report prepared by the front desk at the end of the day's activity indicating the status of all the rooms in the house. This report is sent to housekeeping first thing in the morning.

Nonreusable items Guest supplies that cannot be reused a second time by the hotel, such as soap bars.

Off-peak hours Time of the day (usually in the middle of the night) when the cost of electricity is lowest.

On-call employees Workers who are asked to report to work when extra help is needed.

On-premise laundry Laundry service owned and operated by a lodging property.

On-the-job training Method in which new employees are assigned to watch how the work should be performed before they take over their assignments.

Operating assets Items under the control of the executive housekeeper that are generally used in the day-to-day operations of the department.

Operating budget A budget categorizing items that have a direct relationship to the day-to-day revenue resulting from the sale of guestrooms.

Orientation A sequence of the induction process to acquaint the new employee and the organization with one another.

Other expenses In operating budgets, other expenses include categories other than salaries and wages, such as cleaning and guest supplies.

Outside services Services contracted out to an outside company to be performed at a property, such as area carpet cleaning.

Ozone layer A protective blanket that shields life on earth from lethal ultraviolet radiation from the sun.

Padding Cushion on which the carpet rests.

Panic emotion Uncontrolled anxious behavior caused by threats to individuals such as hotel fires.

Par The optimum number of on-hand items needed for effective operation of a department.

Parcel-pass system A program in which employees leaving the property must show security officers a signed authorization to remove any items from their place of work.

Participative management Practice aimed at creating worker satisfaction by letting employees see themselves as part of the decision-making process.

Part-time worker An employee who is scheduled to work 30 hours or less per week.

Pathogenic germs Disease-causing microorganisms.

Payroll taxes and benefits The operator's share of additional costs related to payroll.

Pay scale A method of compensation that starts with a probationary rate of pay and goes up in accordance with time on the job.

Percale Fabric manufactured with combed fibers.

Perpetual inventory System to keep tight control of valuable items, for example chocolates and perfume, in which items are recorded every time a transaction occurs.

Personal development An effort on the part of the company to provide workers with opportunities to improve their personal potential and the abilities to make changes in their own lives.

Persuasion power A manager's trait of advising (rather than forcing) a worker to do something.

pH scale In chemistry, a measure of the acidity and basicity of a solution.

Physiological needs Basic needs for survival such as food and shelter.

Pile (carpet) The face of a carpet.

Pile warp In bath linens, the yarn making loops on both sides of the material.

Plain weave Textiles made by interlacing the vertical thread with the horizontal yarn.

P.M. guestroom check A physical inspection of all the guestrooms in the house, conducted at the end of the morning shift. A report is generated from this inspection and sent to the front desk for room-status verification between the two departments.

Polisher A heavily weighted machine used to polish marble and other stone floors.

Polycotton A fabric blend of polyester and cotton.

Polyester A synthetic fabric commonly used in blankets.

Polypropylene A synthetic fabric commonly used in carpets.

Prenatal care assistance Help provided to female workers to assist them during pregnancy, such as providing sufficient time for visits to the doctor.

Pre-opening budget Budget that includes the costs of the initial allocation of material and supplies needed to open the property to the public.

Prescreening interview Interview conducted by the human resources department to screen out those applicants who don't meet the criteria for the job advertised.

Preventive maintenance The inspection of guestrooms and other areas on a regular basis to identify repair and maintenance needs before major breakdowns occur.

Premeasured chemicals Ready-to-use chemicals.

Printing and stationery supplies Costs budgeted to cover expenses of guest folios, forms, and other clerical supplies.

Probationary basis Period allowed for first-time employees to learn and perform their jobs efficiently.

Psychological barrier A communication obstacle that occurs when one of the communicators has a preconceived negative perception of the other.

Public areas attendant Cleaner of public areas (formerly known as a janitor).

Purchase order A document stating specifications of a product to be delivered and the conditions involving payment.

Purchasing agent A specialized buyer in charge of procuring products for all departments of large lodging properties.

Quality circles A management technique in which worker involvement in the decision-making process is sought.

Rating scale Tool for employee appraisals consisting of a series of descriptors to which a numerical score is given determining the effectiveness of workers.

Regular maintenance Repairs performed when items break or malfunction.

Relief team In housekeeping, a team that replaces a regular team on days off.

Requisition form A form filled out by departments to request products from the property's main storeroom.

Resort A lodging property near a natural attraction, sporting locations, or in places with balmy, tropical weather.

Retention bonus Extra compensation given to those employees who stay with the company.

Reusable guest supplies Items that can be reused by guests without having to be replaced, such as ashtrays and wastebaskets.

Revenue-generating center A lodging property unit providing services that generate revenue, such as the rooms division.

Reward power A manager's administration of recompense to modify a worker's behavior.

Rinse cycle Washing sequence in which chemicals are removed from the linen.

Room rack A traditional display of the room status of guestrooms at the front desk. Today, the status is provided by computer programs.

Rooms division An operational unit that usually is comprised of the housekeeping and the front office departments.

Rooms division director The person in charge of managing the rooms division of lodging properties. The rooms division director is sometimes referred to as resident manager.

Rooms division operating budget Budget that includes both the front office and the housekeeping departments.

Rooms revenue Amount obtained from selling rooms in lodging operations. The figure is arrived at by multiplying rooms sold by the average daily rate.

Rooms sold The number of rooms sold or projected to be sold for a certain period of time.

Rotational schedule Schedule that rotates forward the team's days off by one day each week.

Safety committee Group of employees organized for the purpose of identifying hazards and investigating accidents in the workplace after they occur.

Safety-training program A plan designed to instruct employees in safe work practices.

Salaries and wages Operating budget allocation for amounts paid to salaried and hourly employees.

Sanforized fabric Linens that have been preshrunk at the source.

Sanitation The practical application of sanitary procedures to prevent the spread of disease.

Scrubber A machine used to scrub hard resilient surfaces.

Sealer A chemical agent used to protect porous surfaces.

Second request A second work order sent to engineering when this department has not promptly addressed the repair need.

Seconds Linen items that have minor imperfections.

Section housekeeper A housekeeping worker in charge of cleaning a section of guestrooms.

Section housekeeper need table A scheduling document showing the number of room attendants that need to be called to work based on occupancy.

Section housekeeper work report A form stating the status of the rooms of each section at the beginning of the shift.

Self-contained extractor A floor cleaner that doesn't require a wand or hoses.

Self-esteem needs Psychological need for recognition and sense of accomplishment.

Selvage The flat narrow side edges of bath linen items with no pile warp.

Shopping form A form that includes products' assigned values for price, quality, and service, used prior to bidding orders.

Short-range objectives Goals planned to be achieved in a short time frame, such as improving worker productivity in the next three months.

Single-purpose cleaner A heavy-duty cleaner used for specific tough cleaning jobs.

Soak sinks Containers for pre-washing treatment of linens for spot and stain removal.

Social needs Maslow's theory in which workers must feel a sense of being accepted by their peers before they can be motivated.

Softners Chemicals added in the final wash cycle to eliminate static cling and smooth wrinkles.

Software In housekeeping, items of a textile nature that are not bed or bathroom linens, such as curtains and bedspreads.

Solar effect The heat-generating impact of sun rays directly hitting windows and walls of buildings.

Source-reduced product A product designed by its manufacturer to prevent waste from occurring before it reaches consumers.

Sours Acidic chemicals used to neutralize any alkaline residues left after washing and rinsing linens.

Spa Originally, a hotel or resort, located near a hot spring, offering water treatments. Today, the term spa refers to the department within a lodging property that provides various personal care treatments.

Space sensor A device used to detect the presence of people in spaces such as rooms and hallways.

Span of control The number of subordinates that a supervisor can oversee effectively.

Spontaneous combustion A fire produced by natural causes, such as by oily rags and lint in dryers.

Standard operating procedures (SOPs) The written operational standards based on each department's function.

Standing schedule A table showing the scheduled days on and off work of employees.

Starch A carbohydrate compound that is added to give linens a stiff appearance.

Statler hotels Hotels built by Ellsworth Statler in major U.S. cities at the beginning of the twentieth century offering conveniences and services not previously available.

Status barrier A communication obstacle in which a manager shows unwillingness to listen patiently to workers who are perceived as having lower social status.

Sterilization The elimination of microbiological organisms by the application of heat.

Stewardship of place An effort dedicated to minimizing or eliminating greenhouse gas emissions by reaching carbon neutrality and achieving sustainability of the planet.

Stripper A chemical compound used to remove old floor finishes prior to rewaxing.

Suggestive power A management technique in which a leader places an idea or proposition before a worker for consideration and possible action.

Sump pump A pump used to remove liquids that have accumulated in a pit commonly found in the basement of buildings below city sewer line level.

Support center A lodging property unit that does not generate revenue, such as engineering.

Sustainability A term implying that biological systems can remain diverse and productive over time.

Team supervisor An employee in charge of the supervision of a designated number of section housekeepers and one houseman.

Team supervisor work report A form informing team leaders of the status of all the guestrooms in their respective sections.

Technical skills A training sequence in which new employees are taught how to perform the tasks listed in their job description.

Temporary help Workers that are hired for a limited time, such as for the summer or skiing season.

Tensile strength The amount of weight it takes to tear a 1 inch by 3 inch piece of fabric.

Terry cloth Common name for bathroom linens.

Therm A natural gas measure of consumption that is equivalent to 100,000 BTUs.

Thread count The number of threads per square inch of material.

Time cards Cards used by employees to clock in and out in noncomputerized operations.

Time-share condominiums Lodging units sold to individual owners who use them or rent them out while having the option of trading them with owners of units located in different parts of the country or the world.

Time sheet A summary of hours worked by hourly employees taken from time cards in noncomputerized operations.

Transportation assistance Financial stipends given mainly to hourly workers to purchase train or bus passes.

Tufted A carpet having the yarn threaded through the backing material to form loops.

Tunnel washer A washing machine capable of processing multiple loads of linen simultaneously.

Turbine A rotary engine propelled by falling water or by wind used to generate electricity.

Turn-down service Procedure provided by some lodging properties that involves unfolding the bed, drawing the drapes closed, emptying the trash, and replacing used towels.

Twill Weft threads woven diagonally in fabrics.

Uniforms Employee work clothes categorized in the operating budget.

Unity of command A management principle that states that workers should be given orders only by one supervisor.

U.S. Green Building Council (USGBC) A nonprofit community of leaders working to make green buildings available throughout the U.S.

Value analysis Identification of a product's essential, desirable, useful, and unnecessary characteristics before it is purchased.

Variance analysis Document with the changes in revenue, expenses, and income from budget by category.

Vendor demonstration Training provided by manufacturing companies on new machinery or products.

Virus An infective agent smaller than common microorganisms, such as herpes and AIDS, that require living cells for multiplication.

Volt A unit of electrical force.

Voltage The electromotive force of electricity expressed in volts.

Warp The vertical thread in fabrics.

Wash cycle A sequence using soil-breaking products to clean the linen.

Water-borne disease An illness caused by contaminated water.

Water cooling tower Units in air-conditioning systems used to cool the warm water flowing from the absorber to the condenser.

Water softener A tank or series of tanks used to purify water before it is used.

Watt A unit of electrical power.

Wattage The watts required to operate an electric device.

Weft The horizontal yarn in fabrics.

Wellness programs A series of incentives provided by companies designed to prevent illness and enhance the well-being of employees.

Wet/dry vacuum A machine designed to pick up on any type of hard flooring surface.

Work order A request to the engineering department for repair or service of items that have broken down or that malfunction.

Zeolite A filtering resin used in water softeners.

C